MAKING LEARNING HAPPEN

Phil Race works with learners to help them improve their learning strategies, and with teachers and lecturers to help them to develop their teaching practices. He is based part-time at Leeds University, but travels around the UK and abroad for the rest of his time working with staff and students towards making learning happen successfully. He is particularly keen to step away from some of the jargon which has dogged teaching, learning and assessment, and help people to adopt practical, straightforward approaches to teaching, learning and assessment.

MAKING LEARNING HAPPEN

A Guide for Post-Compulsory Education

Phil Race

SAGE Publications
London • Thousand Oaks • New Delhi

First published 2005

Apart from any fair dealing for the purposes of research or
private study, or criticism or review, as permitted under the
Copyright, Designs and Patents Act, 1988, this publication
may be reproduced, stored or transmitted in any form, or
by any means, only with the prior permission in writing of
the publishers, or in the case of reprographic reproduction,
in accordance with the terms of licences issued by the
Copyright Licensing Agency. Inquiries concerning
reproduction outside those terms should be sent to the
publishers.

SAGE Publications Ltd
1 Oliver's Yard
55 City Road
London EC1Y 1SP

SAGE Publications Inc
2455 Teller Road
Thousand Oaks, California 91320

SAGE Publications India Pvt Ltd
B-42, Panchsheel Enclave
Post Box 4109
New Delhi 110 017

Library of Congress Control Number: 2005923422

A catalogue record for this book is available from the
British Library

ISBN 1-4129-0708-X
ISBN 1-4129-0709-8 (pbk)

Typeset by Dorwyn Ltd, Wells, Somerset
Printed on paper from sustainable resources
Printed in Great Britain by T.J. International, Padstow,
Cornwall

Contents

Preface

People have been trying to make learning happen throughout the recorded development of the human species – and no doubt for some time before anyone tried to describe it in words. There is now a vast literature about learning and teaching. Some of it is scholarly. There is also an abundant 'how to do it' literature, spanning learning, teaching and assessment. It sometimes feels as though there is a gulf between the two kinds of literature, with at least some academics climbing ever higher up their ivory towers, and at least some practice-based writers ignoring the wisdom which emanates from those towers. This book is my attempt to bridge the gap. In several chapters I have referred to some of what I believe to be the most important scholarship underpinning best practice. However, this book does not set out to be a scholarly text, but rather an attempt to integrate how best we can make learning happen in post-compulsory education by focusing on learners themselves, and on key factors underpinning successful learning.

My problem with at least some of the scholarship is that I think it is adrift! In 2004, the UK government-sponsored review of Coffield et al. posed serious questions about the validity of many of the ways in which teachers in post-compulsory education have been trained to think about learning, and Lindsay (2004) in his thought-provoking and sobering review of two of the best known sources also cast doubt on the foundations of at least some of the approaches to designing learning in universities and colleges. I was heartened by these challenges to traditional approaches, as for some years I too have become dissatisfied (to say the least) with several key elements of the status quo regarding how learning has been believed to happen.

Essentially, this book is rooted in my own experience during the last three decades, where I have been working on four fronts of the interface between teaching, learning and assessment.

- Working with learners, both in subject-related contexts and learning strategy development, has helped me to get closer to how best we can talk with learners about their learning, and help them to prepare for our ways of trying to measure their progress.

- Working with lecturers and tutors in universities and colleges has helped me towards working out how to help them to make learning happen with their students, and how to go about the difficult task of measuring learners' achievement.
- Working with learning resource designers has helped me to see the necessary processes which learning resources (electronic or print based) need to have in place to play their part in making learning happen.
- Most importantly, perhaps, working with trainers on training design has helped me to pick out the useful processes from the spurious artefacts.

During this time I have come to believe that the best way forward on all of these fronts is to address, quite deliberately and consciously, five factors which underpin effective learning:

- *wanting* to learn – often referred to as 'intrinsic motivation' by others
- taking ownership of the *need* to learn – perhaps what others call 'extrinsic motivation'
- *learning by doing* – practice, repetition, trial and error, learning through experience
- learning through *feedback* – from fellow learners, from tutors, from learning resources, from results
- *making sense* of what has been learned – getting one's head round ideas, concepts and theories.

These factors may look obvious – indeed simple. Yet Einstein suggested that 'everything should be made as simple as possible – but not simpler'. *How* these factors interact with each other is indeed complex, as is how best we can set out consciously to address these factors in our bid to make learning happen. My aim in this book is to tackle some of these complexities, based on experience.

I was first alerted to these factors through my work with students on study-skills development. Since then, and in the last ten years in particular, I have continued to develop the links between these factors and just about everything we try to achieve in post-compulsory education, and this book summarizes this work. I have become ever more convinced that addressing the five factors works in practice. I have to date got several thousands of people arguing, debating and extrapolating from the factors at staff development workshops in several countries and cultures, and this book owes much to the wisdom which has been shared and the insights which have developed through these discussions.

Summary of the content

In Chapter 1, 'Setting the scene', I start the book by looking at some of the problems we have got ourselves into with the language that is commonly used about learning. I then give a whistle-stop tour of a number of the models of learning that are currently around, paving the way towards Chapter 2, 'Five factors underpinning successful learning', which is an informal unpacking of the five factors, and the way they continuously affect each other (like 'ripples on a pond') rather than function consecutively in a cycle. In this book I have added for the first time how these factors can be thought to link onwards to the learning pay-off which accompanies the processes of *teaching* and *assessing*, and suggest how useful it can be to involve learners whenever possible in these activities to increase their learning pay-off.

Despite the reservations I have long expressed about learning styles questionnaires, I present in Chapter 3, 'Beyond learning styles?', a new questionnaire aiming to help learners to reflect on how they learn, in terms of the five factors developed in Chapter 2, and illustrating how the questionnaire can be used to provide learners with individual feedback on their reflections, to help them to further develop their approaches to learning. This questionnaire, however, is different from the usual 'yes/no' format, in that it allows learners four choices for each of 100 statements about how they *feel* they learn. Notwithstanding my reservations about 'scoring schemes' for such devices, I have supplied one in Chapter 3 for reasons discussed there. I end Chapter 3 with some suggestions for learners themselves about how they can do their part towards making learning happen, and hope that these suggestions may be a starting point for readers of this book to develop their own discipline-specific guidance for their own learners.

In Chapter 4, 'Assessment driving learning', I start with the premise that for most learners, learning is largely driven by assessment ('when's the deadline?', 'what's the pass mark?', 'what standard is expected?' and so on). I continue by discussing the need to make assessment valid, reliable, transparent and authentic, and then look at some of the things that are presently wrong with assessment in general in post-compulsory education. Two commonly used assessment formats (time-constrained unseen written exams, and essays) are analysed in some detail against the factors underpinning successful learning. In Chapter 5, 'Learning through feedback', I go into more detail about the various ways that learners can be given formative feedback on their own work by lecturers, tutors, teachers and, most importantly, by each other, and how this feedback links to 'wanting to learn, needing to learn, learning by doing and making sense of what is being learned'.

The next two chapters are written in 'question and response' format, addressing in turn some of the most frequently asked questions about large-group and small-group learning. In Chapter 6, 'Making learning happen in large groups', I relate the five factors to large-group teaching contexts such as lectures, large classes and so on, exploring what learners can do to maximize their learning pay-off in such contexts, but also what lecturers and teachers can do to *cause* learners to increase their learning pay-off. In parallel, in Chapter 7, 'Making learning happen in small groups', I aim to get you thinking about your tutorial or seminar groups, and on what we can cause learners to do while working together to increase their learning pay-off.

In Chapter 8, 'Responding to diversity and widening participation', I look at how the learner population is changing as a result of widening participation policies, then move to the related need to put more energy into addressing special educational needs. I analyse some of these needs in terms of which of the five underpinning factors are 'damaged' or 'restricted' by particular contexts, then go on to explore what we can do to compensate for this in our teaching and learner support. A key premise for this chapter is that 'good practice for special needs learners should be good practice for everyone'. In Chapter 9, 'Addressing employability', I use the work of Knight and Yorke (2003) as a starting point for analysing how the various skills and attributes which they have linked to employability can be related to the five factors underpinning successful learning developed in Chapter 2.

In Chapter 10, 'Putting the learning into e-learning', my principal aim is to help readers to interrogate the learning pay-off resulting from e-learning materials. This chapter confronts the status quo where presently much that is called 'e-learning' is no more than 'e-information' and that although 'e-information' is valuable in its own right, it should not be confused with real 'e-learning' where all five factors underpinning successful learning are addressed successfully. I end the chapter with some suggestions about how to go about building e-learning materials, focusing on the learning rather than the associated technologies.

I end the book with Chapter 11, 'Making workshops work', which tries to bridge another gulf – that between education and training. In the context of interactive small-group teaching and learning, I believe that designing training workshops well sums up much of the practical side of making learning happen in post-compulsory education. In a way, workshop design embraces sharply many of the most important aspects of curriculum design in general, not least formulating intended learning outcomes well, and monitoring and reviewing what actually happens in practice. This discussion explores in detail how best we can strive to increase the learning pay-off of participants at training workshops, particularly by getting them involved in 'learning by doing' and 'feedback' processes, and by causing them to reflect on their actions. In this chapter, I have provided several checklists as a starting point for planning and refining your own efforts to design appropriate learning environments for small-group learning in workshop contexts, and as an aid to your reflections on the extent to which you are succeeding to make learning happen.

Further material is available online at www.sagepub.co.uk/resource/race.pdf.

Acknowledgements

I am grateful to countless workshop participants for their permission to share the products of our combined thinking and discussion in several parts of this book. I am particularly indebted to my better half, Sally Brown, for innumerable relevant day-to-day discussions about formative feedback, assessment design, and fit-for-purpose approaches to teaching and learning in universities. Thanks also to John Cowan, who over the years has helped me to think deeper into the substance of what is now this book, especially about what we can do as teachers to make learning happen. I dedicate this book to all the students who have helped me to learn about learning, and to the memory of my sister Muriel from whom I learned a great deal about many other parts of life, but who sadly did not live to see this book come to fruition.

Phil Race
January 2005

1

Setting the scene

Why this book?

There is a massive literature about teaching, learning and assessment, referring to all levels of education and training. Some of this literature is about scholarship and research into how human beings learn, and how best to cause them to learn more effectively. Some of this literature is more practical in nature, advocating ways to go about designing our teaching, and monitoring how learning is happening. So what is intended to be different in *this* book?

Perhaps the main difference is that this book aims to get back to straightforward language about teaching and learning, and avoid some of the jargon which so often gets in the way of helping teachers in post-compulsory education reflect on their work. Also, at the time of writing, robust and well-argued criticism is appearing in the scholarly literature, questioning many of the ideas, concepts, theories and models which have been around for many years, some of which have been found to arise from limited studies in specific contexts, then been extended beyond reason to broader contexts where they cease to be useful. The reviews published by Coffield et al. (2004) are among the most significant critical analyses made to date of factors relating to how learning happens in post-compulsory education (and, indeed, help us to question how learning happens at all stages of life).

In short, the approach I am using in this book is to leave aside most of the questionable thinking about learning styles, and theories and models of learning, and probe much deeper into the factors underpinning *all* learning. It can be argued that these factors are actually quite easy to identify. Moreover, once identified, they are relatively straightforward to address in the design of all manner of teaching-learning contexts and environments. 'Learning styles' can then simply be regarded as the different ways that individuals respond to the main factors underpinning successful learning, and learners themselves can be liberated from the threat of being trapped in some sort of predetermined mould regarding how their brains go about the processes of making sense of themselves and the world around us.

Starting with Einstein

Einstein is reported to have said: 'Everything should be made as simple as possible, but not *too* simple.' It can be argued that much of what has been written about learning in the last half-century or more has not been as simple as possible in the words and language used, but at the same time has been *too* simple in terms of many of the models proposed.

Another Einstein maxim is 'Knowledge is experience – everything else is just information'. We are now in an age where information is more abundant than could every have been imagined. It is also easily obtained – in other words it is plentiful and cheap. When I myself was a student, most students left most lectures with about as much *information* as they could write in an hour or so, a few hundred words or equivalent, from what the lecturer said, did and showed. Nowadays, students are likely to emerge from an hour's learning with several thousands of words or equivalent in handout materials, downloadable files from an intranet or the web, but it is all still just information until they have done things with it to turn it into the start of their own *knowledge* about the subject concerned, and link it up to other things they already know about that subject and about the rest of the universe.

So perhaps at one level the quest to make learning happen in post-compulsory education boils down to how best can we help our learners to turn information into their own knowledge. I argue in this book that we can go a long way towards achieving this mission by carefully and systematically addressing the five factors underpinning successful learning identified in Chapter 2. But first, I would like you to think a little more about the problems we've made for ourselves with the over-complex language that is so endemic at present about the meaning of learning (and, indeed, the learning of meaning).

Minding our language

Learning? Knowing? Understanding?

In a book with the words 'making learning happen' in the title it is probably useful to stop and reflect upon what we really *mean* by 'learning' and, since the words 'knowing' and 'understanding' (among others) naturally creep into any such reflections, to try to work out what we're really about when we attempt to 'make learning happen'.

For a start it is, of course, *learners* who learn, we can't do it to them, we can't do it for them. One way or another they have to do it themselves. We can, however, structure the environment – let's call it a 'learning environment' – so that learning becomes easier, more productive, more efficient, more likely and so on. In other words, our actions can increase the probability that learning will happen.

Understanding

Knight and Yorke (2003) acknowledge that there is a problem with 'understanding', and also point out that the kinds of assessments learners meet in post-compulsory education have a significant effect upon the extent to which learners develop understanding.

> There is uncertainty about what counts as understanding. Side-stepping some important philosophical issues, we suggest that a student who understands something is able to apply it appropriately to a fresh situation (demonstration by far transfer) or to evaluate it (demonstration by analysis). Understanding cannot be judged, then, by evaluating the learner's retention of data or information; rather, assessment tasks would need to have the student *apply* data or information appropriately. This might not be popular in departments that provide students with a lot of scaffolding because their summative assessment tasks only involve near transfer, not far transfer. Where far transfer and evaluation are the hallmarks of understanding, assessment tasks will not be low-inference, right or wrong tasks, but high-inference ones, judged by more than one person with a good working knowledge of agreed grade indicators. (Knight and Yorke, 2003: 48, emphasis in original.)

Perhaps we have a problem in the English language in that words such as learning, knowing and understanding overlap so much in their everyday usage. If we intend learners to become able to soft-boil an egg, it is normally enough that they become able to soft-boil an egg, and do so successfully most times they attempt the task. We could say then that they have learned to soft-boil an egg, and equally we could say that they then 'know how to soft-boil an egg'. But we wouldn't (I trust) say that they 'understand' about soft-boiling eggs until a lot more had happened in their brains, not least all of the chemistry of the colloidal processes varying with temperature within the egg, the physics of the differences in boiling temperature of water at different heights above sea level, the meteorology of the effects of the variation in air pressure under different climatic or weather conditions, not to mention the zoological considerations of the differences between different kinds of egg, and so on. But such knowledge is not necessary to boil an egg (fortunately), though for some people such knowledge may indeed enrich the thinking which might just accompany the routine process of making a soft-boiled egg.

A musical diversion

When the subject matter becomes more complex, the dangers in using words like 'know' or 'understand' inappropriately become more significant. Let's take as an example J.S. Bach's '48 preludes and fugues' written for keyboard instruments of his day, but frequently nowadays also played on various kinds of modern piano. 'Do you know Bach's 48?' is a question which might produce an affirmative answer from a fair number of people. Some of them might be saying 'yes' because they knew *of* Bach's 48, others might say 'yes' because they were able to play one or more of the 48 themselves, or had once been able to, or even had done so successfully only once. (We'll leave aside for the moment what 'successfully' might mean.) Students on a music module might, we think, be expected not just to perhaps become able to *play* one or more of the preludes and fugues, but also to know how the pieces of music themselves actually *work* – in other words to analyse the notes and work out more about what the composer may actually have been achieving when he wrote the notes on manuscript paper – or when he experimented with playing the notes himself prior to writing down his final version of them on paper.

But what might we mean by '*understand* Bach's 48'? Has anyone other than Bach ever achieved this, and how would we know such understanding if we saw it – or, more precisely, *heard* it? Indeed, did Bach himself *understand* what he had achieved in this quite small but important facet of his large output? Now Bach himself would not be in a position to *understand* what changes this set of pieces were to make on the development of instrumental music and, indeed, on what we now call 'tonality' and 'counterpoint'.

So who has (so far) *understood* this tiny corner of the musical world best? Who gets the only first-class degree in the 48? Who gets the PhD or DMus in it? Certainly a likely condition might be that this someone should be able to play all of them successfully. This might be interpreted to mean 'note perfect' – in other words without hitting any wrong keys on the keyboard. But that is relatively simple to achieve – lots of people can play this music perfectly *accurately* and hit all the right notes at the right time in the right order. Many an unwilling and uninterested music student has achieved at least some of this at one time or another, without any real commitment or feeling. We can indeed programme a computer to generate all of the notes in such a way, and it will do so in exactly the same way every time it is required to. So does the computer *understand* Bach's 48? No more, of course, than the person or persons responsible for capturing their own *understanding* of the music into the technology. There are important aspects of *interpretation* to consider – which notes should *stand out* at any given moment? At what *speeds* (tempi) should the different elements of the music be played? How loudly or softly are the notes meant to be heard? What sort of instrument is the best one to bring Bach's conception to realization?

Let's take one musician as an example – Glenn Gould. For much of his relatively short life he was associated with playing the music of Bach, not least the 48. We still have access to his recordings of this music, made over some years, and always since then available in catalogues of available recordings. Anyone, however, who has been involved in making recordings of music (or indeed drama, documentaries or many other 'captured events') knows that the recording studio tends to work in 'takes' and 're-takes' and so on. Often, several attempts at getting a piece 'right' are made, and the best of these preserved or welded together. But those who saw and heard Glenn Gould making his legendary recordings agree with the performer himself that he never played the same piece in exactly the same way twice. All his attempts may indeed have been note-perfect, but the *interpretation* varied every time, as he continued to explore in his own mind the patterns, balances and dynamics of each tiny part of this large set of keyboard pieces. Even on just a single instrument – a piano – there remain infinite possibilities of *realizing* Bach's original composition. Bach himself would, we may speculate, have been the first to welcome this multiplicity of 'getting it right' regarding his music. But we could argue, perhaps, that Glenn Gould had developed a deeper *understanding* of this particular music than most people. But did Glenn Gould *feel* that he had developed a full understanding of this music after playing it for years? He probably would have been the first to say that his 'understanding' was continuously unfolding and developing.

But was Glenn Gould's *understanding* of Bach's 48 the best? And how wise was it to try to realize Bach's conception on a modern piano? Glenn Gould hardly ever touched the sustaining pedal on such an instrument. Different performers have played this music in countless different ways, all note-perfect. Shostakovich was no mean pianist, and no doubt played the 48 to at least some degree of accomplishment. Shostakovich, however, went on to compose 24 preludes and fugues himself, and there is little doubt that he was influenced – or perhaps a better word is *inspired* – by Bach's work. So should we say then that Shostakovich, too, *understood* the 48? And what of a present-day musician who is able to play both Shostakovich's 24 *and* Bach's 48 – is this a pathway to a greater *understanding* of either or both works?

Then there's another problem. Suppose Glenn Gould's *understanding* of the Bach 48 was in some way deemed to be 'the best', and was taken to be the benchmark for this particular achievement. Would all the critics *agree* with this decision? Surely not. And sooner or later this benchmark would be replaced, or go out of fashion, as different ways of thinking about the 48 came into prominence. So perhaps this boils down to understanding being ephemeral as a concept in any case?

Back to learning, and mapping it out for learners

One of the problems of formulating a curriculum is that in the English language people tend to use the word 'understand' much too loosely. Intended learning outcomes are too often badly phrased along the lines 'by the end of this course students will understand x, y and z'. Nor is it much use to soften the outcomes along the lines 'this course will help students to deepen their understanding of x, y and z'. Yes, the course may indeed help students to *deepen* their understanding, but do they know how much they are deepening it, and can we measure how much they have deepened it? In short, we can't measure what students *understand*. We can only measure the evidence that students produce to *demonstrate* their understanding. That evidence is all too easily limited by techniques of demonstrating understanding – their written communication skills perhaps. Or whether they are note-perfect in music. We can measure such things, and give students feedback about them, but we can't ever be sure that we're measuring what is present in learners' minds. In some religions, blessings are phrased along the lines 'the peace of mind which passes all understanding'; perhaps in education we need to be aware of 'the piece of understanding which passes all attempts to measure it'! Or, when it comes to under-standing, 'if we *can* measure it, it almost certainly isn't *it*'.

Similar problems surround the words 'know', 'knowing' and 'knowledge'. I've already quoted Einstein's 'knowledge is experience; everything else is just informa-tion'. Think of a person you know. What do you *mean* by know? There are all sorts of levels of knowing someone. Even at the closest levels, people often find out (usu-ally too late) that they never *really* knew whoever-it-was.

So where does this leave us with 'making learning happen'? Developing learners' understanding may well be a useful direction to go in, but we need to be really care-ful to spell out exactly *how far* learners are intended to develop their understanding, and what *evidence* they need to be aiming to produce to prove that they have devel-oped their understanding, and what *standards* this evidence must measure up to, to indicate that they have successfully developed their understanding sufficiently. We also need to think hard about which *processes* are best to help learners to develop their understanding, and to recognize that different processes and environments suit different learners best. We can use similar arguments about knowing and knowledge. We only measure what learners *know* as far as we can assess the evidence which learners produce. In other words, we can only measure what learners *show* of what they know.

Even more difficult words? Another excursion!

The word 'metacognition' pervades the scholarly literature about learning, not least in post-compulsory educational contexts. Knight and Yorke (2003: 50) quote from Pellegrino et al. as follows:

> One of the most important features of cognition is metacognition – the process of reflecting on and directing one's own thinking. Metacognition is crucial to effective thinking and problem solving and is one of the hallmarks of expertise in specific areas of knowledge and skill ... *Assessment should there-fore attempt to determine whether an individual has good metacognitive skills.*
> (Pellegrino et al. 2001: 4, emphasis in original.)

The above definition of metacognition as 'the process of reflecting on and directing one's own thinking' is fine of course – we really do want our learners not only to get their heads round the subject matter they encounter, but also to become much more aware about how their brains actually work.

Unfortunately, I believe that metacognition has turned out to be one of those words which has led to confusion and problems in helping practitioners to increase the probability that learning is made to happen. Being provocative, I would suggest that in perhaps nine out of ten instances when I see the word metacognition being used, one or both of the following two purposes seems to be served:

- An attempt to appear to be suitably scholarly and austere, and thereby achieve credibility;
- An unwillingness to probe into which aspect of metacognition is really being considered – in other words, the use of the word as a cover-all, to avoid explaining *exactly what* is intended to be meant by it in the particular circumstances in which the word is used.

Asking subject practitioners in higher education to 'define' the word 'metacognition' in simple language – and to speculate on what the word might mean if they did not know – gave me the following phrases (gathered in Swansea and Leeds, and reproduced with the permission of the contributors). I have included all the responses I gathered, so the extent of overlap and duplications can be seen, but also so that you can notice that at least some of the guesses are way out! The list does, however, show that this particular word means quite different things to different people – and that more often than not attempts to define 'metacognition' lead backwards to that other word which means different things to different people – 'understanding'.

- Analysis and evaluation of thought around a particular subject.
- Navel-gazing?
- Understanding how we understand. The process of learning in review – usually by considering an example of how one comes to understand something.
- Convergence of understanding (thinking).
- A combination of the views of lots of people about a subject.
- Criteria that determine most fundamentally how our processes of understanding operate.
- Thinking about thinking – how you think about what you think.
- Maybe it means how you interpret a learning objective – something may be different to what is expected of you – therefore leads to problems.
- Understanding understanding – knowledge of what is known.
- Understanding, expressing.
- Applied understanding?
- Understanding various aspects of a concept.
- Knowing how to understand.
- Higher order thinking, that is, analysing/theorizing – drawing many strands of thought together.
- Every way that things are learnt.
- When learners think about how they learn and what they have learned.
- Knowing a medium amount of all the knowledge there is.
- Collaboration.

- Meta = about everything, cognition = to know.
- The outcome of an abstraction process on existing cognition.
- A wide/broad understanding of own thought.
- Thinking about thinking.
- A large combination of mental processes, thought, emotion, memory, and so on, – thinking.
- Learning and understanding by all possible means.
- The act of thinking about thinking processes.
- Advanced thinking.
- How the brain processes our thinking in patterns and behaviours.
- Being aware of one's mental cognitive processes.
- Expansive thought processes.
- Informed knowledge.
- Consciously reflecting on the processes of thinking and gaining knowledge.
- All the processes which make us think and feel.

As you can see from these attempts to define metacognition, there is a tendency for academics to retreat into the comfort zone of other academic language – notably 'understanding' when trying to communicate the idea of a complex word like 'metacognition'. Andrew Morgan of University of Wales, Swansea, recognizes this as a problem which often happens when a student says 'I don't understand this' about a concept, and academics, though trying to help, end up by making it even less understandable, going deeper into the concept instead of (as needed) trying to simplify it.

One workshop participant responded to the task of trying to guess what 'metacognition' might mean by quoting A. Conan Doyle in *Sherlock Holmes*: 'I never guess. It is a shocking habit, destructive of the logical faculty.' This touches on an important nerve in thinking about how learners develop their thinking about complex concepts. They too often feel that guessing is somehow of little value, and will only lead them into trouble if done in any assessment-related context. They may need to be persuaded that the process of guessing, followed by interrogation of the various resultant guesses to see which are credible and which are not, is a useful way of developing thinking. In our efforts to make learning happen in post-compulsory education, we need to make sure that we legitimize creativity and originality – which often begins with guessing. I assert that we can cause learners to develop creativity and originality.

Long ago, in one assessed task I happened to allocate 10 of 100 marks for 'originality' – not least because I had already used up the other 90 marks for things which related directly to the intended learning outcomes associated with the task. I was surprised – and delighted – by the quality of learners' work on the task. They went to considerable lengths to deserve some or all of those 10 marks for originality – and no doubt deepened their thinking and learning significantly in the process. Needless to say, thereafter I tended to allocate at least some marks simply to 'originality', or 'creativity', or 'lateral thinking approaches', and so on.

Metacognition, and metacognitive processes can mean many things to many people. For example, one or more of the following overlapping dimensions may be involved in the following attempts to explain the concept *without* recourse to the word 'understanding'.

- Thinking about learning.
- Working out what has been learned, and how this happened.
- Learning about thinking.
- Thinking about thinking.
- Becoming more able to 'reflect' and working out what 'reflecting' actually means in practice.
- Reflecting upon learning.
- Reflecting upon thinking.
- Thinking about experiences.
- Deepening learning by thinking about feedback.
- Thinking about the past when planning future actions.
- Working out how some learning actually happened.
- Working out what stopped some learning from happening.
- Learning from mistakes, and becoming more conscious of the value of learning from mistakes.

All these interpretations of metacognitive processes fit readily into the *making sense* factor underpinning successful learning discussed in more detail in Chapter 2, and many of them could be regarded as *making sense of making sense*. Each in its own way is part of 'digesting' or getting one's head round some subject matter and, more importantly, getting one's head round the process of getting one's head round the subject matter.

Adherents of the use of words like metacognition, argue the case that the word is being used as a precise, shorthand term to use just one word to communicate the desired idea, rather than a whole string of words. However, I would argue that in fact the use of the word (as I have also argued about the word 'understand') is in fact *less* precise – and, indeed, often sloppy in the quest to use language well to communicate meaning.

A short tour of the territory

Having argued the case that we need to be careful with our language when thinking about learning (and especially when helping our learners to think about their own learning so that they can take more control over it), I would like to continue this book by summing up, sometimes with critical comment, a selection of the terms and models which are in common use in the context of post-compulsory education.

Andragogy (Malcolm Knowles)

Post-compulsory education is naturally about adult learning, and the topic of andragogy has grown up specifically about grown-ups and their learning. However, some doubt whether such age-based distinctions are well founded, for example, Cotton argues:

> I believe that the concept of an adult learning style as distinct from a childlike learning style is fundamentally flawed ... Children learn through play, repetition and experimentation supported by some guidance and occasional correction. (Cotton, 2004: 22–7)

and he argues that so indeed do adults, and that differences are more about different teaching styles than learning preferences.

Knowles (1975) is regarded by many as the founder of andragogy, and he argues that adults:

- need to know *why* they need to learn something
- learn experientially
- approach learning as problem-solving
- learn best when they see that the topic is of immediate value to them.

Knowles further argues that adults are:

- self-directed and autonomous
- able to bring to learning their own stock of experience and knowledge
- goal-orientated – know what they want to get out of an episode of learning
- seeking relevance to their everyday lives

and that adults need to be shown respect.

All this is fine when people are in a position where they *want* to learn, but in post-compulsory education we do well to avoid the assumption that people intrinsically are wanting to learn at all times – indeed, it is often the case that they may *need* to learn something, but don't particularly want to learn it.

Processes of thinking and learning

Litzinger and Osif (1993) explored the different ways in which adults and children think and learn, breaking down learning into three sub-processes:

- Cognition – acquiring knowledge (but is this too often just acquiring information?).
- Conceptualization – processing information (I would equate this with 'turning information into their own knowledge').
- Affective processes – to do with values, motivation, ways of going about decision-making, emotional preferences, and so on.

But what is missing here? There is no mention of learning through feedback. I agree with the many commentators about post-compulsory education who regard formative feedback as just about the most important ingredient in any effective learning environment – be the environment face to face, distance education or virtual. Furthermore, although Litzinger and Osif refer to motivation, they miss out on the *purposeful* side of motivation, which can be thought of in terms of taking on board the *need* to learn at a particular time and place.

Kolb's learning cycle, and associated work

Kolb's work was originally based on the non-conscious development of psychomotor skills, and does not necessarily extend readily to other types of learning. It has been criticized (for example, Cotton, 2004) for not taking into account cultural factors, age, educational experience, socio-economic and other variables. Nonetheless, Kolb's four cornerstones can be summed up as:

- concrete experience – involvement in a new learning experience
- reflective observation – developing personal observations about the learning experience
- abstract conceptualization – forming theories to explain the observations
- active experimentation – using those theories to make decisions or to solve problems.

Honey and Mumford (1982) can be regarded as extending Kolb's approach to identify four distinct *styles* of learning:

- Activists – people who enjoy immediate experiences, such as exercises, problems, drama and excitement, but do not enjoy mere observation.
- Reflectors – people who like to view things from different standpoints, and seek time to think, and make notes as a way of capturing their own thinking.
- Theorists – people who approach learning in an analytical, objective way, seeking structure, clarification, explanation.
- Pragmatists – looking for new ideas and trying them out.

My problem with learning styles questionnaires, however, is that they too often end up pigeon-holing learners. In other words, people feel that they have been shown to have (for example) a tendency towards being a pragmatist – as though they were incapable of using any of the other approaches at will.

A different approach (at least different at first sight) is that of McCarthy (for example, 1987), who identified four types of learners as follows:

- Dynamic learners – directing their own discovery, teaching themselves and others, enjoying role-play, games, simulations.

- Analytical learners – acquirers of facts, wanting to deepen their understanding of processes and concepts, enjoying lectures, research and data analysis.
- Common-sense learners – seeking to know how things work, and enjoying trying things out, hands-on learning experiences.
- Innovative learners – linking learning to their own experience, needing good reasons to learn things, seeking relevance to their daily lives, enjoying brainstorming, collaborative learning and making connections between things they learn.

However, one could argue that for successful learning to occur, and the cycle to be completed, the learner would need to be all things – dynamic, analytic, common-sense and innovative, and play activist, reflector, theorist and pragmatist at different stages on each learning journey. But in this book, I'm concerned with 'making learning happen' – how on earth can we systematically help or cause learners to be all these things at exactly the right time?

Multiple intelligences

And what about *intelligence*? Gardner (1993) starts by regarding intelligence as 'the capacity to solve problems or to fashion products that are valued in one or more cultural setting'. Whatever *intelligence* may be, it should not be thought of as simply the capacity to perform well in particular assessment-related contexts or environments – for example, intelligence must be much more than merely the capacity to do well in time-constrained, unseen written examinations. Gardner's work usefully subdivides *intelligence* into multiple facets:

- Linguistic – use of language, words.
- Mathematical-logical – patterns, deductive reasoning.
- Musical – compose, perform and appreciate musical patterns.
- Bodily-kinaesthetic – use of whole body or parts of the body, co-ordination of movements.
- Spatial – recognizing and using patterns of space, parking the car, crystallography.
- Interpersonal – working with other people, understanding their motivations, intentions and desires.
- Intrapersonal – understanding oneself and recognizing one's feelings, fears and motivations.
- Spiritual – embracing aesthetic, unseen and spiritual dimensions.
- Bestial – communicating effectively with animals.

Any one person's intelligence can be regarded as a fairly unique blend of several of these facets. Any learning experience is likely to involve several of these, adding to the picture of each individual learner being quite unique in their overall approach to learning (and putting such ideas as 'pragmatist', 'theorist', 'reflector' and 'activist' onto a much less significant plane perhaps).

Neurolinguistic programming

In short, this can usefully remind us that, in many learning contexts, language is a primary conduit for our thoughts and is important in the ways that knowledge and information are expressed and exchanged. Thinking is based on our primary senses – seeing, hearing, feeling, smelling and tasting. We may indeed have a favoured sense out of these, leading to:

- visual learners – thinking primarily in pictures and images, perhaps colours
- auditory learners – learning through remembered and imagined sounds, tone, pitch, speed, and deriving much of their learning through listening and hearing
- kinaesthetic learners – processing information primarily through physical and emotional feelings.

Degrees of learning?

A further small vocabulary of descriptors has become associated with learning:

- 'Deep' learning is regarded as the 'best' form of learning. But how can we set learners up so that they adopt 'deep' approaches, and achieve deep learning? How best can we measure 'deep' learning? Deep learning can be thought of as being fired by a strong 'want' to make sense of what is being learned – to get one's head round it fully, to really 'understand' it.
- 'Surface' learning is easier to describe. It can be regarded as 'shallow', transient, ephemeral, temporary and 'reproductive'. Surface learning may be induced by the ways in which learning achievement is seen to be assessed. If it's just a matter of regurgitating information into an exam script, surface learning seems to be perfectly satisfactory for the purpose. If there's no need to hold on to the learning after an assessment occasion, likewise.
- 'Strategic' approaches to learning are more complex. The result may be 'deep' for some things learned, and 'surface' for others. 'Strategic' implies a conscious choice about which things are learned deeply and which are only afforded surface learning status. Strategic learning is target driven. Feedback is likewise used strategically, and exploited for what help it can give in preparing for particular measurement contexts such as exams.

In most of the literature about learning, deep learning is idealized. Working with students on developing their learning skills, I find myself sometimes cautioning them about deep learning, however. For example, a significant danger deep learners fall into is spending too much time and energy on particular elements from a syllabus, at the expense of the bigger picture. In assessment contexts, people who have learned some things deeply may gain well-deserved credit for having done so, but this may not be enough to compensate for all the other things they learned much less successfully because of having concentrated their energies and time on the narrower cross-section of the overall picture.

Slow learning, repetition and building on what learners already know

Perhaps when in two or three decades we look back at the development of post-compulsory education, in the UK in particular but often enough elsewhere as well, we may be surprised at the speed with which we rushed into modular provision in the 1990s. In many higher education institutions, this was coupled with semesterization, splitting the academic year into two main sections (rather than three terms), with what has often turned out to be an awkward and uncomfortable inter-semester break, towards the end of January. Many institutions are now moving back in some subject disciplines to the design of 'long thin modules' which last a full year.

Claxton (1998) referred to the idea of 'slow learning', suggesting that some learning takes weeks, months or even years to construct. Knight and Yorke (2003: 53) argue that 'complex learning is almost invariably slow learning, taking longer to grow than most modules last'. They also suggest that 'an advantage of monodisciplinary programmes is that, almost without the need for curriculum planning, some of the learning can take place over the full span of the programme' (ibid.: 140).

Another problem which can be exacerbated by too wide-ranging a mixture of available modules is that learners begin any element of study with widely differing amounts of existing knowledge. Ausubel (1968: 235) stated: 'if I had to reduce all of educational psychology to just one principle, I would say this: The most important single factor influencing learning is what the learner already knows. Ascertain this, and teach (him) accordingly'.

Knight and Yorke (2003) go further into the assessment implications of some learning being 'slow', and the problems this causes when the curriculum is too fragmented. Practising teachers in post-compulsory education can often cite aspects of their own subject which seem to be necessarily learned slowly. In my own former discipline, the Second Law of Thermodynamics is one such topic. It has to be 'lived with' for quite a while before it begins to make sense. It is often quite some time after being able to *use* it successfully, and solve problems with it, that the meaning of it gradually dawns. This is not just because historically it tends to have been expressed in rather forbidding terminology, perhaps following on from the precedent of Newton's *Principia* (containing his Laws of Motion) in the 1690s, of making concepts intentionally difficult to understand, leading to his masterpiece being described as 'one of the most inaccessible books ever written'. Notwithstanding, Dennis Overbye (adapted by Bill Bryson, in *A Short History of Nearly Everything*, 2004) is not far from simplifying the truth when he sums up the three main laws of thermodynamics as (1) you can't win (that is, can't create energy from nothing), (2) you can't break even (that is, there is always some energy wasted) and (3) you can't get out of the game (that is, can't reduce the temperature to absolute zero).

In our target-driven systems of post-compulsory education, there seems little room for *not-yet-successful* learning. Yet the more elusive ideas and concepts which can only be learned relatively slowly, often need to be re-learned several times during that pathway where slow learning leads to successful achievement. It is in fact useful to encourage learners to celebrate *forgetting* things, as part of the natural process of becoming less likely to forget them next time round. The most complex ideas probably need to be grasped then lost several times before they are gradually retained more permanently and safely. Learners, however, often feel frustrated and disappointed when they have mastered something one moment, and then find that it has slipped shortly afterwards. For example, the light may dawn during a lecture, then be found to have 'gone out again' when learners try to do the same things on their own as they seemed to be doing perfectly successfully during the lecture.

One way of helping learners take ownership of the benefits of slow learning when appropriate, is to point out to them that repetition not only pays dividends in the permanence of learning, but can be a very efficient way of using time and energy as part of an intentional learning strategy. For example, if a particular concept takes one hour to get one's head round first time, but then slips away, it may only take 10 minutes to regain the ground a few days later. If it slips away again, it may only take five minutes to get it back a few more days later and so on. By the twentieth time round it may only take a minute or less of re-learning and it will be safely recaptured. Encouraging learners that 'it's not how long you spend learning it, it's how *often* you've learned it and lost it and regained it that counts' is a way of allowing them to feel ownership of a successful strategy for approaching those things which are best learned slowly. It is also worth encouraging them *not* to spend too long on trying to learn anything the first time round, but to come back to it frequently until it begins to make sense. Meanwhile, rather than struggling to force the brain to make sense of a difficult concept, they can spend the time more productively between attempts refreshing their learning on things already learned successfully, and ensuring that these don't just slip away.

The Mexican hat approach

This way of thinking developing learning was described by Robinson and Udall (2003; 2004) in the context of engineering education. The model focuses on the analysis of learners' state of learning, with reference to the following three questions:

- How do I know if I am doing what I should be doing?
- How do I know if I have gained understanding from what I am doing?
- How do I know if the understanding I have gained will result in success?

and describes learners as respectively:

- Not yet participating (that is, not yet learning by doing)
- Participating but not yet achieving (that is, learning by doing, but not yet making sense)
- Participating and achieving (that is, doing, making sense, and learning through feedback)

The proportions of learners in a group in the respective positions they likened to the three 'regions' of a Mexican hat.

Trying to sort out the picture

I quoted Einstein earlier as advocating 'everything should be made as simple as possible – but not *too* simple'. I argue that the plethora of terms and processes that have arisen in the models summarized above are not at all simple enough to describe adequately something as fundamental as how our species learns – but perversely that the 'going around in a circle' idea in a particular direction is much *too* simple. In other words, though all of the processes may have a part to play in successful learning, they are unlikely to follow on from each other in a neat cycle. In fact, they are much more likely to interact with each other, and affect each other and to occur concurrently rather than consecutively.

How then can we simplify the picture, but at the same time enrich it? My belief is that the way ahead is to find out what factors are involved in all the main processes involved in learning – what is the underlying picture?

Perhaps the most detailed review to date of models of learning in general, and learning styles approaches in particular, is the work of Coffield et al. (2004) which can be downloaded from www.lsrc.ac.uk. The cover text on their report is as follows:

> **Learning styles and pedagogy in post-16 learning – A systematic and critical review**
>
> This report critically reviews the literature on learning styles and examines in detail 13 of the most influential models. The report concludes that it matters fundamentally which instrument is chosen. The implications for teaching and learning in post-16 learning are serious and should be of concern to learners, teachers and trainers, managers, researchers and inspectors.

In the conclusions they refer back to their original aim as follows:

> This report has sought to sift the wheat from the chaff among the leading models and inventories of learning styles and among their implications for pedagogy: we have based our conclusions on the evidence, on reasoned argument and on healthy scepticism. For 16 months, we immersed ourselves in the world of learning styles and learned to respect the enthusiasm and the dedication of those theorists, test developers and practitioners who are work-

ing to improve the quality of teaching and learning.

We ourselves have been reminded yet again how complex and varied that simple-sounding task is and we have learned that we are still some considerable way from an overarching and agreed theory of pedagogy. In the meantime, we agree with Curry's summation (1990, 54) of the state of play of research into learning styles: 'researchers and users alike will continue groping like the five blind men in the fable about the elephant, each with a part of the whole but none with full understanding'. (Coffield et al., 2004: 157)

They continue by voicing various concerns, including:

Fortunes are being made as instruments, manuals, videotapes, in-service packages, overhead transparencies, publications and workshops are all commercially advertised and promoted vigorously by *some* of the leading figures in the field. In short, the financial incentives are more likely to encourage further proliferation than sensible integration. It also needs to be said that there are other, distinguished contributors to research on learning styles who work in order to enhance the learning capabilities of individuals and firms and not in order to make money.

They conclude their large-scale report as follows:

Finally, we want to ask: why should politicians, policy-makers, senior managers and practitioners in post-16 learning concern themselves with learning styles, when the really big issues concern the large percentages of students within the sector who either drop out or end up without any qualifications? Should not the focus of our collective attention be on asking and answering the following questions?

- Are the institutions in further, adult and community education in reality centres of learning for *all* their staff and students?
- Do some institutions constitute in themselves barriers to learning for certain groups of staff and students? (Coffield et al., 2004: 157)

It is with these conclusions and questions resounding in my own mind that I set about the task of preparing this book about making learning happen in post-compulsory education.

Conclusions

In short, we have got to be really careful about the language we use to *describe* learning. In some instances, it takes a great deal of adjustment to put into words what might at first sight appear to be a perfectly reasonable learning target. Such targets only work well when everyone who sees the words knows exactly what those words are intended to mean. Different teachers teaching the same module need to be able

to agree with each other about the standards and evidence descriptors that are associated with intended learning outcomes. Much more importantly, learners themselves need to be able to 'know' what the words mean. They more than anyone else
need to be able to make realistic and accurate interpretations of the wording of our
intended learning outcomes.

A small but vital part of 'making learning happen' is to get our wording right
when we try to describe what we intend learners to become able to do. This is why
learners find it so valuable to be shown evidence of successful achievement – and
evidence of *not-yet-successful* achievement – so that they become more aware of the
directions in which they are intended to be moving and more aware of the nature
of the intended destination of each element of their studies.

Finally, we need to think about the *processes* of learning, and avoid the danger of
oversimplifying them. This leads nicely towards the purpose of Chapter 2 – to think
about learning in straightforward language which we can share with our learners,
so that all of us can co-operate and play our respective parts in making learning
happen, but to avoid oversimplifying the processes an instrument as complex as the
human brain uses when learning.

2

Five factors underpinning successful learning

Background

In this chapter, I introduce you to how we can identify that there are five factors which underpin successful learning, and to a discussion of how they overlap and interact with each other. This way of thinking about learning has been developed from asking tens of thousands of people four questions about their learning – successful as well as unsuccessful learning. These people have come from the following main groups:

- students I work with on developing their study skills approaches to further and higher education
- lecturers and teachers in higher and further education, during courses and workshops on the design of teaching, learning and assessment
- trainers I work with on the design of training processes and resources.

I've often developed the discussion of these factors at conferences, as well as in training workshops and staff development programmes. The ages of respondents spans 18 to 80, and I've worked through the analysis which follows widely around the UK and Ireland, but also in Australia, New Zealand and, occasionally, in Singapore, Canada, Sweden and Switzerland. I therefore feel able to argue that the common ground which emerges is about fundamental processes underpinning successful learning by adults from several cultures, rather than pertaining only to a relatively focused cross-section of learners.

Basically, I ask people four questions, each in two parts. The first part of each question asks them to identify an element related to one instance of their own learning, whether formal or informal. I then ask them to jot down their answers to the second part of each question, in only a few words – I normally suggest up to six.

To enter into the spirit of this book, however, I prefer not to say anything more about these questions or the factors which emerge from people's answers to them, until you have had a go at answering them yourselves. (If, however, you've already noticed them from the Preface, please see whether you think that they link to the four questions in Table 2.1.) Please therefore jot down your own responses in Table 2.1.

Table 2.1 Four two-part questions about how you learned well – and less well

Four questions about your own learning

Please use this page to revisit four aspects of your own learning. The first part of each of the four questions which follow is to get you thinking about particular instances in your own learning. The second part of each question asks you to put pen to paper to capture some of the processes which led to the success – or otherwise – of the respective instances of your learning.

1   Think of something you are good at – something which you know you do well. (This may be an academic subject, but equally could be a hobby or skill – in short, anything at all that you're good at.)

Next, jot down a few words about *how* you became good at this.

2   Think of something you *feel* positive about – something which you like about yourself. This could be anything about yourself which you're proud of.

Now jot down a few words about how you *know* that you can be proud of this – in other words, upon what evidence is this positive feeling based?

3   Think of something which you *don't* do well! This could be the result of an unsuccessful learning experience, maybe long ago or maybe recently. If you've nothing in this category, you can miss out question 3 – no one has so far, however!

Now jot down a few words about each of the following: what went wrong, do you think, in your learning relating to this thing you do not do well? And who, if anyone, might have been to blame for this?

4   Think of something you can indeed do well, but that you didn't *want* to learn at the time you learned it. This could be something like 'driving', 'swimming', 'cooking' or, equally, it could relate to a particular area of academic study – perhaps 'statistics' or 'economics' and so on. Whatever it is, you're probably pleased *now* that you succeeded with it – it's likely to be useful to you now.

Finally, jot down a few words about what kept you going, so that you did indeed succeed in this particular episode of learning.

Now that you've answered the four questions and noted down your own replies to the second parts of each of the questions, look back over your answers and see if you can pick out what these answers can tell you about how you yourself learn best – and, indeed, worst.

After pausing to reflect on your learning as illustrated by these four facets of it, please press on to read my account of most people's answers to the same questions. You can then compare to what extent your answers are mirrored by those of other people.

Towards the factors underpinning successful learning

In the next section of this book, I summarize the responses I have had to these questions and draw from them the factors which underpin successful learning.

I How most people become good at things

Most people's answers to the second part of question 1 are along the lines:

- practice
- learning through getting it wrong at first
- experimenting
- trial and error
- repetition
- experience
- having a go

and so on. 'Practice' is by far the most common of these responses. All of the above answers have one thing in common – they're about 'doing' of one kind or another.

There's nothing new about this of course. The ancient Greeks and Chinese knew a lot about the importance of learning by doing – Sophocles is reported to have said words to the effect that 'though one thinks one can do something, one has no certainty until one tries to do it' – indeed, many of the Ancients could have said this.

Ancient wisdom about learning is worth revisiting. *How* we learn has not changed much over the millennia. Even though there have been vast changes in *what* we learn, and indeed in the resources and tools we learn *with*, those essential processes of 'learning by doing' remain. Or, in other words, there may have been huge changes in our learning environments over the years, but the human brain evolves very slowly, and the processes underpinning successful learning are slow to evolve.

Learning by doing can be learning through mistakes too. Niels Bohr, the nuclear physicist, is reported to have defined 'an expert' as follows: 'someone who has made all of the mistakes which it is possible to make – in a very narrow field!' Sadly, at present we often seem to undervalue the potential of learning through mistakes. There's a tendency to take note of people's mistakes and use these against them in evidence.

Although most replies about how people became good at things relate to *doing* of various kinds, at least some relate to ways in which they were affected by other people. In particular, there are usually some responses about how other people caused or enabled practice or repetition, and even 'training' comes up occasionally – but quite rarely 'being taught'. 'Being inspired' comes up rather more often, along with 'being enthused'.

2 How people come to feel good *about* things

Question 2 yields very convergent replies to 'how you *know* that you can be proud of this – in other words, upon what evidence is this positive feeling based?' Typical answers include:

- feedback
- other people's reactions
- praise
- compliments
- people come to me for help
- seeing the effect on other people
- seeing the results.

All these can be summed up as 'feedback' of one kind or another. Feedback clearly plays a vital part in helping people to develop positive feelings about things they do, and things they are. The majority of such feedback arises from other people, including fellow learners, tutors, teachers, trainers, mentors, friends, just about everyone or anyone. Some feedback is also linked to self-assessment or self-evaluation, for example, the 'seeing the results' replies often refer to looking at the *evidence* arising from the learning – the visible side of the achievement (including drawings, paintings, musical compositions, sculptures, and many other artefacts which are products of the learning concerned).

While most people readily accept that feedback plays a vital role in helping them to learn, there are two key problems which can get in the way of feedback reaching its optimum value:

- The feedback needs to be provided very soon after the actions which it is based.
- Feedback needs to be 'received' and not rejected or dismissed.

In Chapter 5 I go into much more detail about how adjusting the timing of feedback can make a lot of difference to its value to learners, and about how a wide range of feedback processes can be analysed in terms of which are the most 'receivable' by learners in various contexts.

3 Learning going wrong!

Question 3 yields a rich harvest of causes of learning going wrong. People's replies to the questions; 'what went wrong, do you think, in your learning relating to this thing you don't do well? And who, if anyone, might have been to blame for this?' show that a wide range of things can be the causes of unsuccessful learning – 'things people aren't good at' – and that though many people accept the 'blame' for this, even more blame other people. In fact, the blame is often directed at particular teachers and lecturers at virtually any stage of learning.

Many replies link back to the overlap between question 3 and the previous two questions. For example:

- Didn't get enough practice.
- I didn't work hard enough at it.
- I got poor feedback.
- Poor communication between myself and teachers (or trainers, tutors, fellow-learners).
- I was made to feel small about it.
- No one explained to me how to become better at it.

And so on.

But many replies bring in some important further factors:

- I didn't want to learn it in the first place.
- I couldn't see the point of it.
- I couldn't see what I was supposed to be aiming to do with it.
- I couldn't get my head round it.
- I just didn't understand it.
- The light wouldn't dawn.
- I couldn't make sense of it.

A further, even more common factor is:

- Poor teaching!

When running this exercise with learners themselves, they often write down the *names* of teachers here.

A further dimension underpinning successful learning is clearly to do with 'getting one's head round it', or *'making sense'* of it. This is all about developing deeper understanding of what is being learned. In addition, replies to question 3 often bring in aspects of motivation. In particular, when learners don't really *want* to learn something, we should not be surprised that they may be unsuccessful at learning it well. Conversely, when learners *really* want to learn something, little will stop them from succeeding. There are countless tales of learners who had a very strong *want* to succeed in learning difficult and complex things, who succeeded even when people around them did not think they would make it.

It can be useful to think of the *making sense* process as mentally *digesting* the experience of learning, and *digesting* the feedback being received. The everyday use of the word 'digesting' is about extracting what we need from what we eat and drink – taking what will sustain us for the next few hours or days. But just as important in normal 'digesting' is discarding what we don't need – 90-odd per cent of the total amount eaten and drunk no less.

We can think of *digesting* as being a parallel process where the human brain sorts out the floods of information sent to it by the various senses, and keeps just a little of this information in one form or another, discarding perhaps 99.9 per cent of it quite rapidly. We can therefore regard the process of *digesting* to be turning information into knowledge. I use *digesting* and *making sense* quite interchangeably in many parts of the discussion in this book.

The metaphor linking *making sense* to digesting food and drink can, of course, be extended much further. We can think of mental *indigestion* arising from various conditions and environments. We can think of some *ailments* which can be caused by exposure to adverse kinds of information or inappropriate amounts of information, or failure to *digest* caused by poor reception of feedback or even total lack of feedback. Too much of one kind of information may be bad for us. Low-quality information can't be good for us. Incomplete processing of important information decreases the amount of *making sense* we achieve.

4 What keeps learners going, when the going is tough?

Just about everyone to whom I have posed question 4 has no difficulty in thinking of something they did learn successfully, but didn't actually *want* to learn at the time. Often they are now glad that they did succeed – whatever it was has proved worthwhile in the long run. The things people have learned in this way include just about everything imaginable, for example:

• swimming
• driving
• cooking
• ironing
• keyboard skills.

Moreover, all sorts of academic learning come into this category for many learners, not least:

- statistics
- calculus
- thermodynamics
- critical theory
- counterpoint

and so on.

But what then keeps learners going, when they don't really *want* to learn something? People's answers to the second part of the question reveal at least three factors.

- Some learners are kept going by strong support and encouragement. Such support often comes from teachers or tutors, but also from mentors, friends, family and just about anyone. In a large group, however, it is usually only about one in 10 people who attribute their 'being kept going' to strong support and encouragement. For these people, that support is indeed critical, and without such support they probably would not have succeeded – or would have taken much longer to succeed. This has implications for the feedback we give learners on their work. It is all too easy for carelessly phrased feedback to stop such learners in their tracks.
- Rather more learners are kept going by something which at first sight seems rather negative – not wanting to be found lacking, or not wanting to be humiliated, or wanting to prove to other people that they can indeed do it – sometimes to people who may have implied that they did not expect them to succeed. Some learners need to prove to *themselves* that they can succeed – they take ownership of the challenge and put everything into meeting the challenge head on. The implications of feedback are more profound when learners don't want to be seen to fail, however. Any critical feedback can all too easily stop them in their tracks, and we need to be particularly careful with the wording of feedback when they have not yet accomplished something. In practice, this range of 'negative' drivers of learning is surprisingly common – about one in three learners seem to be kept going by not wanting to be seen to fail.
- The majority of learners – six out of 10 – however give different accounts of what kept them going when they didn't actually *want* to learn something. The common factor is 'need'. People say 'I kept going because I needed to become able to do it' or 'it was a necessary step in the pathway I was heading along' or 'I needed this to open the door to what I really *wanted* to do' and so on. But it's not just about 'need', it's usually about people accepting *ownership* of the need. This is all perfectly *rational* of course. Learners who take ownership of a particular *need* to learn are quite robust – they are not easily stopped, even by critical feedback when they get things wrong.

Five factors underpinning successful learning

From people's answers to these four questions, the following five factors can be seen to be involved in successful learning.

- *Wanting* to learn. We could call this 'intrinsic motivation' but no one has yet used these words in answer to any of the questions. Such language may *mean* the same, but remains cold, remote and academic-sounding. Everyone knows what a 'want' is, and that if the 'want' to learn is powerful enough, success is likely to follow.
- *Needing* to learn – or, to put it more precisely, *taking ownership* of the need to learn. This could be called 'extrinsic motivation' but again learners don't use this sort of language when describing what kept them going when the going was difficult.
- *Learning by doing* – practice, experience, having a go, repetition, trial and error. This fits well with all that has been said about 'experiential learning', but includes both 'concrete experience' and 'active experimentation' which in practice overlap so much with each other that in my opinion it is not wise to think of them separately, and much more satisfactory to think of them all simply as learning by doing.
- *Learning through feedback* – other people's reactions, confirmation, praise, compliments and simply seeing the results. Constructive critical feedback helps too, particularly in the context of learning by trial and error. Feedback, of course, is directly connected to everything under the 'learning-by-doing' banner. The quicker the feedback the better it helps learning.
- *Making sense of things* – or *'digesting'*. This process is perhaps the most important in most learning situations. This is about 'getting one's head round it' or 'the light dawning' or 'gaining understanding' and so on. But this is very firmly linked to any or all of the other factors in the list above. For example, *feedback* plays a vital part in helping most people make sense of the results of their *learning by doing*. If there was already a strong *want* to learn, it is not surprising that the *making sense* is catalysed dramatically. Even if there is only a distinct *need* to learn, *making sense* is aided.

So how do these five factors work together?

It has already been argued that they all affect each other. They don't just follow on from each other in a particular order, nor are they necessarily *different* stages of an ongoing process. My argument is that they all affect each other, and all occur more or less simultaneously. One way of thinking about this is to imagine them as ripples on a pond, bouncing backwards and forwards and interacting with each other in the same way as ripples do when a pebble falls into a pond.

Imagine that initially the water on the surface of the pond is mirror-smooth. Then a 'pebble' falling into the pond starts the water rippling. The energy to start learning happening can arise from *wanting* to learn. It can also arise from *needing* to learn. Better still, both may be involved. When learners really want to – *and* need to – learn, it is very likely that some learning will take place. See Figure 2.1.

Figure 2.1 Wanting to learn and/or needing to learn starting the 'ripple'

But how often do we know that we *want* to do something – or indeed *need* to do something – but we don't actually get round to it? All too easily, if we do nothing more, the *want* or *need* just fades away. We could think of this as the pond smoothing itself out again as if nothing had happened. However strong the *want* or *need* to learn may be, nothing tangible happens unless some *learning by doing* happens next. This can take many forms – practice, trying something out, experimenting, trial and error, repetition, application and so on. Figure 2.2 illustrates this.

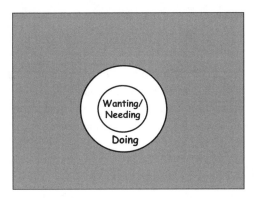

Figure 2.2 Learning continuing by doing – practice, repetition, trial and error

However, just *doing* something is no guarantee that learning is happening. For example, I often talk to learners coming out of other people's classes, and ask them about what they feel has happened during the last hour or so. They often say that they have *enjoyed* the last hour, and feel inspired and empowered to go on learning whatever it was. But all too often when I ask them to tell me a little about what they learned during the session, their replies are along the following lines: 'Sorry, I haven't actually *read* it yet, I've just taken down the notes, or collected the hand-outs' and so on. In other words, they've got the *information* but they haven't yet really started on converting it into their own knowledge.

Put bluntly, they've been wasting their time during the session. They may have been *taking* notes, but often without even thinking about what they were writing down. They've been copying things down from the screen or board, and copying things down verbatim that the teacher or lecturer said, but without thinking about what the meaning was. There has been precious little *making sense* going on. Some-times they have been far too busy trying to capture all the information and they have not even had time to try to make sense of what they have been writing. Now if they had been *making* notes rather than *taking* notes, things might have been much better and they would then be able to tell me a lot about what had been going on in their minds during the session.

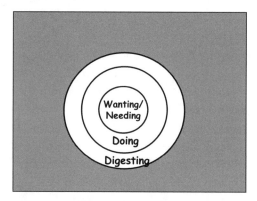

Figure 2.3 Learning continuing with digesting or making sense of what has been done

So for effective learning to be taking place, *doing* needs to be accompanied by *mak-ing sense* or *digesting*, as illustrated in Figure 2.3. Learners need to be *processing* infor-mation and turning it into their own knowledge, not just capturing information.

But how can learners know that they've *made sense* of the subject matter they have met? It's one thing to *feel* that they've made sense of it, but another thing to *know* that they've made sense of it. That's where *feedback* comes in. If they have been getting a lot of feedback on their thinking *during* a teaching session or while working through learning resource materials, they are in a much better position to know whether they've got their heads round the subject matter that has been the content of the session.

Feedback from whom? The lecturer or teacher of course, but also from each other, and from comparing their own thinking with what's on handout materials and other learning resources associated with the session.

The feedback helps them to *make sense* of their own *learning by doing*. The feedback helps them to digest the information they have been processing, and turn it into a start towards building their own knowledge from it. The feedback also clarifies the *purpose* of the information – for example, by linking it to the frame of reference provided by the intended learning outcomes for the session. Feedback allows learners to see *why* an element of learning will be useful to them or relevant to them. It helps them to gain a sense of ownership of what they *need* to learn. If they already *wanted* to learn it, feedback may confirm that they have succeeded or help them find out what they still need to do to achieve the intended outcome. See Figure 2.4.

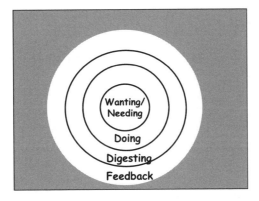

Figure 2.4 Feedback flowing in from the outside

In many ways, feedback is perhaps the most important of these factors underpinning successful learning. Thinking of ripples on a pond as a metaphor, we can imagine the feedback ripples bouncing back towards the middle of the learning ripple, strengthening the *making sense* process, causing more *doing* to occur, clarifying the *need* and, when constructive and helpful, enhancing the *want* to continue learning. Without feedback, much less *making sense* is likely to occur – perhaps none at all.

Making learning happen by addressing the five factors

It is useful to think of these five factors as continuously affecting each other, not just in a particular sequence, but simultaneously and concurrently, just as ripples bounce backwards and forwards on a pond. More importantly, all five of these processes are tangible and easily understood by teachers and learners alike. However, perhaps the real breakthrough is that these five factors can be addressed and harnessed both by teachers and by learners themselves.

As teachers, we can set out to:

- enhance or initiate the *want* to learn
- clarify the *need* to learn, and help learners to take ownership of this need

- cause learners to *learn by doing* – practice, trial and error, repetition and so on
- help learners to *make sense* of what they are learning, rather than just store information for later processing that may never happen
- cause learners to receive *feedback* on what they do, and on what they think about what they have done, and so on.

Several parts of this book refer to much more detail of what we can do to make learning happen in learners' minds.

'Look – no teacher!'

Learners, too, can be involved in taking charge of how these five factors work for them. In my work with learners developing study skills, I encourage them to:

- explore their own motivation, seeking good reasons which will fuel their *want* to learn – in other words, building their own rationale for *why* they are learning and what they want to *become* as a result of their learning
- clarify exactly what they *need* to learn – in other words, identify exactly what they need to become able to do as a result of their learning, taking ownership of the real purpose of the intended learning outcomes involved
- recognize that *learning by doing* is how it all happens in practice, encouraging them to put their energy into practice, repetition, trial and error and so on
- accept that *making sense* of what is being learned is important, and thereby trying harder to *digest* information, selecting from it the really useful parts, rather than just collecting and attempting to store as much information as possible
- make the most of *feedback* on their learning from all possible sources – from each other, from teachers or trainers, from books and articles, and from anyone else who can give them feedback on their actions, their evidence, their *making sense* and so on.

Learners find it perfectly understandable that the actions listed above all affect and enhance each other, and that any combination or, indeed, all of the actions can be happening at any instant during their learning.

Since learners themselves can take control of all these factors and develop them for themselves, it is not surprising just how much learning takes place without any teaching, training, instructing or tutoring processes. The phrase 'self-taught' is in widespread use, often in contexts where particular people have reached outstanding levels of achievement without teaching interventions. It could often be said that the people concerned have simply found their own ways of mastering how they learn, and have developed their own ways to address the factors described above.

Imagine you yourself needed to learn something new, and there was no one to help you to learn it. Imagine you found yourself in a library, surrounded by books, articles, videos, web access and so on – in other words adrift in a sea of information about the topic. This taxes our imagination rather weakly, because most people have been exactly there! What do we do about it? What works is to start *processing* all that information – finding out what the important parts really are, finding out what they mean and rearranging the information in ways where we can handle it. We learn by doing – practice, repetition, trial and error. We reduce the vast sea of information down to manageable proportions – summarizing it. We try to get feedback on how our learning is going. We gradually digest and make sense of the information.

Perhaps, therefore, in our bid to make learning happen in post-compulsory education, we need to be spending much more time helping learners to see how learning really happens. I firmly believe, of course, that we should be starting to help people to be in control of their own learning long before they reach post-compulsory education. Developing learners' control of their learning is already happening under a variety of labels – key skills, transferable skills and so on – but, possibly because we so often use the word 'skills' for such things, people don't yet quite realize that these are exactly the 'skills' which underpin even the most sophisticated levels of knowledge or understanding. And perhaps the most important outcome of any element of learning is that of becoming a better *learner* bit by bit.

But what can we do if there isn't a want, and if learners are not even conscious of a need?

Partly as a result of policies to increase participation in post-compulsory education, many groups of learners nowadays contain at least some learners who don't really *want* to learn anything at a given moment in time, and who may also be quite oblivious of any real *need* to put in the effort to learn something. We can try to initiate a *want* but that can be an uphill struggle. We may, however, be able to convince at least some of the 'unwilling' learners that they have a *need*. One of the most useful ways of approaching this task is to remind ourselves that we may need to convince learners of the benefits which will accrue when they have put in some effort to achieve some learning.

When faced with an array of disinterested, bored-looking faces in a class, it can be worth asking ourselves 'What station am I broadcasting on just now?' The most appropriate one is 'WIIFM' I sometimes suggest to staff – 'what's in it for me?' In other words, we need to try to help our students to take ownership of the *need* to learn, and spelling out the benefits they will derive from having learned something successfully can sometimes win them round. We can point ahead to:

- what they will be able to do when they have learned something successfully
- what doors this may open for them in their future lives and careers
- how learning this bit will make the next bit achievable

and so on.

But even these tactics leave some learners unmotivated, especially if they are there against their will in the first place. So what else can we try?

Experience suggests that the best approach is to get them *doing* something. Choose something that:

- does not take long
- is interesting in its own right
- can be linked back at least in some way to a relevant intended learning outcome
- will stretch them a bit, but not intimidate them
- may win them over to the idea of doing something more very soon.

This is illustrated in Figure 2.5.

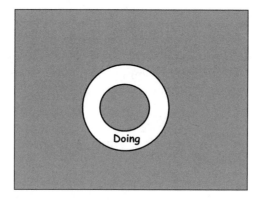

Figure 2.5 Starting the whole process with learning by doing

Then, as soon as possible, get them *making sense* of what they have been doing by getting them to compare with each other, argue, discuss, debate – in other words, deepen their learning through feedback and digesting, as shown in Figure 2.6.

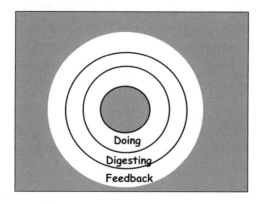

Figure 2.6 Following doing by feedback and digesting

If they enjoyed the episode of learning by doing, found that making sense of it was interesting too and liked gaining and giving feedback about it, the ripple can 'bounce back' right to the centre and alert them to the *need* they have now addressed. In other words, we can help them to realize that the small increment of learning they have just done links to something worthwhile and relevant to them. The more they enjoyed it, the more likely they are to be willing to engage in the next element of learning by doing – in other words, they now have at least some degree of *wanting* to continue learning, as illustrated in Figure 2.7.

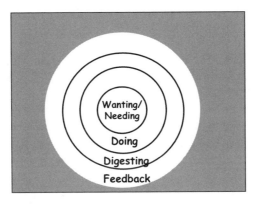

Figure 2.7 The 'want' or the 'need' now present

Thinking further about *teaching*

I'd like you to think back to the very first time you taught some particular topic. Then I'd like you to decide your own response to the following question: 'Did you understand the topic a lot better *after* you taught it that first time, than *before* you taught it that first time?' I've now asked thousands of teachers this question, and the vast majority replied in the affirmative – usually strongly so. We can interpret this as evidence for the process *teaching* yielding high learning pay-off for teachers. We can also think of this as a further ripple in the model discussed so far, as shown in Figure 2.8.

The old cyclic models of learning did not really lend themselves to demonstrating the full power of learning through teaching. Looking at it as a further ripple in the model in Figure 2.8, however, it can be seen *why* we learn so much when we teach – and particularly when we teach anything for the *first* time.

- We gain vast amounts of *feedback* as we teach. All the eyes in a classroom or lecture theatre are feedback to us. All the work our learners do give us feedback – everything they do successfully as a result of our teaching and their learning is feedback to us; even more so, all the mistakes they make are further feedback to us. It is not surprising that all this feedback helps us to deepen our own learning while we teach.

- We're *digesting* ourselves all the time we teach. How often have you found yourself, while in the middle of explaining something to learners, *making sense* of it as you go? It is often halfway through the process of explaining things to other people that the real meaning dawns in the mind of the explainer.
- We're also *doing* when we teach. We're not only learning by doing things ourselves, but we're learning by getting other people doing things too. So teaching is full of experiential learning for us, let alone for our learners.
- We're addressing the *need* as we teach. We are trying to help learners to see the point of what they're learning. We're trying to help them to see what it's for, what it will do for them and where it fits in to the bigger picture. We're trying to convince them that the intended learning outcomes are for them, not just for us.
- And we're confronting the *want* all the time we teach. More acutely, often we're confronting the *lack of want* as we teach, and using all our skills to try to 'warm up' learners so that they take ownership of the need to learn *and* want to learn as well.

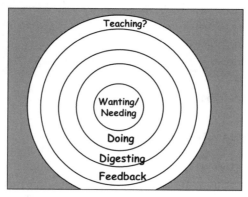

Figure 2.8 Teaching: another ripple?

It therefore should not surprise us how much we learn as we teach. And particularly that *first* time we try to teach something, we're plotting our own course in uncharted territory regarding *how* we explain things to learners, *what* we get them to do, *how* we help them to get feedback, and so on.

If teaching is so good in terms of learning pay-off for us, the obvious question is 'should we be getting our learners themselves to maximize their learning pay-off through teaching?' My answer is 'Definitely!' Imagine, for example, a maths lesson, where the teacher has explained a proof or derivation to the extent that a third of the learners in the room have seen the light. That is the time, I argue, for the teacher to stop, and get the learners into threes, each containing one who has seen the light and can now *do* it, and two who haven't yet seen the light and can't yet do it. Then get the one who can do it to talk the other two through until they too can do it. When one does this, the *explainers* remember it for ever! It's one of the deepest learning experiences there is, to see the light about something, then within minutes, talk a couple of fellow human beings through it until they too can do it. The explainers are benefiting from the high learning pay-off associated with teaching.

The 'explainees' are having a good deal too. They are *now* having it explained to them by someone who remembers how the light dawned. For us as teachers, all too often we've known things for so long that we've forgotten how the light dawned that vital first time round. Perhaps the moral is that we are better able to teach things that we can clearly remember *not* understanding? If it seems that we've always understood something, we probably are not the best person to try to teach it to others.

Are there any more 'ripples'?

I think there is one more important ripple – *assessing*.

Let me ask you another question. 'Thinking again back to that first time you taught a particular topic, did you understand it even better *after* marking the first pile of learners' work after that teaching element?' Again, most people agree that this was indeed the case. When we mark that *first* chunk of learners' work, we find out several things – and very quickly:

• We find out all the mistakes that we never imagined anyone would make.
• We discover the different ways in which individual learners have made their own sense of whatever it was.
• We gain a great deal of feedback about how to go about teaching the same thing next time round, to minimize the mistakes learners will make and maximize their learning pay-off.

We can think of the act of *assessing* as causing all the other ripples to strengthen in our own learning of what we're assessing, as in Figure 2.9.

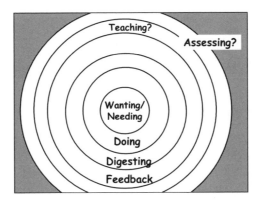

Figure 2.9 Learning being further deepened by assessing

• We're getting a great deal of feedback on how our learners' learning has gone.
• We're finding out a lot about how our teaching has gone, and what to do to make it better next time.

- We're continuing to make sense both of the topic, and of other people's disasters and triumphs as they learn the topic.
- We're learning by doing yet again – this time particularly by applying criteria and designing feedback for learners about their achievements and their problems.
- We're gaining yet more information about their *need* to learn, and their *want* to learn.

In short, the whole process deepens our own learning every time we assess learners' work, but particularly those first few times we engage in the process, where we find out a great deal very rapidly.

Once more, we can ask 'if the process of *assessing* yields such a high learning pay-off, should we be causing *learners* to assess rather than just assessing their work for them?' I believe that we should indeed do so. Causing learners to self-assess their own work leads to deepening their learning in ways which just don't happen if we do it all for them. Moreover, causing learners to peer-assess each others work achieves even more:

- They may get a great deal more feedback than we ourselves would have been able to give them.
- They may find it easier to take feedback from a fellow learner than from figures of authority such as teachers or tutors.
- They deepen their own learning by applying assessment criteria to fellow learners' work.
- They find out about things that other learners did better than they did themselves.
- They see mistakes that they themselves avoided making, and increase their awareness of what to avoid doing in future.

Once learners are convinced of the value of self- and peer-assessment, it can become one of our strongest teaching tactics to set this up and facilitate it. However, there are always some learners who will argue 'this is *your* job, not mine' or 'you're paid to do this, not me!' We therefore have to work hard sometimes to convince learners that the act of assessing is one of the best ways to deepen their own learning, and a useful pathway towards their own success and achievement.

In at the deep end?

We explored earlier how *doing* can start off the whole process, when there isn't a *want* or a *need*. What about *teaching* and *assessing*? Every teacher has tales to tell of how quickly they learned things they had previously never encountered when they were plunged in at the deep end and given a new topic to teach at short notice. This can be very frightening, but it often works surprisingly well. We can easily examine the situation and draw out that there is indeed a great deal of *learning by doing and trial and error* in teaching a new subject, and a great deal of *feedback* gathered in action. This in turn causes a lot of *digesting* or *making sense* and so on.

Similar arguments can be applied to *assessing*. Suppose you were appointed as an examiner for a major examining body, and your first big pile of exam scripts included one or two topics that were quite new to you – a scary prospect. However, many examiners report that this has happened to them quite often, though they would have been wary of admitting this to a Chief Examiner at the time! Nevertheless, the act of applying assessment criteria to other people's evidence of *doing* (even when that 'doing' is just writing things down in exam halls) causes accelerated *making sense* to occur. Those unfamiliar elements of the syllabus may take considerably more time and energy to mark, but where is all that extra energy going – into *digesting*.

This flexibility is perhaps the most significant aspect of a way of thinking about learning which allows the process to begin at quite different starting points. That said, I would hesitate to suggest that as teachers or trainers our approach to making learning happen should be intentionally to drop learners into the deep end of the pond! However, we would do no harm in alerting them to the fact that they can indeed survive and prosper when they unexpectedly find themselves in these deeper waters.

So where does 'understanding' come in?

Earlier in this book, I've suggested that the word 'understand' is not a particularly useful one for various reasons – especially that it's unsuitable as a key word when we express intended learning outcomes. However, perhaps it's the next ripple? Please see Figure 2.10.

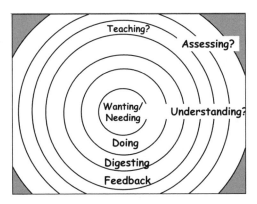

Figure 2.10 'Understanding' at last?

It can be argued that one never really *understands* something till one has learned it, then taught it, then assessed it.

In other words, *understanding* something can perhaps be regarded as the cumulative effect of:

- knowing what it's for – identifying and clarifying the *need* – taking ownership of the intended learning outcome
- *wanting* to achieve the learning outcome
- all that *doing* – practice, trial and error, repetition, teaching, assessing
- all the *feedback* obtained when learning, when teaching and when assessing
- all the *making sense* or *digesting* which accompanies learning in the first place, then explaining and teaching, then assessing.

The value of 'time out'

But *understanding* does not usually just 'stop'. As we continue to teach something over the years, continue to assess learners' work on it and continue to refine our teaching through all the feedback we get in these processes, it is not surprising that our own understanding continues to deepen. However, even this is not as straightforward as it seems. For example, if we just continue teaching and assessing, we get to a certain level in our own understanding. But if we move on to different things for a year or two and *then* revisit the original topic in our teaching and assessing, we are often surprised at how much *more* we feel that we now understand it. We could think of this as 'different' ripples in our own learning adding to 'previous' ones – or the whole pond becoming more agitated. It is not surprising that industrious teachers sometimes feel that they are learning so much that it's almost like becoming seasick – a good excuse to laze on a beach somewhere to recharge our batteries now and then!

A 'slice' of the pond?

We've now looked at the five factors underpinning successful learning, and the additional ways in which teaching and assessing can increase learning pay-off. But what about the documentation – the paperwork associated with some of these processes?

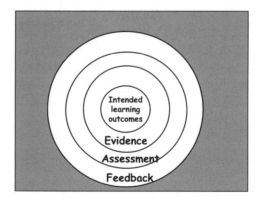

Figure 2.11 A cross-section of the pond?

We can think of intended learning outcomes as right at the centre of the picture, as in Figure 2.11. These should define the *need* to learn. Better still, if the outcomes can be designed in such a way that learners find them attractive, we may even manage to link them more strongly to their *want* to learn.

Learning by doing: this becomes *evidence*. This evidence can take many forms:

- written assignments done by learners – essays, reports, problem sheets and so on
- practical work – laboratories, studios, fieldwork, work-based learning and so on
- written test and exam answers
- performances, interviews, presentations, discussions, debates and so on.

The *making sense* or *digesting*: the extent to which these processes have taken place needs to link to our assessment criteria, defining the expected standards of achievement of the intended learning outcomes we are aiming towards.

Feedback: this should help learners to see to what extent their *evidence* in all its different forms has demonstrated their achievement of the *intended learning outcomes* to the standards specified by the *assessment criteria*. This can be regarded as one way of visualizing what Biggs (2003) means by 'constructive alignment' of the curriculum.

But even this can be seen to be an oversimplification. What about the *emergent* learning outcomes, as well as the *intended* ones? In just about everything we do as human beings, there are emergent outcomes as well as intended ones. Sometimes the emergent ones turn out to be even more important than the intended ones. For example, the emergent learning outcomes associated with teaching and assessing can be thought of in terms of all those *extra* things which link to these respective processes, as discussed above.

So what about *assessment* of the emergent learning outcomes? We can't really do this! This would be unfair. These are not part of the overt targets – even when they are important and desirable. And besides, the emergent learning outcomes are going to be different for different learners. But we can still give learners *feedback* on their *evidence* of achievement of their own emergent learning outcomes, alongside giving them feedback on the extent to which their evidence demonstrates their achievement of the *intended* learning outcomes. It would be tragic to refrain from congratulating learners on particular aspects of their achievement, just because these aspects weren't part of the picture as defined by our curriculum.

How well do learners know how to use the intended learning outcomes?

I've included a self-assessment checklist which you can give to learners (or better still, fine-tune and adapt for your own learners) to help them get a sense of how well they're using your intended learning outcomes. In practice, the reflection that such a checklist can start off may alert learners to the fact that they *can* actually make good use of the outcomes.

Putting learning outcomes to work

Please tick one or more of the columns for each row, as appropriate.	This is what I do.	I would like to do this, but do not manage to.	I don't think this necessary.	This just is not possible for me.	I'll try to do this in future.
1 I locate the intended learning outcomes in my course documentation.					
2 I already use the intended learning outcomes as a frame of reference for my studying.					
3 I find it easy to work out exactly what the intended learning outcomes mean in practice.					
4 I carefully work out exactly what I'm supposed to become able to *do* to show my achievement of each learning outcome.					
5 I keep the intended learning outcomes to hand, so I can see how each study element relates to them.					
6 I know how to link learning outcomes to assessment, and to what I need to be able to do in assignments and exam questions to show I've achieved them.					
7 I find it useful when tutors give me feedback about the extent to which I've demonstrated my achievement of each learning outcome involved in an assignment.					
8 I ask for clarification when I'm not sure about the standards I need to meet in the context of an intended learning outcome.					
9 I discuss the meaning of intended outcomes with fellow students, helping me to get a better idea about which are the really important outcomes.					
10 I've made sure that the intended learning outcomes for each lecture are included in or with my notes.					
11 I've checked how well I reckon I've already achieved each of the intended learning outcomes, and marked these decisions against the outcomes for future reference.					
12 When I can't find out exactly what the intended learning outcomes are, I design some myself and check with tutors and fellow students whether I've made a good attempt at this.					

Conclusions

The five main factors underpinning successful learning, as developed in this chapter, form an agenda for much of the rest of this book. Their strength lies in their simplicity – at least in terms of the language we can use to describe them. This language is easily shared by teachers and learners alike. But the strength of this way of thinking about learning also lies in its complexity – the way the factors all interact with each other and don't need to occur in a set order or pattern. And perhaps the most significant factor is that any or all of these factors can be going on at any instant in our learning – and we can choose to address any or all of them quite intentionally at any moment in our teaching.

3

Beyond learning styles?

I referred in Chapter 1 to the work of Coffield et al. (2004) on 'Learning styles and pedagogy in post-16 learning'. Their review was quite critical of the work of Kolb's 'Learning Styles Inventory' (LSI) for example, as follows:

> Kolb clearly believes that learning takes place in a cycle and that learners should use all four phases of that cycle to become effective. Popular adaptations of his theory (for which he is not, of course, responsible) claim, however, that all four phases should be tackled and in order. The manual for the third version of the LSI is explicit on this point: 'You may begin a learning process in any of the four phases of the learning cycle. Ideally, using a well-rounded learning process, you would cycle through all the four phases. However, you may find that you sometimes skip a phase in the cycle or focus primarily on just one' (Kolb 1999, 4). But if Wierstra and de Jong's (2002) analysis, which reduces Kolb's model to a one-dimensional bipolar structure of reflection versus doing, proves to be accurate, then the notion of a learning cycle may be seriously flawed.

Coffield et al. also reviewed in detail the strengths and weaknesses of various learning styles instruments and models. Of the popular Honey and Mumford work in the area, particularly the 'Learning Styles Questionnaire' (LSQ), they said:

> Perhaps the more fundamental problem is the implicit assumption that one instrument of 80 statements can capture all the complexities and the multi-faceted nature of learning as well as the cycle of learning. In addition, Honey and Mumford based their LSQ on Kolb's model, but because they found its bipolar structure untenable, they designed the LSQ so that the style preferences are aligned to the stages in the learning cycle. They have not, however, produced an alternative to Kolb's bipolar theory. For all these criticisms, the LSQ remains very popular as a self-development tool with practitioners, is used extensively – for instance, by industrial trainers and FE tutors – and can now be completed online.

Coffield et al. go so far as to ask:

> Should research into learning styles be discontinued, as Reynolds has argued? In his own words: 'Even using learning style instruments as a convenient way of introducing the subject [of learning] generally is hazardous because of the superficial attractions of labelling and categorizing in a world suffused with uncertainties' (Reynolds, 1997: 128).

This chapter is built around a new questionnaire aiming to put learners in the driving seat of the vehicle which is their own learning. The 100 statements in the questionnaire are intended to be seen as learner-friendly language, rather than remote pedagogic terminology. The intention is to allow people to reflect on their own individual ways of learning, and their preferences and dislikes.

More importantly, the instrument is not designed just to be a one-off snapshot of people's learning at a given moment in time, but something that learners can return to and revisit their entries, and see how they change as their experience of learning widens and develops. This allows them to gain control of their learning and steer it in particular directions based on experience, and to accelerate particular processes which seem likely to be productive and relevant, and indeed to put the brakes on regarding aspects of their learning which are not proving useful or enjoyable.

Publishing this questionnaire in this particular book, my aim is to make it freely available in the public domain, and I hope that people will feel free to photocopy the questionnaire pages and put them to use with learners. More importantly, perhaps, I hope that people will feel free to use the questionnaire as a starting point and fine-tune the statements to the contexts of particular learning situations, and improve the statements and make them more relevant to known cross-sections of the learning community. Moreover, it will be even more worthwhile to design questions which are directly relevant to the particular subject areas or disciplines which learners are studying, particularly if the main intention remains to use the device as a catalyst to giving feedback to learners about how best to adapt their approaches to meet the needs of the discipline concerned.

As you will see from the decision-making columns, this questionnaire is not just another of the 'true–false' instruments. The problem with those is that, more often than not, a given statement is neither completely true nor completely false for an individual learner in a specified context. When forced then to make a 'true–false' or 'yes–no' decision, the validity of the decisions are compromised and learners end up using a 'surface' rather than 'deep' approach to their decision-making. People using drafts of this questionnaire have often reported that it takes them a lot longer than they thought it would, because they are pondering quite deeply whether a statement is 'very like me', 'often like me', 'sometimes like me' or 'not at all like me'. This range of choices helps respondents not to feel trapped by particular statements or forced to make compromised choices.

	Statements	(a) This is very like me.	(b) This is often like me.	(c) This is sometimes like me.	(d) This is not at all like me.
1	I'm really eager to get everything I can out of anything I'm learning.				
2	I always put everything I've got into anything I'm learning.				

In effect, the questionnaire sets out not to be a 'learning styles' instrument, but more a vehicle for allowing learners to explore their *feelings* about a range of aspects of their learning. This helps people actually to work out – perhaps for the first time – what they actually feel about various factors about their 'want' to learn, and the extent to which they have ownership of the need to learn and the learning targets or intended outcomes associated with their learning. Many people who have filled in draft versions of this questionnaire have reported that they thought more about their learning in doing so than at any time before, and indeed found out a lot about how they learned just from making decisions about the various statements in the questionnaire. Often they have said that they found out about things which had been going on quite unconsciously in their learning, and that making sense of these things changed how they were likely to approach the next element of their learning. In other words, the questionnaire can be regarded as a formative device rather than merely a summative one. It is intended to help people to make sense of how they learn, rather than just to give them a snapshot of their learning at a particular point in time or on a particular day when they are in a given frame of mind about their learning at a specific stage.

Looking at the five different sections of the questionnaire, you will notice that there are several statements which overlap between sections, and have a bearing on one or more of the *other* underpinning factors and not just on the factors overtly referred to in the section headings. For example, the statements numbered 1 to 40 sometimes relate both to the self-motivation (or 'wanting') dimensions of learning and to the 'taking ownership of the learning need' dimensions. Similarly, several statements in the 41–100 sections relate to more than one of 'learning by doing', 'learning through feedback' and 'making sense of what is being learned' dimensions.

The language used in this questionnaire aims to be learner-friendly throughout, and avoids relating to particular associations with formal learning, college-based learning, formal training and so on. This is so that they can explore how their minds work, rather than just how they respond to particular learning contexts, environments or scenarios. That said, the concept of this kind of questionnaire can be regarded as a starting point rather than an end in itself. For example, the idea of devising statements and decision-making processes can easily be extended to specific teaching-learning scenarios, and separate sets of statements can be devised relating to such dimensions as:

- lectures
- reading
- e-learning
- group work
- work-based learning
- practical work
- distance learning
- supported self-study
- project work
- action learning
- research

and so on.

No hidden agendas!

The questionnaire published in this book is *overtly* based on the five factors under-pinning successful learning as expounded earlier in the book. It is deliberately *not* based on any of the specific pedagogies of learning available in much of the scholarly literature about how human beings learn, not least because of serious criticisms of many of these pedagogies – for example, that at least some of them are based on rel-atively narrow research with particular kinds of learners in specific (often rather aca-demic) contexts. I played with – but soon rejected – the idea of mixing up the respective statements into a 'blind' list and then allowing the five factors to be linked to learners' responses after the event. In other words, the approach I used is that of no surprises, no hidden agendas and no 'sudden death' diagnosis. My principal rea-son for deciding to make the agenda for each part of the checklist quite overt is that I have no wish to keep learners in the dark about what the respective statements are pointing towards. For example, when they *know* that the agenda may be to do with the extent to which they *want* to learn, they are much more likely to be making sense of their own want to learn when they choose particular columns for their responses. They are much better informed about answers to 'what's going on here?' and 'why is this statement included?' as they make their decisions.

E Making sense of what I'm learning: getting my head round it

	Statements	(a) This is very like me.	(b) This is often like me.	(c) This is sometimes like me.	(d) This is not at all like me.
85	I find that I need other people around me to talk to, to work out whether I've understood something or not.				
88	It really annoys me when I can't get my head round a particular idea.				

This questionnaire is designed to open up further feedback to learners about their decisions. For example, in addition to being a self-evaluation instrument, a great deal of added value can become available when learners gain additional feedback on their decisions from significant others in the context of their own learning, for example, tutors, lecturers, trainers, mentors, fellow learners and so on. Such people can, for example, bring further legitimization to 'not at all like me' decisions, and can help learners to interpret and analyse particular decisions they have made as strengths or weaknesses or opportunities or threats. Even simple comparison of the choices made by a group of learners can lead them into useful discussion of the individual differences in their approaches to learning, and can help them to broaden their own understanding of what learning is all about by comparing their approaches to those of fellow learners. This, of course, is likely to *change* the way they approach their own learning – another example of the intention to use the questionnaire as a formative rather than summative tool.

What's the score?

Most learning styles instruments, whatever their purpose, seem to have been accompanied by scoring schemes of one kind or another. With a formative device which is intended to help learners to reflect on their approaches to learning, and cause them to *change* how they learn, such scoring may be seen as being quite inappropriate. However unwise scoring might be, there is an expectation that some form of diagnosis or feedback will result from adding up some numbers at the end of the exercise, and it is for this reason that I have included a scoring scheme, which in a rough and ready way gives some indication of:

A   The degree and intensity of learners' 'want' to learn – their self-motivation.
B   The extent to which learners feel ownership of their need to learn, and of the targets involved.
C   The extent to which learners feel that practice, trial and error, and repetition helps them to learn.
D   The value which learners derive from a wide range of kinds of feedback they may experience.
E   The ways in which learners feel that they make sense of what they are learning, and develop their understanding of what they learn.

This attempt at scoring could be considered to be more valid than when simple 'yes–no' or 'true–false' decisions are made, in that in this questionnaire there are the four options available for each statement, and respective scores of 3, 2, 1 and 0 are available for each statement. However, I must point out that there remains a serious flaw with even this philosophy of scoring, in that one particular statement may be much more significant than another in the context of an individual's own learning, and that to afford each statement the same scoring range is clearly a gross over-simplification. In other words, I have serious reservations about the numbers which result from scoring *any* instrument exploring how people learn, but believe that the approach is a little less flawed when the scoring is not just 'black and white' but includes two shades of grey as well.

There is, however, one distinct benefit of making scoring an option. This is that for some learners (and, indeed, for some facilitators of learning) there is increased likelihood that the whole process of filling in and reflecting upon the agendas addressed by the questionnaire will be completed, rather than started and then dropped. In other words, the scoring can be a useful end point, even when the journey is much more important than the destination.

It is therefore for these reasons alone that I have included a table showing how the various statements can be scored as the penultimate section, 'To score, or not to score?', in this chapter. As with other aspects of the questionnaire, the scores I have indicated should not be regarded as the *correct* ones for each statement. Indeed, as you will see from the scoring grids, some of the statements could be regarded as not being directly related to the main factors overtly addressed in the particular sections in which they are located, for example, when the question is primarily designed to help learners to reflect on a particular aspect of their learning and, perhaps, gain feedback by comparing their thinking on that aspect with that of fellow learners or of significant others in the context of their learning. Also, sometimes I have allocated the scores in a direction which indicates just one of a number of possible interpretations of the statement concerned. In those cases, the real intention is to enable fruitful discussion between learners, where possible, about the different roles which the particular statements may play in their own learning contexts. 'Why on earth is "very like me" getting a "3" here?' is exactly the sort of discussion starter I am sometimes intending particular elements of the scoring scheme to cause. I would also hope that the distrust of scoring schemes which this particular scheme may foster, might be usefully extended to various existing questionnaires where respondents end up with scores arising from their responses.

I have included at the start of the questionnaire, which follows, a brief explanation of the purposes of the questionnaire and enough detail to let learners know how it is intended to work.

Analyse how *you* learn

There has been serious criticism in recent years of most of the instruments and devices which claim to measure 'learning styles'. Frank Coffield, David Moseley, Elaine Hall and Kathryn Ecclestone (2004) analyse the problems in *Should We Be Using Learning Styles? What Research Has to Say to Practice* (Learning and Skills Research Centre, accessible through www.LSRC.ac.uk).

In *Making Learning Happen* one of my aims is to help learners (and teachers and trainers) get *behind* learning styles, into the factors which underpin successful learning. Different learning styles can merely be regarded as different balances between the strength and influence of these respective factors. In this way, I believe we can all move *beyond* learning styles.

This questionnaire aims to help you to find out more about your own learning – in other words, to become more aware of how it works – and how to make it work better.

The five sections of the questionnaire relate to:

A Wanting to learn: self-motivation
B Needing to learn: taking ownership of the targets
C Learning by doing: practice, trial and error, repetition
D Learning from feedback: other people, scores, marks, grades
E Making sense of what I'm learning: getting my head round it

---

Think of any of the following:

- something you're presently learning
- something you've recently learned
- something you may be about to start learning
- your own ways of learning in general.

In other words, it doesn't matter, as long as it's about how *you* learn and how you *feel* about learning. In the questionnaire which follows, I'm using the word 'programme' to mean a piece of learning. This could be a whole course or, equally, a small bit of learning that has nothing to do with a formal course. So, every time you see the word 'programme', just think of the bit of learning you're thinking about – past, present or future. The questionnaire is written in the present tense, however, so whatever the case try to capture each situation as if you were right in the middle of learning whatever it is, will be or was.

The questionnaire consists of 100 statements, 20 of each grouped more or less around the agendas of the five factors underpinning successful learning mentioned above. There are four columns for you to select;

(a) This is very like me.
(b) This is often like me.
(c) This is sometimes like me.
(d) This is not at all like me.

Sometimes 'this is very like me' may seem to be a good choice relating to a particular statement, but on other occasions the same choice may be felt to be an unsatisfactory one, so don't be tempted just to tick the same column each time. Remember that only *you* know which column is the most appropriate one to tick. Don't just try to tick the ones that you think are the *best* ones to tick. This is *your* questionnaire.

When you've had a go at the questionnaire, read on for a discussion about what it's all about, and various different things you can do to find out more about what your choices entered on the questionnaire may boil down to. This should help you to find out quite a lot about how you yourself learn – and may give you many ideas for possible ways to fine-tune and develop your ways of learning.

A Wanting to learn: self-motivation

	Statements	(a) This is very like me.	(b) This is often like me.	(c) This is sometimes like me.	(d) This is not at all like me.
1	I'm really eager to get everything I can out of anything I'm learning.				
2	I always put everything I've got into anything I'm learning.				
3	When I'm learning something, I'm doing it for me – not just because other people expect me to do it.				
4	I don't worry about what anyone else thinks regarding whether I succeed or not.				
5	I usually get involved in learning things because I've been put onto a learning programme by my boss.				
6	I'm learning because it is expected that I will get myself skilled up in this particular area.				
7	I'm learning because other people I know have done similar programmes, and I want to keep up with them.				
8	I'm doing this programme because other people I know said they found it really useful.				
9	Once I start on learning something, I keep going, even when the going gets tough.				
10	I'm very good at starting things, but I tend to give up on things if I don't like them much.				
11	I'm a finisher! When I start something, I finish it, even if I'm not enjoying it.				
12	I need quite a lot of encouragement to keep me going when I'm learning something new.				
13	I'm perfectly happy learning on my own, and it doesn't matter to me if no one else I know is learning alongside me.				
14	I might find myself rather lonely learning on my own, and prefer other people around me to be learning too.				
15	I'm always learning something or other – life without learning is just not possible for me.				
16	I need to do this programme for my job – it will open up other possibilities for me.				
17	I need to do this programme to escape from my present job – it's my passport to better things.				
18	Learning this programme is a welcome relief from the normal day-to-day business of my work.				
19	I'm doing this programme because I'm really fascinated by the subject material.				
20	I'm doing this programme because it's a challenge to me, and I can't resist challenges.				

B Needing to learn: taking ownership of the targets

	Statements	(a) This is very like me.	(b) This is often like me.	(c) This is sometimes like me.	(d) This is not at all like me.
21	I'm doing this learning because I need it for my job.				
22	I'm doing this programme because it will be useful for my future career.				
23	I find it essential to have clear targets, so that I know all along what I'm aiming to achieve.				
24	I'm doing this programme because I need to keep up with other people around me at work.				
25	I'm doing this programme because I need to keep up with other people around me at home.				
26	My boss told me to do this programme.				
27	Everyone at my place is put on this programme, and it's my turn to do it now.				
28	I'm not actually very keen to learn this programme, but I know that I'll need it.				
29	I'm doing this programme because I have a weak spot, and this will help me to put this right.				
30	I'm actually doing this programme against my wishes, but I've just got to make the best of it.				
31	I'm doing this programme to keep up with someone else who is better at the subject than I am.				
32	I'm doing this programme to prove to other people that I can do it.				
33	I'm doing this programme to prove to myself that I can actually do it.				
34	I really like to know in advance exactly what I'm going to become able to do.				
35	I've started this programme, and I'm the kind of person who finishes what I've started.				
36	Although I need to complete this programme, I may give up if I get bored with it.				
37	Although I need to complete this programme, if I get discouraged I'm quite likely to quit.				
38	I'll be perfectly happy as long as I get by with this programme – I'm not aiming for the skies with it.				
39	This programme is only of limited relevance to me, and I don't expect to get all that much out of it.				
40	This programme is exactly what I need – it could have been designed just for me.				

C Learning by doing: practice, trial and error, repetition

	Statements	(a) This is very like me.	(b) This is often like me.	(c) This is sometimes like me.	(d) This is not at all like me.
41	What works best for me is lots of practice.				
42	I need to do things over and over again to keep them in my mind.				
43	For me, I don't learn much just by looking at a book or handout.				
44	I need to be making my own notes to learn anything really well.				
45	I can look at a piece of paper for ages, but not actually take anything in from it.				
46	I learn most by getting things wrong, then finding out why they were wrong, and trying again till I get them right.				
47	I learn a lot from other people's mistakes, and I try to avoid making the same kinds of mistake.				
48	I don't learn much from listening to teachers or trainers talking about it – I've got to have a go myself to learn.				
49	I like learning at my own pace, rather than when the pace is set by teachers or trainers.				
50	I learn best when I can choose when and where to learn, rather than in fixed places at set times.				
51	I like to learn by myself, with no one around to distract me.				
52	I like the comfort of privacy to make mistakes, and to learn from my mistakes without anyone else seeing them.				
53	I like to press ahead with whatever I'm learning, without going back and polishing up what I've already covered.				
54	I prefer to get one thing really mastered, and don't like to go on to new stuff until I'm sure I've cracked the old stuff.				
55	I'm not at all happy working just with learning materials, I prefer to get my hands dirty and put theories into practice.				
56	I only feel I've learned something when I go away and have a go at it for real.				
57	I really like learning things at a computer, as I can get my head round things better without all the other distractions.				
58	I prefer to learn things with other people rather than sitting on my own.				
59	I never remember what I'm told, but usually remember things I've done.				
60	I only really understand things after I've done them again and again.				

D Learning from feedback: other people, scores, marks, grades

	Statements	(a) This is very like me.	(b) This is often like me.	(c) This is sometimes like me.	(d) This is not at all like me.
61	When I get something right, I really like to be told 'well done'.				
62	When I get something wrong, I like people to explain exactly what was wrong, and what I can do about it.				
63	I don't like to be told I've got something wrong – I'd much rather find out for myself.				
64	When I've had a go at something, I want to find out straight away whether I got it right or not.				
65	Once I've done something, that's it – I'm not particularly bothered to find out whether it was bad or brilliant.				
66	If I have to wait for days to find out how I did, I'm past caring, and don't take much notice of any feedback I get.				
67	I like working with other people around, and comparing notes on how I'm doing with how they're doing.				
68	I find that it's really useful for me to have fellow learners explaining things to me as I learn.				
69	I like there to be a tutor or trainer around – someone to ask, when I don't understand things.				
70	I prefer not to ask people when I'm stuck, but to try everything to sort it all out for myself.				
71	I find I learn a lot myself by explaining things to other people who can't yet get their heads round them.				
72	The first thing I look at when I get marked work back is what score or grade I was given.				
73	I like to find out how I'm doing very soon after I start learning anything.				
74	I prefer to wait till I've finished something before finding out how well I've done – or not.				
75	I learn a lot more when I get face-to-face feedback from people rather than just written comments or emails.				
76	I prefer to forge ahead with the programme, rather than stopping to explore my success with each bit I tried.				
77	When I get things wrong, I want to know why I got them wrong, not just what the right answer might have been.				
78	I prefer to get feedback in writing rather than face to face, to avoid embarrassment.				
79	For me, feedback is the most important thing – I need to know how I'm doing every step of the way.				
80	It really cheers me up every time I get something right, and get this confirmed.				

E Making sense of what I'm learning: getting my head round it

	Statements	(a) This is very like me.	(b) This is often like me.	(c) This is sometimes like me.	(d) This is not at all like me.
81	I'm never really satisfied until I feel that I really understand what I've been learning.				
82	I don't worry too much about whether I understand something or not, as long as I can do what I need to do with it.				
83	I find I only really understand something when I can explain it to other people.				
84	I'm worried that I may be sailing along without understanding what I'm learning.				
85	I find that I need other people around me to talk to, to work out whether I've understood something or not.				
86	When I can't understand something, I tend to get stuck, and can't press on until I've sorted it out.				
87	When I can't understand something, I simply press on, and often the understanding comes along quite soon as I continue learning.				
88	It really annoys me when I can't get my head round a particular idea.				
89	I find that some things have to be lived with for a while before the light really dawns.				
90	My problem with teachers and trainers is that they don't seem to be able to believe that there are some things I just don't understand when they try to explain them.				
91	The advantage of learning with a computer is that it will explain things again and again until I've got my head around them.				
92	Understanding things is overrated! All I want is to be able to be good at doing what I need to do.				
93	I sometimes feel that I understand something, then get disappointed when I realize that I hadn't yet understood it properly.				
94	For me, the light dawns slowly, and only when I'm doing things, rather than reading about them.				
95	I feel really great when the light dawns on something I've been struggling with for ages and ages.				
96	I'm patient with my brain, and don't try to force it to make sense of everything all at once.				
97	I find that one day I've got my head right round something, then next day it's gone again, and I have to start all over again.				
98	For me, something has got to have gone through my brain several times before it really stays there.				
99	I'm worried about how much I forget.				
100	I no longer worry about forgetting things, as next time round it takes far less time to get to grips with them again.				

Providing feedback on respondents' decisions

Another possible way of extending the use of the content of this questionnaire would be to compose feedback responses to each of the choices respondents make. Imagine, for example, that this time the 100 questions were placed on a computer-based learning system (or, better still, online), which 'fired' the questions in random order to learners, who then picked options from 'this is very like me' to 'this is not at all like me' using a mouse or touch-screen system. Feedback responses could be pre-programmed to come up automatically, aiming to deepen learners' thinking about the significance of options they had chosen, and also designed to increase their confidence where some particular aspect of learning did *not* seem to be doing much for them.

These feedback responses would of course be quite different for 'this is very like me' or 'this is not at all like me', with intermediate responses for the 'often' and 'sometimes' options. However, it could be argued that the most important feedback would be for the two more extreme choices, as that is where learners' feelings are most deeply held or their view most clearly defined.

Ideally, these feedback responses would be best if designed in the particular context of a known course or programme of study, where the feedback could relate not only to the processes underpinning successful learning, but also to the subject content. However, some generic feedback could also be useful, and to illustrate the kinds of feedback which may be designed, I have selected a few different options from the questionnaire, and provided indicative feedback responses to one or other of the 'stronger' choices below.

	Statements	(a) This is very like me.	(d) This is not at all like me.
2	I always put everything I've got into anything I'm learning.	Well done – you've clearly got no problems regarding the energy you invest into your learning.	You probably need to see clearly 'what's in it for you' to cause you to invest time and energy into your learning – that's perfectly natural for many people.
5	I usually get involved in learning things because I've been put onto a learning programme by my boss.	This is fine so long as your boss makes sure that you are indeed put onto the learning programmes which are going to be good for you.	So you don't have to wait for your boss to cause you to do some learning – good. Or perhaps you've got a boss who doesn't think enough about the learning which might be good for you – not so good.

	Statements	(a) This is very like me.	(d) This is not at all like me.
10	I'm very good at starting things, but I tend to give up on things if I don't like them much.	You're in good company – it takes a lot to keep going when learning things we don't like. However, sometimes it's worth it – make sure you know how valuable your learning might prove before you give up on it.	So you're the sort of person who finishes what you start? This can be really useful, but make sure you don't just end up spending too much time and energy finishing things which are not proving valuable to you.
20	I'm doing this programme because it's a challenge to me, and I can't resist challenges.	This is fine, as long as you continue to find your learning sufficiently challenging. But might you give up if you come to an easier bit that doesn't challenge you?	Yes, now YOU think of a response.
23	I find it essential to have clear targets, so that I know all along what I'm aiming to achieve.	Most people feel that clear targets help them – keep the intended learning outcomes clearly in mind as you learn, and get the most value you can from them.	It can be worth you paying more attention to the targets associated with your learning, to avoid you wasting time and energy on things which are not really important enough to spend time on.
30	I'm actually doing this programme against my wishes, but I've just got to make the best of it.	Sadly, most people have to learn things against their wishes sometimes. However, try to find some good things *you* will get out of your learning too.	Good, you're not trapped learning things just because other people want you to. This may well mean you have strong reasons of your own for spending time and energy on your learning.
38	I'll be perfectly happy as long as I get by with this programme – I'm not aiming for the skies with it.	This is fine if all you need to do is to become reasonably competent with what you learn, and don't need to turn yourself into an expert on the topic concerned.	It's always useful to be aiming as high as you feel comfortable when you're learning something – but don't invest more time and energy than the programme is going to be worth to you in the long run.

	Statements	(a) This is very like me.	(d) This is not at all like me.
40	This programme is exactly what I need – it could have been designed just for me.	You're lucky. Enjoy your learning programme, and make the most of it.	Don't worry, it's a luxury when a learning programme seems absolutely ideal. It doesn't mean that you're not going to be able to succeed, even if the programme seems not quite tuned in to what you need.
42	I need to do things over and over again to keep them in my mind.	Fine – for most people repetition is a very useful part of getting their heads round things – as long as it doesn't just become boring repetition.	You're lucky – most people need at least some repetition to get things firmly in their minds. Keep making sure, however, that things are not in fact slipping away due to lack of practice now and then.
46	I learn most by getting things wrong, then finding out why they were wrong, and trying again till I get them right.	Good – learning through mistakes is indeed a valuable way of learning. The more mistakes you make – at the right time – the more you can learn from them.	Don't underestimate how useful it can be to get things wrong (at the right time) and then learn why they were wrong. This can save you making the same mistakes when it could count against you.
53	I like to press ahead with whatever I'm learning, without going back and polishing up what I've already covered.	This is fine, as long as what you've already covered is indeed staying with you. However, it's worth deliberately checking now and then to make sure things aren't slipping away from you as you press on.	It is indeed useful to go back and make sure things you've already mastered remain with you – that helps to make sure that what you learn *next* will have a solid foundation.
60	I only really understand things after I've done them again and again.	Yes indeed, most people find that repeated practice is the key to developing genuine understanding.	Beware! It's easy to think one understands something, but then find oneself unable to do them for oneself. A bit of practice and repetition can work wonders.

	Statements	(a) **This is very like me.**	(d) **This is not at all like me.**
61	When I get something right, I really like to be told 'well done'.	This is fine – most of us do like a little praise when we've got something right. But make sure that you give *yourself* credit too – don't become too dependent on other people giving you positive feedback.	Don't let praise irritate you. The important thing is to know yourself when you've done something well, and to build upon it as you go further with your learning.
63	I don't like to be told I've got something wrong – I'd much rather find out for myself.	This is understandable, but the danger is that you may not find out for yourself. Better be sure, and use *all* the chances to find out what you do wrong, so you can put these things right as you press on.	Good, all feedback is useful, including when you get things wrong. It can, indeed, take too long to find out for yourself what you get wrong, so make the most of other people's feedback whenever it is available.
70	I prefer not to ask people when I'm stuck, but to try everything to sort it all out for myself.	This is all very well, but it can sometimes be much faster to get people to help you when you're stuck – and can help you to find out *why* you were stuck.	Good, other people can save you a lot of 'banging your head against a brick wall' when you're really stuck.
71	I find I learn a lot myself by explaining things to other people who can't yet get their heads round them.	Yes indeed, this is one of the very best ways of learning new things. Explaining them to other people helps you get your own head firmly round new things.	You may be missing out on a very good way of deepening your own learning – there's nothing better than explaining things to other people to help you get a really good grip on them yourself.
77	When I get things wrong, I want to know why I got them wrong, not just what the right answer might have been.	Absolutely. When you've worked out *why* you got something wrong, you're much less likely to get it wrong ever again.	The trouble is that you may not remember what the right answer was, and it can be really useful to keep in mind *why* you got something wrong to avoid it happening again.

	Statements	(a) This is very like me.	(d) This is not at all like me.
81	I'm never really satisfied until I feel that I really understand what I've been learning.	This is all very well as long as you're able to understand everything you learn. But some things take quite a long time before understanding really dawns, so don't expect this satisfaction straight away every time round.	Good – understanding doesn't always come straight away, and it's useful to be patient enough with your brain to allow understanding to develop in its own time when necessary.
86	When I can't understand something, I tend to get stuck, and can't press on until I've sorted it out.	This can be a problem. Some things take time for the light to dawn, yet the *next* thing might be much easier to understand – and may indeed help the first thing to become clearer. It can often be worth pressing on.	Good, it's useful to press on when you can't understand something, in case the next bit is much more straightforward and throws light in its own way on that difficult earlier bit.
93	I sometimes feel that I understand something, then get disappointed when I realize that I hadn't yet understood it properly.	This is normal. We think we understand something today, only to find out tomorrow that today's understanding wasn't very good anyhow. Understanding usually develops, rather than coming all at once.	It's good not to be disappointed when you find out that you hadn't understood something properly – it's all part of gradually getting your head round things, particularly complex ideas and concepts.
96	I'm patient with my brain, and don't try to force it to make sense of everything all at once.	Good. Human brains don't like to be forced to do anything too fast – continue to give your brain time and opportunity to work at its best.	Don't be cruel to your brain. The user's manual (if there were one) would point out that human brains work best when given time and space to work properly.
98	For me, something has got to have gone through my brain several times before it really stays there.	This is perfectly normal. For most of us, we have to grasp then forget complex things a few times before we get a real grip on them.	Don't be surprised when a complex idea doesn't stick first time before you've really got your head around it – many things need to go through the brain a number of times before we really get a grip on them.

	Statements	(a) This is very like me.	(d) This is not at all like me.
99	I'm worried about how much I forget.	Don't be too worried! The more we forget, the more we learn. It's always much faster to re-learn something you've forgotten twice than something you've only forgotten once – and so on.	Good. Forgetting is a perfectly normal part of learning things. With complex ideas we often need to 'lose' them a few times and re-learn them until they don't slip away so easily again.

Putting learning through feedback to work

You can see from the range of responses given above to 'this is very like me' and 'this is not at all like me', how feedback can be provided to learners who have made their own decisions regarding selected elements from the questionnaire. You can also see how the appropriate feedback responses can be quite different from learners who made the respective choices.

Furthermore, most learners are naturally curious and, even when they pick (for example) a statement as being 'very like me', while looking at any feedback we provide to them on making this choice, they are interested too in what we might have said to them if they'd rated the same statement as being 'not at all like me'. When they get both feedback messages, they are helped to think more deeply both about the meaning of the statement upon which they have made a decision and the decision itself that they have made thereon. So, most importantly, stopping to ponder such feedback helps learners to reflect on the real agendas which the successive statements represent, and to think more deeply about whether their existing approaches are fine as they stand or whether it could be worth fine-tuning their learning techniques to make the most of the various factors underlying the statements in the questionnaire. You are invited to think how best *you* can devise similar feedback responses to many of the other statements in the questionnaire, and indeed to extend the whole picture by adding new statements which are more directly relevant to your own learners' subject matter, and the contexts in which they are learning.

I hope that from these feedback responses you will feel that the scores which can be derived from this questionnaire (and, indeed, other instruments to diagnose learning styles or preferences) are of very limited significance, validity or reliability compared with the deepening of learners' own thinking which is possible by giving them individual and intimate feedback on the underlying factors influencing their approaches to learning in various contexts. It is feedback responses, rather than scores, which enable learners to reflect upon their learning, and on decisions they have made which indicate their own feelings and attitudes about how they learn best – or how they learn unsatisfactorily. This reflection is what enables learners to move in their approaches and attitudes to learning, and to add to their approaches further dimensions they would not even have thought about without having been made to take stock of their learning by taking decisions based upon what they knew about it – or *believed* that they knew about it.

To score, or not to score?

I've already shared my thoughts on the pros and cons of trying to 'add up' the meaning of decisions made about different statements, and particularly the fact that in no way can a bank of such statements be of equal importance or significance.

That said, people *like* to try to use numbers to work out more about the meaning of data, and may engage in deeper thinking about what the data means in their bid to make sense of what the numbers are telling them. It is for this reason that I am including a scoring system. But don't take it too seriously. I may even have deliberately skewed the odd score here and there in the 'wrong' direction, just to keep you on your guard and to minimize the chance that you'll take the scoring dimension too seriously.

Self-evaluation questionnaire scoring grids

A Wanting to learn: self-motivation

	(a)	(b)	(c)	(d)
1	3	2	1	0
2	3	2	1	0
3	3	2	1	0
4	3	2	1	0
5	0	1	2	3
6	0	1	2	3
7	0	1	2	3
8	0	1	2	3
9	3	2	1	0
10	0	1	2	3
11	3	2	1	0
12	0	1	2	3
13	3	2	1	0
14	0	1	2	3
15	3	2	1	0
16	0	1	2	3
17	3	2	1	0
18	0	0	0	0
19	3	2	1	0
20	3	2	1	0

B Needing to learn: taking ownership of the targets

	(a)	(b)	(c)	(d)
21	3	2	1	0
22	3	2	1	0
23	3	2	1	0
24	3	2	1	0
25	3	2	1	0
26	0	1	2	3
27	0	0	0	0
28	3	2	1	0
29	3	2	1	0
30	0	1	2	3
31	0	1	2	3
32	0	1	2	3
33	3	2	1	0
34	3	2	1	0
35	3	2	1	0
36	0	1	2	3
37	0	1	2	3
38	0	1	2	3
39	0	1	2	3
40	3	2	1	0

C Learning by doing: practice, trial and error, repetition

	(a)	(b)	(c)	(d)
41	3	2	1	0
42	3	2	1	0
43	3	2	1	0
44	3	2	1	0
45	3	2	1	0
46	3	2	1	0
47	3	2	1	0
48	3	2	1	0
49	3	2	1	0
50	3	2	1	0
51	0	0	0	0
52	3	2	1	0
53	0	1	2	3
54	0	1	2	3
55	3	2	1	0
56	3	2	1	0
57	0	0	0	0
58	0	0	0	0
59	3	2	1	0
60	3	2	1	0

D Learning from feedback: other people, scores, marks, grades

	(a)	(b)	(c)	(d)
61	3	2	1	0
62	3	2	1	0
63	0	1	2	3
64	3	2	1	0
65	0	1	2	3
66	3	2	1	0
67	3	2	1	0
68	3	2	1	0
69	3	2	1	0
70	0	1	2	3
71	3	2	1	0
72	0	1	2	3
73	3	2	1	0
74	0	1	2	3
75	3	2	1	0
76	0	1	2	3
77	3	2	1	0
78	3	2	1	0
79	3	2	1	0
80	3	2	1	0

E Making sense of what I'm learning: getting my head round it

	(a)	(b)	(c)	(d)
81	3	2	1	0
82	0	1	2	3
83	3	2	1	0
84	3	2	1	0
85	3	2	1	0
86	0	1	2	3
87	3	2	1	0
88	3	2	1	0
89	3	2	1	0
90	3	2	1	0
91	3	2	1	0
92	0	1	2	3
93	3	2	1	0
94	3	2	1	0
95	3	2	1	0
96	3	2	1	0
97	3	2	1	0
98	3	2	1	0
99	0	1	2	3
100	3	2	1	0

Helping learners to make learning happen

There are numerous sources of study skills advice for learners, many suggesting tried and tested approaches to learning. I have chosen to end this chapter with a set of 20 key suggestions, which you may find useful to copy for your learners – or, better still, adapt for them, tuning the suggestions in to the particular contexts of their own studies in your own discipline.

1 *Want to succeed.* Don't just *hope* to be successful. Be determined to get your result and to do everything you need to do to make it happen. Think positive. Think ahead to how much better your life will be *having* succeeded. More choices available in your career. A better developed brain.

2 *Make good use of the intended learning outcomes.* These tell you a lot about what you need to become able to do to actually get to your target. These help you to sort out what to learn from what not to learn. These help you to find out about what is fair game as an exam question and what is not. These help you to work out what your assessors are looking for in assignments.

3 *Don't bury your head in the sand.* Getting your learning to work for you is a big job, but like any big job, is done one little bit at a time. Keep doing little bits of the job all the time, rather than hiding from the enormity of the whole task. You get your result for doing all the *little* jobs, not just for tackling the whole task.

4 *Confront your work avoidance tactics.* It's all too easy to put off the evil moment of starting a task. Meanwhile, you could have got the task well under way. Don't waste time feeling miserable about all the backlog of work you've got – just do one thing from the backlog and you'll immediately feel better. Then do another thing, and you'll feel ahead of the game.

5 *Don't mix up 'important' with 'urgent'.* The danger is that if you're too busy doing things that seem urgent, you'll miss out on things that are really important. Do one short important thing *before* you do the urgent thing you've got to do that day. That's one less thing that will become urgent. Revising last week's lecture for 10 minutes is often more important than the first 10 minutes you will spend writing up this week's assignment.

6 *Don't confuse being busy with working effectively.* It's all to easy to be busy working at something which will only contribute a mark or two towards your overall result, when you could have spent the same time on something that would count for a lot more. Being busy can actually become an advanced work-avoidance tactic. Keep your eye on the big picture, not the small detail.

7 *Don't spend too long on any one thing.* Don't get so involved in writing a particular essay or report that you miss out on spending time getting your head round the important concepts and ideas from the last couple of weeks' lectures. An extra two hours might just get you one more mark on that essay. Two hours spent consolidating the last two weeks' stuff might earn you 10 marks in an exam.

8   *Take charge of your workload.* Don't just respond to the pressures around you. Be your own manager. Do what's expected of you, and what's required of you, but also do things that no one has told you to do – for example, going back over things you've already learned, making sure they're not just slipping away again.

9   *Think questions.* Any important fact or concept is just the answer to a question or two. If you know all the questions, you're well on your way to being able to answer any question that will come your way. Write your own questions down all the time – in lectures, when you're reading, when you're thinking, when you wake up, any time.

10 *Find out the answers to important questions.* Look them up. Ask fellow students. Ask lecturers when necessary. Don't just guess the answers – check whether your guess is good enough. Life is too short to learn 'wrong' stuff.

11 *Learning happens by doing.* Don't just read things or listen to lectures or browse websites or books, handouts and articles. *Do* things all the time. Make your own headline notes. Practise solving problems. Practise answering questions. Do it again – repetition deepens learning. Find out what you need to do *six* times before you get your head round it – this will be more important than something you only have to do once.

12 *Find out how you're doing – all the time.* Get as much feedback as you can – from lecturers, from fellow students and by comparing your own work with what's in books, articles, websites, everything. Don't just wait for feedback to come to you – go looking for it. Don't be defensive when the feedback is critical – learn from it. Don't be glib when the feedback is complimentary, build on it consciously.

13 *Use your friends.* Show your draft assignments to anyone who will read them – fellow students, friends, family members – anyone who can read. Even people who don't know anything about your subject can give you at least some useful feedback – even if just on spelling or punctuation.

14 *Self-assess all the time.* Don't just wait for someone to assess your work. Apply the assessment criteria to your own work before you hand it in for tutor assessment. Cross-reference your work to the intended learning outcomes, and work out which of these you've achieved and which you have not yet achieved. The more *you* know about the standard of your own work, the better you'll fare when others judge your work.

15 *Practice makes perfect.* Exams measure how good you are at answering exam questions under exam conditions. Practise answering questions as your main revision strategy. The more *often* you've jotted down the answer to a tricky question, the *faster* you can do it right one more time in the exam itself. Don't just hope it will be all right on the day in the exam – *make* it all right by practising all the way up to the day itself.

16 *Have a life.* Getting your result isn't *all* hard slog. You need time out for your brain to be refreshed. But build this time out *into* your overall strategy, rather than feeling guilty about it. There's no better way to enjoy some time out than

to take it at the point of just having achieved a useful chunk of learning. So earn your time out, then enjoy it.

17 *Be cue-conscious.* All the time, your lecturers are giving you cues about what's really important and what's less important. The intended learning outcomes give you cues too. You'll get lots of cues from past exam questions. You'll get even more cues by talking to fellow students and finding out what *they* think is important. But don't let all these cues evaporate away – jot them down, preferably in the form of questions you need to become able to answer or things you need to become able to do. When you know where you're heading, you're much more likely to be able to get there.

18 *Take setbacks in your stride.* A low mark for an assignment is a useful learning experience – find out what to avoid doing again so that you don't lose the same sorts of marks next time. Don't just grumble that you deserved better marks. Learn what you can from each setback, then let it go and don't brood over it.

19 *Take pride in your achievements.* Don't just worry about all the things you haven't yet done – learn from things you've done well and build on that learning. There's no way you can ever feel that you're doing *everything* possible towards getting where you're heading – be reasonable with yourself.

20 *Keep becoming better at studying.* At the end of the day, your learning is a measure of how well you've developed your study techniques – not just how much information you've crammed into your brain. Become ever more conscious about *how* you learn best. Explore all the possibilities – find out the techniques which really work for you, and develop them.

4

Assessment driving learning

Why assessment counts

In the context of 'making learning happen' we perhaps need to remind ourselves that *most* learning just happens. It occurs spontaneously as part of people's everyday lives, in their work and their play. People learn a vast amount from television, radio, newspapers, novels, magazines and other sources of information and entertainment. People learn a great deal from shopping, travelling, social contact, sport, entertainment and leisure activities. They learn a lot from any job or career they're involved in. Most of their learning is spontaneous, and isn't formally assessed. Actually, it could be thought of as being assessed in various ways in the normal course of life, but very seldom by (for example) time-constrained unseen written examinations in silent exam halls.

Thinking about 'making learning happen *in post-compulsory education*' is to do with a rather different (and quite small, in fact) sub-section of this vast amount of learning which characterizes the human species. This book is about making *intentional* learning happen – or *purposeful* learning (this is not to say that much of the rest of learning outside post-compulsory education is not both intentional and purposeful too). Perhaps the most significant difference is that learning in post-compulsory education ends up being *assessed* in due course, in various ways. Some of this assessment usually relates to *completion* of stages of learning. Not all learners in post-compulsory education complete their learning programmes. Yorke in Peelo and Wareham (2002: 37) has analysed 'leaving early' in higher education (in other words, non-completion) and finds that around two-thirds of those who don't complete drop out at some time during their first year of higher education study.

> Roughly two-thirds of premature departures take place in, or at the end of, the first year of full-time study in the UK. Anecdotal evidence from a number of institutions indicates that early poor performance can be a powerful disincentive to continuation, with students feeling that perhaps they were not cut out for higher education after all – although the main problems are acculturation and acclimatisation to studying. Having recognised that deleterious

consequences of early summative assessment and that the first year of full-time study is typically only a kind of qualifying year for an honours degree, some institutions are removing from their assessment regulations the requirement that students pass summative assessments at the end of the first semester. This should allow students more of an opportunity to build confidence and to come to terms with academic study, and ought to allow more of the vital formative assessment to take place. (Yorke, 2002: 37)

People lose interest in learning for a range of reasons, and become at risk of dropping out. How and when assessment takes place is one of the more important critical factors which can influence people's decisions to drop out. As we will see in the next chapter, the timeliness, quality and nature of formative feedback is perhaps the most critical of the factors under our control in post-compulsory education, especially when such feedback 'goes wrong' for various reasons, among the causes of non-completion or demotivation of learners.

There are also economics to consider. Making learning happen in post-compulsory education costs money – a great deal of money. Whether it is paid for by governments, or learners themselves or supporters of learners, the costs in time spent learning, teaching, learning resources, learning environments and research and development are high. So it is natural that accountability is necessary. And what therefore should we measure to ensure that value for money is being achieved in making learning happen in post-compulsory education? It would be satisfying if we could reply 'let's simply measure learning'. But it is more complex than this. I've already argued that we can't actually measure *understanding*. We can only measure what learners produce as *evidence* of the understanding that they develop. We can't plug a knowledgometer into our learners and measure how much they know – we can only measure what they *show* of what they know. We can't directly measure the learning which has happened inside learners' heads. We can only measure what they produce as evidence that they have learned successfully. That's where assessment comes in – and, indeed, completion.

'Making learning happen' is not just about causing learning to happen – it's about 'making learning *being seen* to have happened'. It's about results. These affect funding. We're not paid just to make learning happen, we're paid on the basis that we can *show* that learning has happened and that we've played a part in making it happen. 'Teaching excellence' is about making learning happen well. It's really about *learning excellence*. If we're rewarded or promoted on the basis of our teaching excellence, it's actually our learners' achievements which matter. And learners' achievements are measured on the basis of the evidence that they produce to demonstrate their learning. If we've taken due care to express the curriculum in terms of intended learning outcomes and been ever so careful to ensure that our learners will see what these actually *mean* in practice, we've still got to take care with making sure that what we measure is indeed learners' *achievement* of these outcomes, as directly as possible, and not (for example) just a measure of how well learners can communicate with pen and paper in exam rooms how well they may have achieved the outcomes. That would be only an echo of the achievement we are seeking to measure – perhaps only a ghost of the learning. We need to be very careful that our attempts to measure the achievement of intended learning outcomes are not skewed or muffled by filters such as exam technique, which may have little to do with the intended outcomes.

There have been countless scholarly accounts of the importance of assessment as a driving force for learning. Gibbs and Simpson (2002) explain the tendency for assessment to drive learners towards strategic learning as follows:

> Whether or not what it is that assessment is trying to assess is clearly specified in documentation, students work out for themselves what counts – or at least what they think counts, and orient their effort accordingly. They are strategic in their use of time and 'selectively negligent' in avoiding content that they believe is not likely to be assessed. It has been claimed that students have become more strategic with their use of time and energies since the 1970s and more, rather than less, influenced by the perceived demands of the assessment system in the way they negotiate their way through their studies. (MacFarlane, 1992). It is a common observation that students are prepared to do less un-assessed work than they used to, partly due to competing demands on their time such as part time work. (Gibbs and Simpson, 2002)

Gibbs and Simpson share concerns about assessment practices and policies driving learning in the opposite direction to improving learning, as follows:

> When teaching in higher education hits the headlines it is nearly always about assessment: about examples of supposedly falling standards, about plagiarism, about unreliable marking or rogue external examiners, about errors in exam papers, and so on ... Where institutional learning and teaching strategies focus on assessment they are nearly always about aligning learning outcomes with assessment and about specifying assessment criteria. All of this focus, of the media, of quality assurance and of institutions, is on assessment as measure-ment ... The most reliable, rigorous and cheat-proof assessment systems are often accompanied by dull and lifeless learning that has short lasting out-comes – indeed they often directly lead to such learning ... Standards will be raised by improving student learning rather than by better measurement of limited learning. (Gibbs and Simpson, 2002)

This is the main reason that assessment is the principal driving force for learning for so many learners in post-compulsory education. Their exam grades, certificates, degrees and, even, higher degrees depend on them being able to prove that they have met standards, demonstrated achievement and communicated their learning. Learners are rewarded for what they *show*, not just for what they know. Indeed, we can even argue that *showing* is actually *more* important than knowing. In some assessment contexts learners can gain credit by becoming competent at writing *as if* they had mastered something, even when they have not!

Does assessment bring out the best – or the worst – from our learners?

Following on from Chapter 1, much of the discussion about learning revolves around three or four words which describe different (though overlapping) ways of going about the process of learning.

Deep learning gets a good press in the scholarly literature. 'Deep' learning is, we might argue, closer to developing real *understanding*. But we've already seen that this is difficult or even impossible to measure. So deep learning may be the wrong approach to wean our learners towards when our assessment may only be measuring something rather less than deep learning. Deep learning may, of course, be much more appropriate for those learners going on to higher levels, and is doubtless the kind of learning which leads to the most productive and inspired research. Perhaps that is why deep learning is regarded so favourably by educational researchers on the whole. However, 'Save your deep learning for your postgraduate years. For now, your priority is to make sure that you *get* to having some postgraduate years' could be wise advice to give undergraduates!

Surface learning gets a bad press in the literature. However, probably most of the learning done by most people in post-compulsory education is actually only surface learning. Learners learn things 'sufficient to the day' – the exam day or the assessment week or whatever. When it's been learned successfully enough to serve its purpose – pass the module, gain the certificate, whatever – it's ditched. It's not entirely wasted however, something that's been surface learned is a better starting point for re-learning, or for learning more deeply, than something which has not been learned at all. But learners can all tell us tales of the countless things they have learned only well enough to give back when required to demonstrate their achievements, which have been quite deliberately 'eased out' of their minds as they moved on to the next stage of their learning journey. 'You are what you learn' may be a noble sentiment, but it can be argued that our assessment processes and instruments cause learners to learn far too many things which aren't important, diluting the quality of learning that is afforded to those things that *are* important.

Despite the criticisms of surface learning approaches, sometimes it is a fit-for-purpose choice. Where a limited amount of factual information needs to be available at will in a particular scenario, but will not be needed after that scenario is completed, surface learning can be a wise enough choice. There are things that just are not important enough to warrant a lot of time and energy being invested in learning them deeply. An example could be the statistics relating to stopping distances in wet and dry conditions, which need to be learned to pass parts of the driving test in the UK. Few experienced drivers can quote these facts and figures correctly a few years after passing their driving tests, but probably are perfectly capable of judging stopping distances well enough simply based on experience. This aspect of the learning for the test seems to be almost entirely a surface learning business.

What's wrong with strategic learning?

Strategic learning has perhaps had the worst press of all. It's not just *accidental* surface learning. It is perhaps *deliberate* surface learning, consciously engaged in at the expense of deeper learning. Strategic learning is regarded as 'learning for the exam'. It's associated with 'seeking out the marks or credit' quite consciously in essays, reports, dissertations and theses, and extends readily to preparing strategically for job interviews, promotion boards and so on.

Strategic learners tend to be successful, or at least moderately successful. Deep learners may well *deserve* success, but quite often shoot themselves in one foot or the other by mastering *some* parts of the curriculum very very well whilst leaving other parts of the curriculum underdeveloped, and not getting the overall credit that they might have achieved had they spread their efforts more evenly across the curriculum. Surface learners can also fare well enough, if and when all that is really being measured in our assessment systems is surface learning. Strategic learning is often thought of in terms of doing the *minimum* to get by. But there are various 'minima'. In the present degree classification system in the UK perhaps there's the minimum to get by and get a degree at all, the (different) minimum to get by and get a 2.1, the (different again) minimum to get by and get a first-class degree, and perhaps the minimum to get by and get a first-class degree with a margin for safety?

So what *is* strategic learning? We could regard it as making informed choices about when to be a deep learner and when to be a surface learner. It could be viewed as investing more in what is important to learn and less in what is less important to learn. It could be regarded as setting out towards a chosen level of achievement and working systematically to become able to demonstrate that level of achievement in each contributing assessment element.

There is growing recognition that the curriculum in post-compulsory education is content-bound. There is just so much subject matter around in every discipline. Any award-bearing programme of study necessarily involved making informed decisions about what to include in the curriculum, and what to leave out. But is not this the very same thing that strategic learners do? Isn't being an *effective* strategic learner to do with making wise and informed choices about where to invest time and energy, and where not? It can be argued that strategic learning, when done well, is a demonstration of a useful kind of *intelligence* – that of handling quite vast amounts of information, narrowing the information down to a smaller proportion and then processing only that smaller proportion into knowledge.

It can also be argued that those learners who go far are the strategic ones, rather than the deep ones. It can be argued that they know *when* to adopt a deep approach and when it is sufficient to adopt a surface approach.

At the time of writing part of this chapter, there was the annual clamour in the UK about the A level results. This year (2004) some 96 per cent of A level candidates passed. About 20 per cent of candidates attained three 'A' grades. The clamour echoed the usual protests that standards have not fallen, that there has been no 'dumbing down'. Could it not be that A level candidates are becoming better prepared to achieve at A level? Could it not be that they know more about what is being looked for in good exam answers? Could it not be that they are more aware about what is required for good grades in associated coursework? Could it not, indeed, be that they are now better versed in the virtues of strategic learning? And is this really a 'bad thing'?

Things have certainly changed over the last few decades. Widening participation policies are making at least some experience of higher education available for half the population, rather than for a small proportion of learners. Two or three decades ago, a much lesser proportion of A level candidates attained three 'A' grades. I was tempted to conduct a poll of present university vice-chancellors to ascertain how many did indeed get three 'A' grades at A level. A very restricted informal poll of professors indicated that many had reached such status *without* ever having the accolade of three 'A's years ago.

'I'm sorry, but I haven't got a cue!'

As long ago as 1974, Miller and Parlett discussed what can now be thought of as one way of thinking about strategic learning: 'cue-consciousness'. They proposed three approaches which learners can use in the ways that they structure their learning in systems where assessment is a significant driving force – an assessment regime which then in the UK was mainly comprised of written exams. They wrote of:

- cue-seeking learners: more likely to get first-class degrees
- cue-conscious learners: more likely to get upper second-class degrees
- cue-deaf learners: less likely to succeed.

Gibbs and Simpson (2002) expand on, and quote from, Miller and Parlett's work as follows:

> Miller and Parlett focussed on the extent to which students were oriented to cues about what was rewarded in the assessment system. They described different kinds of students: the cue seekers, who went out of their way to get out of the lecturer what was going to come up in the exam and what their personal preferences were; the cue conscious, who heard and paid attention to tips given out by their lecturers about what was important, and the 'cue deaf' for whom any such guidance passed straight over their heads. This 'cue seeking' student describes exam question-spotting:
> *'I am positive there is an examination game. You don't learn certain facts, for instance,*

you don't take the whole course, you go and look at the examination papers and you say "looks as though there have been four questions on a certain theme this year, last year the professor said that the examination would be much the same as before", so you excise a good bit of the course immediately ... '. (Miller and Parlett, 1974: 60)

In contrast these students were described as 'cue-deaf':

'I don't choose questions for revision – I don't feel confident if I only restrict myself to certain topics.'

'I will try to revise everything ... ' (Miller and Parlett, 1974: 63)

Miller and Parlett were able to predict with great accuracy which students would get good degree results.

' ... people who were cue conscious tended to get upper seconds and those who were cue deaf got lower seconds.' (Miller and Parlett, 1974: 55)

Things have not really changed much in three decades. I am, however, readily persuaded by Sally Brown's suggestion that the phrase 'cue-deaf' is unfortunate, and indeed unacceptable – with 'cue-blind' equally problematic, and that 'cue-oblivious' is a better way of thinking about those learners who just don't take any notice of cues about how assessment is going to work, or about how useful the intended learning outcomes may be as a framework upon which they can prepare for assessment, or about how valuable formative feedback on assessed coursework can be to help them improve their techniques for future assessments.

Knight and Yorke (2003) put the matter of cue-consciousness in perspective as follows:

> Learned dependence is present when the student relies on the teacher to say what has to be done and does not seek to go beyond the boundaries that they believe to be circumscribing the task. The construction of curricula around explicit learning outcomes risks the inadvertent building-in of circumscriptions or, for the 'strategic' student seeking to balance study and part-time employment, a welcome 'limitation' to what they have to do. Formal and informal feedback can be interrogated for what it can tell about what is expected, and can become part of a vicious spiralling-in towards 'playing it safe', basing action on perceptions of the implicit – as well as the explicit – expectations. It is a paradox that active 'cue-seekers' (Miller and Parlett, 1974) can exhibit a form of learned dependence, through 'playing it clever' (at least, superficially) by hunting for hints that will help them to maximise the grade received for their investment of effort. Over-reliance on the teacher can thus give achievements a meretricious ring: these may look worthier than they actually are ... (Knight and Yorke, 2003: 134)

It is interesting to think a little more about cue-seekers, cue-conscious learners and cue-oblivious learners, and to analyse how the five factors underpinning successful learning may be at work in their respective cases as they tune in to their differing ways of looking forward to assessment in their choices of learning approaches.

Cue-seeking learners	These could be regarded as strategic learners, who are setting out to find out how assessment works so that they can produce their optimum performances in each assessed situation.
	They are likely to be much more receptive to *feedback*, using critical constructive feedback to fine-tune their learning, and to work out what gets them good marks and what doesn't. They are likely to probe quite deeply into feedback – both positive and critical – to find out as clearly as they can where they are meeting assessment expectations and where their shortfalls presently lie.
	They are likely to be particularly skilled regarding taking ownership of the *needing to learn* dimension, paying close attention to the cues they can draw from published intended learning outcomes, evidence descriptors and assessment criteria. Likewise, they may consciously seek explanation and interpretation of the real meaning of criteria and standards, so that they know more about just how to optimize evidence of their own achievement.
	The *wanting to learn* dimension may still be strong, but steered in the direction of investing time and energy in what they *need* to learn, as above. The *learning by doing* dimension is likely to be governed by their thinking about what is really *worth* doing and what is not. They may indeed invest in practice and trial and error where they see that there are likely to be dividends at the end of the road for them, and may deliberately *not* do things which they see as not paying such dividends in due course.
	The *making sense* dimension is perhaps the most profoundly affected, with cue-seekers making strategic decisions about what they *try* to make sense of, and about what they will be perfectly content to use surface approaches to learn.
	Cue-seeking can therefore be thought of as a rich approach to learning, linking directly to each of the five factors underpinning successful learning explored in this book. It is therefore not surprising that cue-seekers are usually identified to be the learners most likely to succeed well.
Cue-conscious learners	This group of learners may include at least some 'deep' learners, but who are balancing their intrinsic *want* to learn with more strategic approaches to ensure that they do indeed achieve what they believe they *need to learn* as well.
	They are likely to be almost as receptive to *learning through feedback* as their cue-seeking counterparts, but are not likely to go the extra mile to *seek* additional feedback or to ask for clarification of aspects of feedback they are not sure about.
	They may remain conscious of cues in structuring their *learning by doing*, but may be less likely to be as analytical as their cue-seeking counterparts in deciding how much time and energy to invest

	in each element of their studying.
	Cue-conscious learners are likely to use cues to help them to *make sense* of what they are learning, but perhaps gain more from the cues they derive from teaching sessions and learning materials, and are likely to be less aware of cues in assessment contexts than their cue-seeking counterparts.
	Cue-conscious approaches can therefore be seen as relating directly to at least some of the processes underpinning successful learning. There are some parallels with strategic learning approaches, but the strategy could be regarded as underdeveloped. However, the difference between cue-seeking and cue-consciousness may too often end up as a difference in achievement between the most successful and the adequately successful learners.
Cue-oblivious learners	Whatever else, these are probably *not* to be regarded as strategic learners. They can be more like deep learners or, indeed, surface learners.
	Some of these may be learners whose *want* to learn is very high but who perhaps do not make sufficient use of establishing a real sense of ownership of the *need* to learn. They are less likely to draw on published intended learning outcomes, evidence specifications or assessment criteria to structure their learning. Their motivation may, however, be so strong that they learn some parts of the curriculum really deeply, but thereby increasing the risk that they fail to achieve on those parts of the curriculum which interest them less strongly.
	They may derive much less value from *feedback* than their cue-seeking or cue-conscious counterparts and, indeed, may become demotivated by critical feedback, which otherwise they could have used to their advantage.
	Their *learning by doing* may be more haphazard, following their interests rather than attending to the parts of the curriculum in which they may need to invest some practice. They may *make sense* very well of those parts of the curriculum which interest them, and do so much less well where they lack such interest.
	Among the constituency of cue-oblivious learners, however, may be those learners who have not got much *want* to learn at all, and are likely to end up as the casualties of assessment in due course. They, too, are unlikely to take ownership of the *need* to learn, as might have been indicated had they been aware of the cues connected with learning outcomes and assessment criteria.
	All in all, it is not surprising that cue-oblivious learners are not nearly so successful as their cue-seeking or cue-conscious counterparts, as they miss out on the contribution which making use of cues can make to all five of the factors underpinning successful learning.

There are significant implications regarding study-skills training and development. Most successful study-skills programmes address at least some aspects of raising awareness of cues, and developing cue-seeking approaches, to enable learners to prepare for assessment in a more systematic and continuous way than may have occurred if they simply followed their own instincts. Not surprisingly, in voluntary study-skills programmes, cue-seekers take such help most seriously, while the cue-oblivious parts of the learner population do not usually choose to attend – or, if present, tend to let the ideas pass over their heads.

What's wrong with assessment?

We've already seen that it is widely accepted that for most learners assessment drives learning to a quite profound extent. This is particularly the case for cue-seeking learners and strategic learners, and unsurprisingly they fare best in most common assessment processes and procedures. But is this state of things satisfactory?

Institutional policies on teaching, learning and assessment make much of the design of assessment processes and instruments being adjusted to address the following four qualities:

- validity
- reliability
- transparency
- authenticity.

So assessment should be valid, reliable, transparent and authentic. Anyone who cares about the quality of the assessment they design for learners will say how they strive to make it so. We are also *required* in the UK, for example, to make assessment valid, reliable, transparent and authentic by the Quality and Curriculum Authority in secondary and further education, and by the Quality Assurance Agency in higher education.

Most institutional teaching and learning strategies embrace these three qualities in the aspirations of colleges and universities. But hang on – why have we all got 'teaching and learning' strategies in our institutions? Why have most institutions got 'teaching and learning' committees? (Or, indeed, 'learning and teaching' committees – small difference?) Why haven't we got 'teaching, learning and assessment' strategies – or, indeed, 'assessment, learning and teaching' committees, which would be the way round I would name them?

Because assessment is the weakest link, I suggest. It's much easier (and safer) to fiddle around with the quality of teaching or learning than to tackle the big one: assessment. It's actually quite hard to *prove* that some teaching has been unsatisfactory, but only too easy to demonstrate when something has gone wrong with assessment. But, as shown below, there are significant shortfalls in the extent to which many of the most common assessment practices measure up to bringing these qualities to bear on assessment.

Validity?

Valid assessment is about measuring that which we should be trying to measure. But still too often, we don't succeed in this intention. We measure what we can. We measure echoes of what we're trying to measure. We measure ghosts of the manifestation of the achievement of learning outcomes by learners. Whenever we're just ending up measuring what they *write* about what they *remember* about what they once *thought* (or what we once *said* to them in our classes), we're measuring ghosts. Now, if we were measuring what they could now *do* with what they'd *processed* from what they thought, it would be better.

'But we *do* measure this?' Ask learners, they know better than anyone else in the picture exactly what we end up measuring. For a start, let's remind ourselves that we're very hung up on measuring what learners *write*. We don't say in our learning outcomes 'when you've studied this module you'll be able to write neatly, quickly and eloquently about it so as to demonstrate to us your understanding of it'. And what do we actually measure? We measure, to at least some extent, the neatness, speed and eloquence of learners' writing. What about those who aren't good at writing? Or to be more critical, what about those learners who have at least some measure of *disability* when it comes to writing?

In the UK, the writing is on the wall for us regarding any tendency for our assessment instruments and processes to discriminate against learners with disabilities. 'SENDA' (the Special Educational Needs and Disabilities Act, 2001) is causing us to make far-reaching changes to our assessment just to keep it within the law. SENDA came into force in September 2002, repealing the 'education exemption' which had previously applied to the 1995 'Disabilities Discrimination Act' in the UK. SENDA requires us to make 'reasonable adjustments' so that no learner should be unfairly discriminated against by our education provision, not least the assessment-related aspects of this provision. SENDA also requires these reasonable adjustments to be made in an *anticipatory* manner, in other words, not just dealing with instances of discrimination when it is found to have happened.

This is a tricky situation, as in one sense the purpose of assessment *is* to *discriminate* between learners, and to find which learners have mastered the syllabus best, and least, and so on. If we're honestly discriminating in terms of ability, that might be lawful. But if we're discriminating in terms of disability, it won't be lawful. But aren't they the same thing? Where does ability stop and disability begin?

For a long time already, there have been those of us strongly arguing the case for diversifying assessment, so that the same learners aren't discriminated against *repeatedly* because they don't happen to be skilled at those forms of assessment which we overuse (such as, in some disciplines, tutor-marked time-constrained, unseen written examinations, tutor-marked coursework essays and tutor-marked practical reports).

We're entering an era where *inclusive* assessment will be much more firmly on the agenda than it has ever been to date. We now know much more about the manifestations of dyslexia in assessment, and are just beginning to work out the effects of dyscalcula, dysgraphia, dyspraxia and so on. Many of us are beginning to realize for the first time that, even in that packed lecture theatre, we do have learners with disabilities, not just the occasional learner in a wheelchair, but perhaps a quarter or a third of our learners who are affected at some times in their learning by factors which we don't know about and which many of them don't even know about themselves. So is it ever going to be possible for us, in our assessment practices, to be satisfied with the levels of validity to which we aspire?

So we're not really in a position to be self-satisfied regarding the validity of even our most used, and most practised assessment instruments and processes. But the situation isn't new – we've used these devices for ever it seems. That doesn't make them more valid. But we're experienced in using them. Admittedly, that makes us better able to make the best of a bad job with them. But should we not be making a better job with something else?

Reliability?

For many, this word is synonymous with 'fairness' and 'consistency'. Reliability is easier than validity to put to the test. If several assessors mark the same piece of work and all agree (within reasonable error limits) about the grade or mark, we can claim we're being reliable. This is not just moderation, of course. Reliability can only be tested by blind multiple marking. Double marking is about as far as we usually manage to get. And, of course, we agree often enough don't we? No we don't, in many disciplines.

There are some honourable exceptions. 'Hard' subjects such as areas of maths and science lend themselves better to measures of agreement regarding reliability than 'softer' subjects such as literature, history, philosophy, psychology, you name it. By 'hard' and 'soft' I don't mean 'difficult' and 'easy' – far from it. Not surprisingly staff are resistant to the suggestion that they may need to undertake yet more marking. 'But multiple marking just causes regression to the mean' can be the reply. 'And after all, the purpose of assessment is to sort learners out – to discriminate between them – so it's no use everyone just ending up with a middle mark.' 'And besides, we spend quite long enough at the assessment grindstone; we just haven't room in our lives for more marking.'

So why is reliability so important? Not least, because assessing learners' work is the single most important thing we ever do for them. Many staff in education regard themselves as teachers, with assessment as an additional chore (not to mention those who regard themselves as *researchers* with teaching and assessing as additional chores). Perhaps if we were all to be called *assessors* rather than teachers it would help and, perhaps better, if we all regarded ourselves as researchers into assessment, alongside anything else we were researching into? 'Students can escape bad teaching, but they can't escape bad assessment' says David Boud (1995).

In countries with a degree classification system, our assessments can end up with learners getting first-class degrees, or thirds. This affects the rest of their lives. Now if our assessment were really fair (reliable), we could sleep easily about who got firsts or thirds. The learners who worked hardest would get better degrees, and the learners who lazed around wouldn't. This indeed is often the case, but most of us can think of exceptions, where learners got good degrees but didn't really deserve them, or learners who seemed worthy of good degrees but didn't come up with the goods in the assessed components of their courses, so we couldn't award these to them. So perhaps it's not just that our assessment isn't too reliable, it's our discrimination that's sometimes faulty too. In the UK, at last, the question is now being asked 'Is our degree classification system actually fit for purpose?'

When the Burgess Report (Burgess, 2004) was published, Rebecca Smithers, education editor of the *Guardian*, wrote in November 2004:

> The 200-year old system of awarding students degrees classified as firsts, upper seconds and so on could be scrapped under recommendations published by a government-appointed review today. The body set up by the government to evaluate existing ways of measuring students' achievement has concluded that the system fails to provide adequate differentiation of performance and give employers the information they need. (Smithers, 2004)

Transparency?

One way of describing 'transparency' is the extent to which learners know where the goalposts are. The goalposts, we may argue, are laid down by the intended learning outcomes, matched nicely to the assessment criteria which specify the standards to which these intended outcomes are to be demonstrated by learners, and also specify the forms in which learners will present evidence of their achievement of the outcomes. There's a nice sense of closure matching up assessment criteria to intended learning outcomes. It's almost a shame that there's yet another problem: some of the *actual* learning outcomes go way beyond the intended learning outcomes. Patrick Smith (Buckinghamshire Chilterns University College) argues that these are the *emergent* learning outcomes. Some of them are unanticipated learning outcomes. And it could be further extrapolated that there is some tendency for the 'you know it when you see it' extra qualities, which get the best learners the best degrees, are firmly embedded in their achievement of *emergent* learning outcomes and their evidencing of these outcomes within our assessment frameworks.

Leave aside this additional factor, and go back to the links between intended outcomes and assessment criteria. How well do learners themselves appreciate these links? How well, indeed, do assessors themselves consciously exercise their assessment-decision judgements to consolidate these links? Learners often admit that one of their main problems is that they still don't really know where the goalposts lie, even despite our best efforts to spell out syllabus content in terms of intended learning outcomes in course handbooks and to illustrate to learners during our teaching the exact nature of the associated assessment criteria – and sometimes even our attempts to clarify the evidence indicators associated with achievement of the learning outcomes are not clear enough to learners. In other words, learners often find it hard to get their heads inside our assessment culture – the very culture which will determine the level of their awards.

The learners who have least problems with this are often the ones who do well in assessment. Or is it that they do well in assessment *because* they have got their minds into our assessment culture? Is it that we're discriminating positively in the case of those learners who manage this? Is this the ultimate assessment criterion? In systems with degree classification, is it *this* difference which is the basis of deciding between a first and a third? And is this the *real* learning outcome, the achievement of which we're measuring? If so, is this stated transparently in the course handbook?

Therefore, we're not too hot on achieving transparency either. In fact, the arguments above can be taken as indicating that we rather often fail ourselves on all three – validity, reliability and transparency – when considered separately. What, then, is our probability of getting all three right at the same time? Indeed, is it even *possible* to get all three right at the same time?

Authenticity?

This one seems straightforward. It's about (on one level, at least) knowing that we're assessing the work of the candidate, not other people's work. In traditional time-constrained unseen written exams, we can be fairly sure that we are indeed assessing the work of each candidate, provided we ensure that unfair practices such as cheating or copying are prevented. But what about coursework? In the age of the Internet, word processing and electronic communication, learners can download ready-made essays and incorporate elements from these into their own work. Some such practices can be detected electronically, but the most skilful plagiarists can remain one step ahead of us and make sufficient adjustments to the work they have found (or purchased) to prevent us from seeing that it is not their own work.

Plagiarism is becoming one of the most significant problems which coursework assessors find themselves facing. Indeed, the difficulties associated with plagiarism are so severe that there is considerable pressure to retreat into the relative safety of traditional unseen written exams once again, and we are coming round full circle to resorting to assessment processes and instruments which can guarantee authenticity but at the expense of validity.

However, probably too much of the energy which is being put into tackling plagiarism is devoted to *detecting* the symptoms and punishing those found guilty of unfairly passing off other people's work as their own. After all, where are the moral and ethical borderlines? In many parts of the world, to quote back a teacher's words in an exam answer or coursework assignment is culturally accepted as 'honouring the teacher'. When learners from these cultures, who happen to be continuing their studies in the UK, find themselves accused of plagiarism, they are surprised at our attitude. Prevention is better than the cure. We need to be much more careful to explain exactly what is acceptable and what is not. While some learners may deliberately engage in plagiarism, many others find themselves in trouble because they were not fully aware of how they are expected to treat other people's work. Sometimes they simply do not fully understand how they are expected to cite others' work in their own discussions, or how to follow the appropriate referencing conventions.

It is also worth facing up to the difficulty of the question 'where are the borderlines between originality and authenticity?' In a sense, true originality is extremely rare. In most disciplines, it is seldom possible to write anything without having already been influenced by what has been done before, what has been read, what has been heard and so on.

In this discussion of authenticity, I have so far only taken up the matter of *ownership* of assessed work. There is, however, another aspect of authenticity – the extent to which the work being assessed relates to the real world beyond post-compulsory education. In this respect, authenticity is about making assessed tasks as close as possible to the performances which learners will need to develop in their lives and careers in the real world.

But we all try ever so hard!

I would like to assert at the outset that the vast majority of assessors whom I know approach assessment with commendable professionalism, and bring to bear upon it all the integrity, patience and care that they can. They spend a long time adjusting the wording of assessment tasks, and designing criteria with which to measure the evidence which learners deliver to them. Moreover, the decisions they make on the basis of this evidence are made carefully and painstakingly. Their good intentions are unbounded. But the way to hell is paved with such intentions. Perhaps because assessors tend to grow gradually into the assessment culture surrounding us, it is not surprising that they can be unaware of some of the prevailing problems that dominate the scene. At workshops I often liken many of the stalwart efforts which go into designing and implementing assessment as 'tinkering with and fine-tuning the engine of a vehicle which is actually off the road, facing in the wrong direction, and has no wheels left upon it!'

Why is now the time to move towards fixing assessment?

OK, there's a problem, but we've just not got enough time to fix it? *Why* haven't we got time to fix it? Because we're so busy doing, to the best of our ability and with integrity and professionalism, the work which spins off from our existing patterns of assessment, so busy indeed that we haven't left ourselves time to face up to the weaknesses of what we're doing? Or we simply *dare not* face up to the possibility that we may be making such a mess of such an important area of our work? It can help to pause and reflect on just how we got into this mess in the first place.

A couple of decades ago, the proportion of the 18–21-year-old population of the UK participating in higher education was in single figures, now it's well over 40 per cent, and the government waxes lyrical about increasing it to 50 per cent. When there was only 5 per cent, it could be argued that the average ability of those learners who participated in higher education was higher, and they were better able to fend for themselves in the various assessment formats they experienced. Indeed, they usually got into higher education in the first place because they'd already shown to some extent that they'd got at least a vestigial mastery of the assessment culture. Now, there are far more learners who haven't yet made it in getting their heads around our assessment culture, let alone gearing themselves up to demonstrate their achievement within it.

At the same time, when we were busy assessing just a few per cent of the population, we had time to try to do it well, using the time-honoured traditional assessment devices at our disposal. Trying to do the same for five or 10 times as many learners is just not on. We can't do it. We can't do it well enough. We're assessing far too much to do it reliably, for a start.

And what about the learners? Their lives are dominated by assessment. The intelligent response to this (thank goodness our learners remain intelligent) is to become strategic. In other words, if there aren't any marks associated with some learning, strategic learners will skip that bit of learning. If it counts, they'll do it. It's easy to go with the flow, and make everything important 'count' so that learners will try to do all of it. But in the end this just leads to surface learning, quickly forgotten as the next instalment of assessment looms up. We're in danger of using assessment to *stop* learning instead of to start learning. It's no use us bemoaning the increased extent to which learners have become strategic, when our assessment is the cause of this.

Who *owns* the problem of fixing assessment in post-compulsory education?

We can only ever really *solve* problems which we own. But the assessment problem is so widely owned. It's dangerously easy to feel there's just nothing that any one constituency among 'the owners of the problem' can do about it. It's easy enough to identify scapegoats, including:

- professional bodies, in whose name we feel we need to stick to the status quo
- pre-university education systems, which cast the die and train pupils into particular expectations of learning and assessment
- institutional, faculty and departmental assessment regulations, which limit our room for manoeuvre
- teaching and learning strategies, which are so all-encompassing that we can't suspend belief and start afresh again
- heads of department or school, who are often seen (sometimes wrongly) to be content with the status quo
- external examiners who would have to be convinced when radical changes may need to be made
- learners themselves who could or would complain about rapid changes to the level of the playing field or the position of the goalposts (even if the whole is enveloped in thick fog at present)
- the world outside academe, where there's a view about what a graduate should be, and so on
- journalists, broadcasters and editors who would give us a hard time if anything were to be found wrong in the way we did the job we are paid to do
- politicians and policy-makers who got to where they are by succeeding in the system of assessment we already have, and dare not admit that it might have been flawed
- parents, employers, taxpayers and others who foot the bill for education.

However, if we're perfectly frank about it, each assessment judgement is almost always initially made in the mind of one assessor in the first instance. True, it may well then be tempered by comparisons with judgements made in other people's minds, but to a large extent assessment remains dominated by single acts of decision-making in single minds, just as the evidence which is assessed is usually that arising from the product of a single learner's mind at a given time within a given brief. Living on a crowded planet may be a collaborative game, but we tend to play the assessment game in predominantly singular circumstances, and competitive ones at that.

The fact of the matter is that to fix assessment in post-compulsory education will require individuals to change what they do, but that won't be enough to change the culture. Teams of individuals with a shared realization of the problem will need to be the first step.

How can we fix assessment?

We need to work out a strategy. But any strategy has to be made up of a suitably chosen array of tactics. Sometimes it's easier to start thinking of the tactics first. What could be a shopping list of tactics to play with for starters in the mission to get assessment right in post-compulsory education? They include:

- getting learners into our assessment culture, by using peer-assessment and self-assessment more, so that learners are better tuned into our assessment culture when *we* assess them
- reducing the quantity of assessment (say by a factor of three) so that *we* have time to do it well, and learners have time for their learning not to be completely driven by assessment
- increasing the quality of assessment, so that it is fit for purpose, and more valid, more reliable, more authentic and more transparent
- increasing the diversity of assessment instruments and processes, so that learner casualties (where particular learners are discriminated against repeatedly by the same old assessment formats) are not so frequent
- training (yes, training, not just educating) our learners to be better able to play the game of working out where the goalposts are, and practising how to demonstrate their achievement of our intended learning outcomes.

To sum up the problems with assessment, therefore, there are two principal weaknesses in assessment in post-compulsory education at present:

- Assessment often drives learning away from what we might agree would be *good* learning.
- Despite the importance of assessment, we're not very good at getting it right!

So what can *you* do to fix assessment?

Turning tactics into a strategy is a big job, and beyond the scope of a single chapter in a book such as this. I will however offer some concise suggestions at the end of this chapter. Meanwhile, that big job won't even get started unless people are convinced that it needs to be done, and that was the purpose of this chapter. My intention in this chapter has been to employ challenging language to convince you that you've got a problem to adjust assessment so that it makes learning happen in post-compulsory education.

What are *you* going to do about it? I suggest that we can improve things by interrogating our various assessment processes and practices, putting them under the spotlight and looking hard at what exactly they measure but, perhaps more importantly, analysing how they relate to how learners learn in post-compulsory education. This is the way forward to adjusting our assessment to contribute positively to making learning happen, rather than to continue to allow surface or reproductive learning to be the outcome of post-compulsory education. With this in mind, I would like you to consider how the assessment processes and instruments which you use contribute to making learning happen for your learners.

Linking assessment processes to the factors underpinning successful learning

In the analysis which follows, I am selecting two of the most common assessment processes, traditional exams and essays, and suggesting how they may impact on the five factors underpinning successful learning. Although I am only interrogating two of the available assessment processes and instruments, they presently represent a large proportion of the assessment in post-compulsory education in the UK for example, and I hope that this may help you to look in a similar way at other assessment processes you employ, and think through the implications in parallel to my analysis below. The analysis which follows is based not just on my work helping teaching staff in post-compulsory education to develop assessment processes and instruments, but even more on my parallel work over three decades in helping learners to develop the skills they need to demonstrate their optimum performance in a range of different assessment conditions and environments.

Traditional exams

In particular, let's take the example of time-constrained unseen written examinations. In other words, candidates don't know the questions till they see them in the exam room. They work against the clock, on their own, with pen and paper. Assessment systems in the UK are quite dominated by this kind of assessment, usually at the end point of increments of learning. The assessment can therefore be described as summative.

As an assessment process, exams can be *reliable* – if there is a well-constructed marking scheme each candidate can be reasonably confident that the marking will be fair and consistent.

The main problem with many traditional exams is that they don't rate highly on *validity*. In other words, too often they measure what the candidate can *write* about what they have learned, in the relatively artificial conditions of solemn silence, against the clock. Where, however, exams are based on problem-solving, case study analysis and so on, validity can be much higher.

Exams can be improved in terms of *transparency* where candidates have been involved in applying assessment criteria to their own or other people's exam answers, and have found out all they need to know about how the examiner's mind works.

One of the major advantages of exams is that we are reasonably certain (with due precautions) that the work of the learner is being marked – in other words, that side of *authenticity* is assured. The other side of authenticity, however – the extent to which the assessed performance relates to the normal conditions in which the learning is intended to be applied – is less assured, and in some traditional exams the conditions under which achievement are measured are quite alien.

Wanting to learn	For many exam candidates, the 'want' to learn is damaged by the mere thought of looming exams. Many learners, if given the choice, go for learning modules that are continuously assessed rather than assessed by examination, because of their fear – and even dread – of exams. Few assessment processes induce such high emotions. This is not the case for everyone, however. Some candidates love exams – and are very good at preparing for them and doing them. Not surprisingly, the cue-seekers mentioned earlier in this chapter are among those who are good at traditional exams. Their cue-seeking approach is thus rewarded by this pervasive assessment format.
Needing to learn	This is where the intended learning outcomes should come into their own. Ideally, if learners have systematically prepared to demonstrate their achievement of these outcomes, and practised doing so sufficiently, they should automatically remain able to demonstrate the same achievements under time-constrained written exam conditions. However, there is often a gulf between the intended learning outcomes as published, and what is *actually* measured by traditional exams. Due attention to achieving constructive alignment can overcome this problem. But there is another side to needing to learn. Candidates who prepare successfully for exams by mastering the intended learning outcomes so that they can demonstrate their achievement in answering likely exam questions, often concentrate very firmly on what they perceive they need to learn, and don't invest time or energy in things they decide can't (or won't) come up in the exams. We are therefore favouring strategic learners by the use of exams (and, of course, cue-seeking strategic learners do best).
Learning by doing	There is plenty of learning by doing *before* traditional exams. But not much further learning by doing happens *during* traditional exams. It can, however, be claimed that a looming exam is as good a way as any of causing learners to get their heads down and do some learning. We could argue, however, that preparing for an oral exam (viva) would have just as much effect on learning by doing.
Learning through feedback	This is where traditional exams do really badly. As far as feedback is concerned, they are mostly lost opportunities. By the time the scripts are marked, learners have often moved on to the next part of their learning, and are no longer really interested in which questions they answered well and why, or (more importantly) in where they lost marks and why. Many learners were *very* interested

in these matters immediately *after* the exam, and spent some hours in post-mortem mode trying to work out how their answers measured up to what was being looked for by their examiners.

All the feedback that most learners receive – after some time – is their score, or their grade, or simply whether they passed or failed; feedback of a sort, but hardly formative feedback. We can, of course, argue that exams are intended to be summative measures, but they still seem to represent lost feedback opportunities. Where feedback *is* provided very quickly after an exam (for example, in computer-marked multiple-choice exams, where a feedback print-out can be handed to each candidate on leaving the exam room), feedback can, indeed, play a much more powerful role even in summative testing.

Making sense of what is being learned

This, too, links badly to traditional exams. As with learning by doing, a great deal of making sense of the subject matter occurs *before* an exam and, indeed, could be argued to be happening *because of* the exam. But few exam candidates report later that the moment when the light dawned was *during* the exam. More often, they report that they only found out that the light *had not* dawned during the exam.

And then we need to ask whether traditional exams are measuring the extent to which learners have made sense of what they learned. Too often, exams seem to measure what learners can *reproduce* rather than what they can *do*. Many learners can tell us about the frequent occasions where surface learning was all that they needed to engage in to address the task of answering a particular exam question.

Traditional exams: summary

The picture painted above of the links between traditional exams and the factors underpinning successful learning is very bleak. It does not *have to be* so bleak, however. With care, for example, exams can be designed which are much better at measuring 'making sense' than suggested above. Problem-solving exams and case study exams are much better at *not* rewarding reproductive learning. But the concerns remain about the damage that can be inflicted on many candidates' *want* to learn, the artificial way that exams can skew the *need* to learn and the fact that so much work may be done by examiners making sure that the exams have been fair and reliable, yet very little feedback usually reaches learners. In some ways, it seems that traditional exams are diametrically opposed to the factors underpinning successful learning! Couple this to the problems of achieving validity, reliability and transparency, and it is surprising that in some assessment cultures (including much post-compulsory education provision in the UK) traditional exams continue to hold sway to the extent that they do.

Other kinds of exams

The discussion above focused on the most common kind of exams – against the clock, written and with candidates not seeing the questions until they sit at their exam desks.

There are however many other kinds of exam, which overcome some of the problems about reliability, validity, transparency and authenticity in suitable contexts and discipline areas. These alternatives also can be thought of in terms of the five factors underpinning successful learning, and some 'food for thought' implications are summarized below for several of the alternatives.

Computer-marked multiple-choice exams

Wanting to learn can be less threatened than with traditional exams, as candidates are aware that it is their decision-making which will be measured rather than their ability to put their knowledge into words in writing. Ownership of the relevant *need* to learn can also be improved, so long as learners become practised and rehearsed regarding *which aspects* of their achievement of the intended learning outcomes can indeed be measured by this sort of exam. *Learning by doing* in such exams is primarily of the decision-making variety, but with skilful attention to the design of questions and option choices, decision-making can cumulatively be used to yield a good measure of the extent to which learners have *made sense* of what they have learned. At least we can be assured that the *learning by doing* that is measured by computer-assisted assessment is not skewed by such mundane factors as the speed of handwriting or its legibility. Perhaps the most significant link between computer-assisted assessment and making learning happen is *feedback*. There are many possibilities. Learners can be provided with on-screen feedback as they go through a computer-based exam, allowing them to avoid the possibility of carrying forward errors of thinking into their answers to the next questions they meet. Or they can be given feedback on-screen or in printouts at the end of each exam, when at least the feedback is quick enough for them to still remember what their thinking – and their decisions – were as they answered the questions. The availability of speedy and specific feedback can help learners to *make sense* of the subject matter they have been working with, admittedly too late for the computer-based exam they have just undertaken, but better late than not at all.

In-tray exams

These can take place in a normal exam environment. The main difference is that the amount candidates *write* is normally much less than in a traditional exam, while the amount they *think* may be considerably more. Candidates sitting in-tray exams typically take their places at their exam desks to find a range of paperwork already there. For example, health care professionals studying hospital ward management may find paperwork summarizing the patients presently in the ward, the staff available and so on. Then after some time to read and make sense of the paperwork, a critical incident occurs – they are given, for example, a slip of paper with details of three emergency cases which will arrive at their ward due to an accident at the airport, and are asked to make decisions about how they will adjust the staffing and bed allocations to deal with the emergencies. They hand in their decisions within the next half-hour or so, by which time they will have the next element of case study data to respond to, and so on. Such exams rate highly on validity – it is exactly this sort of thing that ward managers need to be skilled in handling. The reliability of such exams is also high, in that it is the quality of the decision-making which is measured, rather than the eloquence with which the decisions are expressed on paper.

These exams link favourably to the factors underpinning successful learning. *Wanting* to learn is enhanced by the relevance of the exam context and agenda to the real work involved. Similarly, candidates take much more ownership of the *need* to learn, when what is being measured relates so clearly to the intended learning outcomes associated with the exam.

Learning by doing is also much less artificial than in traditional written exams, as even though the decisions are written down on paper, it is the decisions rather than the writing that are assessed. *Feedback* is not so directly addressed, but can be provided with a little forward planning. For example, there is no reason why candidates leaving such an exam can't be given some pre-prepared paperwork illustrating some of the options they might have chosen in addressing the exam tasks.

Perhaps the strongest advantage of in-tray exams is that they really do come close to measuring how well candidates are *making sense* of the subject matter involved, in the context of being able to handle it 'on demand'. Knowing that they are heading for an exam of this sort undoubtedly causes candidates to adopt a *making sense* approach in their preparation. In other words, they are less likely to engage in rote learning for regurgitation purposes when the exam will be focusing on their speed and depth of making sense of the case study data they encounter in the exam itself.

OSCEs

Objective structured clinical examinations (OSCEs) are widely used in medical education and health care studies, and lend themselves to many other disciplines where practical *doing* is important in the intended learning outcomes. Essentially, OSCEs are exams where each candidate *does* something at each of a number of assessment stations located around the exam room. In medicine, for example, candidates may visit successive stations and perform a series of assessed tasks such as:

- interpreting some X-rays
- looking through a set of notes on a patient, and approaching a diagnosis
- prescribing medication for a given condition in a given context
- briefing a ward sister about the pre-operative preparation of a patient
- talking to a patient to diagnose a condition (though in practice the 'patient' is an actor, as it is hard to get real patients to tell the same story to successive doctors).

The key claim made for OSCEs is that the assessment is valid, in that candidates are assessed on exactly the sorts of things they have been intended to become able to *do* in practice and not just on what they may have written in traditional exams about hypothetical cases.

Clearly, OSCEs link closely to learning by doing – practice, repetition and trial and error. Furthermore, the more feedback candidates get on their practice before such an exam, the more they can improve their performance. OSCEs also link strongly to well defined *needing to learn* agendas, and as practitioners can see the relevance of developing their skills and knowledge to cope with such situations, the *want* to learn is enhanced. The variety of tasks which can be built into an OSCE add to the depth of *making sense* of what is being learned and assessed, as triangulation is possible, approaching key tasks from different angles. While it can take a considerable amount of time to design a good OSCE, when candidate numbers are large this is time well spent, and the time spent *marking* an OSCE can be much less than a corresponding written exam, not least because most of the assessment decisions can be made at the assessment stations while the exam is in progress.

Essays

In some subject areas (notable exceptions include maths, science and technology based disciplines) essays are key elements of both coursework and exams. We can again pose questions about how successfully essays relate to validity, reliability, transparency and authenticity. Essays do not do very well as an assessment method on such interrogation.

There are particular problems with *reliability* where subjectivity in marking is all too easily present, and inter-marker reliability is a problem (different markers giving the same essay different marks) as also is intra-marker reliability (the same marker giving the same essay different marks on different occasions – for example, among the first half-dozen marked or the last half-dozen marked).

Validity is perhaps the weakest link for essays as an assessment device. If we look hard at 'what are we *really* measuring?' it is often essay-writing *skills* rather than mastery of the subject matter concerned.

Transparency can be improved a lot by involving learners in self- and peer-assessing essays, so that they become much more aware of how marks are earned and lost, and how the assessment criteria work in practice – and, indeed, how the assessment links to the associated intended learning outcomes.

Authenticity is more problematic. At least in exam-based essays we can be reasonably certain whose work is being marked, but in coursework essays we can't. However, in time-constrained essay-type exams we are perhaps penalizing the slower learners – perhaps by measuring speed rather than quality of thought. The other side of authenticity – the link between essays and the context in which learning may be intended to be applied – is also problematic. There are many learners in post-compulsory education who will never again put pen to paper (or fingers to keyboard) to compose an essay after leaving education.

Meanwhile, let's continue with our analysis of how essays may relate to the five factors underpinning successful learning. I should point out at once that there are *very* significant differences here between coursework essays (with feedback in due course) and exam-based essays. As many factors relating to the latter overlap with what I've already said about traditional exams, the discussion which follows is mostly about the coursework essays.

Wanting to learn	The affects here are widely variable. Some learners really enjoy 'sorting out their minds' by putting pen to paper to construct essays, particularly when they then get detailed and helpful feedback on their learning. Such feedback is unlikely to be forthcoming for exam-based essays. For other learners, actually getting round to putting pen to paper (or fingers to keyboard) is a major challenge. Ask a group of learners 'what was your best work-avoidance tactic which you used to delay starting to put together that essay?' and you will soon see how, for some learners, the task of getting started was the daunting part.
Needing to learn	On one level, essays help learners to take ownership of the need to learn, by giving them something to do to cause them to get their heads into the books and resources relating to the task. However, the agenda of taking ownership of the intended learning outcomes is less successfully addressed, as all too often the links between these outcomes and a particular essay-writing task are not spelled out clearly enough in the briefings learners receive.
Learning by doing	Essays certainly involve learning by doing. There are several kinds of *doing* in play, including information retrieval and sorting, planning, communicating in writing, comparing and contrasting ideas, making decisions and judgements and summarizing. So this aspect of learning can be regarded as being satisfactorily addressed by the use of essays. Similarly, during the processes of drafting and redrafting an essay, a great deal of reflection and deepening of ideas can take place,

and the act of writing the essay becomes much more than simply learning by doing.

However, it is worth asking how many of the same aspects of learning by doing are involved in constructing *essay plans* rather than fully fledged essays. Such plans may miss out on some of the finer points of communicating in writing and on the reflective dimension, but making essay plans can involve many of the other important aspects of learning by doing. And if, let us suppose, 10 essay plans can be produced in the same time as it takes to write one fully-fledged essay, the learning pay-off associated with writing essay plans becomes all the more attractive.

Where, however, essays are primarily being used to train learners in the arts of marshalling their ideas, presenting them coherently and logically, and coming to a well thought out conclusion or summary, and these are the primary intended learning outcomes, writing full essays will meet these aims to a much greater extent than simply preparing essay plans.

Learning through feedback

Coursework essays can be very valuable in the context of making feedback available to learners. Feedback in general is discussed in more detail in the next chapter of this book; meanwhile it is worth bearing in mind that the timing and nature of the feedback on formative essays need to be managed well for optimum learning through feedback. It can be well worth considering ensuring that at least some of the feedback can be intentionally developmental.

For example, if an essay is 'marked' three times, once where feedback is given on an essay plan, again when a rough draft is submitted and, finally, when the last version of the essay is completed, feedback on the first two stages can lead to much higher quality in the final products. This clearly takes extra assessor time, but the two earlier feedback stages do not need to be quantitatively 'marked', and can be required simply as conditions to be satisfied before the final essay version is submitted.

Making sense of what is being learned

Coursework essays coupled with formative feedback can be very valuable in helping learners to get their heads around ideas and concepts, and also in helping them make sense of other people's ideas from the literature. It is often the act of trying to communicate an idea which causes the human brain to clarify it and put it into perspective. This is equally true of oral responses, but writing out ideas and progressively making them more coherent is probably one of the best ways of causing reflection and deepening learning. 'I don't know what I think until I've written about it' is said by many authors, who recognize the value of putting ideas down on paper as a way of helping the brain to make sense of them.

Coursework essays can also cause learners to find and retrieve information from the literature and from other sources, and then to sift it and analyse it, and distil from the source materials their own conclusions or thinking about a topic, issue or question.

Essays: summary

As can be seen from the above analysis, essays used formulatively in a coursework context (rather than summatively in exam contexts) can involve all five factors underpinning successful learning. Perhaps partly because they are time-consuming to plan, draft, and polish, they are perhaps better than many assessment-related artefacts in enabling reflection and consolidation (important aspects of 'making sense'). They are, however, often solitary learning journeys, at least until the points where feedback is received. Peer-review, peer-assessment and peer-editing processes can be used profitably to enable learners to benefit from feedback along the way.

What other assessment choices could we think about?

Brown and Knight (1994) identified over 80 alternatives to exams and essays. I will only list a few alternatives here, with just the briefest of indications about how these may link more successfully to some or all of the factors underpinning successful learning.

Question banks

Question banks are where learners compile a list of a specified number (for example, 300) of short, sharp questions about a topic or subject, and make a parallel list of answers to the questions or clues leading towards the answers. My own experience shows that this increases learners' *want* to learn, as it helps them break down the daunting task of getting to grips with a topic area into the more manageable steps of working out what questions they need to become able to answer, and linking the questions to the answers. Those learners who do not revel in trying to write in sophisticated language like the fact that the questions are intended to be short and direct, and the quality of a question bank depends on the relevance of the questions rather than the use of language. Question banks also give learners a high sense of ownership of the *need* to learn, as they translate the meaning of the intended learning outcomes into a practical tool which they can use to develop their ability to achieve the outcomes. *Learning by doing* is involved in making a question bank in the first place, then it lends itself to practice, repetition and trial and error as learners put it to use. What is more, they have control and ownership of all stages of the learning by doing. Learners get immediate feedback as they use their question banks, especially when they use them with fellow learners quizzing them with the questions and checking whether their answers are satisfactory. All this practice and repetition does a great deal to help learners to *make sense* of the subject matter covered by the questions and answers, at least to the extent of equipping them to be better able to answer questions in traditional exam contexts.

Using a question bank instead of a conventional coursework assignment can get learners to build themselves useful learning tools, where high learning pay-off results both from making the tools in the first place, then practising with them from there onwards.

Annotated bibliographies

Learners can be asked, for example, to select what they consider to be the best 20 sources on a topic, and write just a few lines relating to what they think is most useful (or most important) in each source in turn. This then equips them with a useful learning tool and gives them valuable practice at referencing sources accurately.

The task of making an annotated bibliography involves a lot of learning by doing – for example, finding the sources, making decisions about which are the most appropriate sources, then working out what is special to each source.

This in turn causes learners to *digest* the subject matter, as they compare and contrast the different viewpoints or emphases of the various sources. As with question banks, there can be much more thinking per hundred words in making an annotated bibliography than just writing an essay or an exam answer. In other words, learning pay-off can be much higher. Annotated bibliographies can be an excellent way of breaking down a lot of information into useful summaries, and can serve as useful learning tools, aiding revision and preparation for traditional exams.

Presentations

These are often part of an assessment mix. Learners can be asked to prepare a presentation with supporting materials (handouts, slides, sometimes posters) and then give the presentation to an audience of their peers (including tutors). Usually presentations are followed by a question and answer session with the audience. When the presentations are peer assessed, and especially when the learners themselves have been involved in designing the assessment criteria and establishing their respective weighting, they learn not only from preparing and giving their own presentations, but also from applying the criteria to each others' presentations.

Learners often take presentations very seriously, and to some extent preparing and giving their first presentation might damage their *want* to learn at least temporarily. When learners have ownership of the criteria, however, they feel more positive about the *need* to try to achieve them. There are several aspects of *learning by doing* involved, not least researching the content, preparing the support materials, rehearsing the presentation itself and preparing to be able to answer questions after giving the presentation.

Perhaps the most significant link between presentations and learning is the *making sense* which occurs as a result of their preparation and delivery. Learners are usually able to answer questions on the topic involved long after the event, and their learning about the subject matter can be said to be much deeper than if they had just written an essay or assignment on the topic.

Learners can also gain a great deal of *feedback* during the various processes, not least from fellow learners during rehearsal and during the presentation itself. Further feedback can be provided by tutors or other assessors.

The skills which learners develop as a result of preparing and giving presentations, and answering questions about the topic concerned, link strongly to employability. In particular, oral communication skills can be developed and practised alongside the subject-matter learning going on.

Towards assessment becoming a *better* driver for learning

Let me end this chapter by returning to some tactics which can play their part in helping to bring assessment closer to the intention to make learning happen.

1 *Diversify assessment more, and move away from overuse of just two or three assessment formats.* In particular, we need to ensure that our assessment systems do not end up just measuring how skilled (or unskilled) our learners are in a limited range of assessment contexts, such as *just* a mixture of time-constrained unseen written exams, tutor-marked essays and reports.

2 *Make assessment fit for purpose, so that we measure what we really should be measuring – not just ghosts of learners' learning.* We need to revisit the validity of each and every form of assessment we employ, and choose those which are good at measuring what students have really learned.

3 *Make assessment a high-learning pay-off experience for learners by making the most of feedback to students.* We need to think ahead to how we will give feedback to students after each element of assessment, and to how useful that feedback can be, even when the main purposes of assessment are summative rather than formative.

4 *Reduce the burden of assessment for learners and for ourselves.* We have got our education systems into a state where assessment all too often militates against deep learning and takes much of the enjoyment out of learning. Reducing the amount quite dramatically – by a factor of three or four perhaps – can be part of the pathway towards increasing the quality of assessment and the usefulness of associated feedback to learners.

5 *Assess evidence of what learners have learned, not just what we have tried to teach them.* It may be instinctive to try to find out what students have learned as a direct result of what we have tried to teach, but there should be more to assessment than just this. We need to be able to credit learners for their achievements in learning they have done for themselves and with each other.

6 *Assess students' evidence of their learning more reliably.* Most assessors are aware that assessment is rarely an exact science, yet with so much depending on the marks and grades we award learners, we need to be constantly striving to make each assessment element as reliable as we can, so we can make learners feel more assured that they are being assessed fairly – and so that employers and others can have more trust in the results of our assessments.

7 *Focus learning outcomes on 'need-to-know' rather than 'nice-to-know' material – and stop measuring things which are 'nuts to know'!* Too often, it is possible to look at what is *really* being measured by an exam question or assignment and find ourselves asking 'why on earth are we causing learners to learn *this* bit?' Sometimes, our reply to ourselves – if we're honest – is as banal as 'well, at least this lends itself to being measured!' Not a good enough reason. What is measured by assessment should be easily recognized as being important, not just interesting.

8 *Measure 'know-how' and 'know-why' much more, and 'know-what' much less.* In other words, move learning away from information recall and regurgitation, and strive to use assessment to encourage learners to make sense of what they have learned, and towards being able to explain it and apply it rather than merely describe it.

9 *Involve learners in assessing their own and each others' work to deepen their learning, and help them to get their heads round how* we *conduct assessment.* The more learners know about how assessment really works, the better they can do themselves justice in preparing for it and demonstrating their learning back to us. There is no better way than helping them to develop self-assessment and peer-assessment skills, to deepen their learning and acclimatize them to the assessment culture they are part of.

10 *Get our wording right – in our outcomes, briefings, tasks and criteria – write them all in English, not in 'academese'.* Too often, whether in exams or other assessment contexts, learners who are skilled at working out exactly what our assessment tasks actually *mean* achieve better results than equally deserving learners who are not so skilled. Teaching is about effective communication, not playing word games.

5

Learning through feedback

Already in this book, feedback has been identified as one of the five principal factors underpinning successful learning. Feedback should interact with the other factors continuously, as follows:

- Feedback should help learners to *make sense* of what they have done.
- Feedback should help learners to clarify and take ownership of the *need* to learn as defined by the intended learning outcomes they are working towards achieving.
- Feedback ideally should enhance learners' *want* to learn by increasing their self-esteem and confidence whenever possible, and by helping them to believe that they can indeed achieve the intended learning outcomes *and* demonstrate this in ways where they will be duly credited for this achievement.
- Feedback should motivate learners to move forward into their next episodes of *learning by doing*, and focus their efforts more sharply towards bringing the experience from their past work to bear on making their next work better.

Feedback or feed-forward?

Some writers already use the term 'feed-forward' to describe those aspects of feedback which particularly point towards what to do next, rather than merely looking backwards at what has (or has not) already been achieved by learners. Feed-forward can offer help along the following lines:

- details of what would have been necessary to achieve better marks or grades, expressed in ways where learners can seek to improve their future assignments or answers
- direct suggestions for learners to try out in their next piece of work, to overcome problems or weaknesses arising in their last assignment
- suggestions about sources to explore, illustrating chosen aspects of what they themselves are being encouraged to do in their own future work.

Feed-forward can be regarded as *formative* – in other words pointing towards improving and developing future work. This contrasts with *summative* feedback, referring back principally to what was – and what was not – achieved in past work. Ideally, feedback needs to achieve both purposes, but the danger is that it sometimes is not sufficiently formative and is too dominated by summative comments.

Feedback, achievement and failure

There is now a substantial and rich literature on the potential role of feedback in formative assessment contexts. This section of the chapter picks on just a few important sources of wisdom and expertise on using feedback to make learning happen in post-compulsory education. Positive feedback brings few problems to learners or to staff giving it. However, it is the feedback on unsuccessful work which causes most heartache to staff and learners alike. Peelo (2002: 2) writes tellingly on the difficult subject of failure as follows:

> Failing is not a popular subject. Even though failing, in some shape or form, is an everyday occurrence, it remains a subject rarely discussed. This silence occurs as much in the world of education as in the world generally, even though many educational assessment procedures are intended to discriminate, separating those students deemed unsuccessful from the rest ...
>
> To use the word 'failing' seems, superficially, to be a negative approach to education. Indeed, in universities this unpopular word has overtones of the taboo, with the suspicion that using the word itself invites failure. Yet integral to all discussions of standards and access is the practice of failing students. All competitive systems have losers. The practice of teaching and examining in universities includes the activity of finding some students wanting – it is part of the job ...
>
> Just as important as the idea of students failing, is the need to question whether or not the system itself is doing the best for its students or is, indeed, failing the students it's trying to educate ...
>
> Failure in universities, whether of staff or students, is a matter of discomfort and embarrassment and yet is seen as an essential demarcator of successful work. It is an integral part of institutional structures, yet it is often experienced individually and in isolation. (Peelo, 2002: 2)

However, she continues:

> However correctly dealt with by the system, a student who is failing in a system which is built on academic success may well experience a sense of isolation and strangeness. Similarly, few students suddenly and unexpectedly fail academically – there is usually prior warning. For many *failing is not an event*

but a series of hesitations, a combination of moments of failure. For others *experiencing failure is not about external criteria, but about falling below their own, personal standards.* Externally, everything may be fine and they may well be passing their courses successfully. But internally, the pressure and striving can be enormous. If something else goes wrong in life then the fragile structures which support such students through university assignments can begin to crumble (original emphases).

The key to all this is of course timely, helpful and supportive feedback. Bowl (2003: 93) illustrates poignantly, through student quotes, the need they have for such feedback. For example one of the case studies around which her book is written includes the following scenario:

Planning assignments is my worst, it's my weakness definitely. I can say what I want to put in it, but it's how do I do it? What comes top, second, third? I know I can write. It's just that initial help to say that should go first, second or whatever. Once I've got that, I can do an assignment ... Some give you guidelines, and some don't. It's like, how do you want us to write this? How do you want us to do it? I would go out and know how to work practically. But writing, it's like – what do you want? ... It's getting it structured the way that it suits them and suits their needs. (Sandra, first year student.)

But what makes feedback work to make learning happen? Knight and Yorke (2003: 135) explain it thus:

Formative assessment can clearly be said to have 'worked' if the student demonstrates having learned as a result of the feedback provided. This requires that the student has a concept of learning that allows them to take in what the assessor has sought to convey and they then act on the basis of this developed understanding.

They also quote Stowell (2001) in discussing the role of formative assessment as follows:

Formative assessment is concerned with maximising the learning of each individual student. In theory, each student should receive feedback that is most appropriate to their learning needs. Feedback should therefore be differentiated. The problem occurs on the assessor's side when time and resources are constrained. The assessor then has to make choices regarding the amount of feedback that should be given to each individual. The choices they make will reflect personal value judgements about the purposes of education: some teachers will opt for 'levelling up' in the interests of social justice, whereas others will give priority to 'high flyers', seeing their action in Darwinian 'survival of the fittest' terms.

It is also argued that it is the lower fliers who are most in need of feedback, for example Bandura (1997) argues: 'The less individuals believe in themselves, the more they need explicit, proximal, and frequent feedback of progress that provides repeated affirmations of their growing capabilities' (Bandura, 1997: 217).

Knight and Yorke (2003) have a wealth of useful food for thought concerning the role of feedback in formative assessment. They argue:

> Complex achievements take time. This implies practice but it also implies feedback on practice, whether it be self-generated or comes from other learners or experts. Without feedback, the learner is like someone learning to play chess blindfolded, wearing earmuffs, and beyond any helpful tactile contact. When achievements are complex, careful thought is needed about the nature of feedback. When the aim is improving future performances, the most useful feedback is about improvement strategies: what are the most important two or three things on which to work if performance on a similar task is to be improved? Unless there is a requirement that learners master particular detail, there is a danger that too much correction of specific detail will take attention away from improvement strategies. (Knight and Yorke, 2003: 126)

They describe the purposes of formative assessment in general as follows:

> Three purposes of formative assessment
> 1 To give credit for what has been done, with reference to the expected standard.
> 2 To correct what is wrong, thereby helping the student to avoid repeating the error (hence merely saying that something is wrong is insufficient).
> 3 To encourage emancipation by alerting the student to possibilities which they may not have hitherto discerned. (Knight and Yorke 2003: 35)

They also argue that:

> Although all feedback can evoke learning, it is helpful, from the outset, to declare an interest in feedback that draws attention to actions that, if taken, have the power to make a difference to future work on different topics. Although many teachers give a lot of feedback on specifics, it is *general* feedback that has the greater power to stimulate learning. If general feedback relates to the learning intentions declared in course and programme specifications, then this is a clear benefit to the coherence of student learning. (Knight and Yorke 2003: 32–3)

It can be argued that giving learners feedback is just about the most important dimension of the work of teachers in post-compulsory education, second only perhaps to that of making assessment judgements which can affect the future careers and lives of our learners. But perhaps all told, formative feedback is *the* vital dimension as, given at the right time and in the best possible way, it can lead learners steadily towards successful achievement in summative assessment contexts.

Varieties of formative feedback

What sorts of feedback can help to make learning happen more successfully? There are many ways in which feedback can reach learners, each with advantages and disadvantages. Perhaps the more *different* ways we use to get feedback to learners, the more likely we are to ensure that they receive at least some feedback in ways which suit their own personal approaches to learning.

Written and printed feedback

Such feedback can take many forms, including:

- handwritten comments directly entered onto learners' work
- summary overall comments on learners' assignments – handwritten, word processed or emailed directly to learners
- model answers or specimen solutions, giving feedback to learners on what may have been looked for in their own work
- generic feedback on a batch of learner work, in print, emailed to all learners, or put up on an electronic discussion list, virtual learning environment or computer conference
- sheets listing 'frequently occurring problems' specific to a particular assignment, allowing learners to see feedback on some of the problems they may themselves have encountered, but also alerting them to other potential problems they may not have been aware of themselves, but which may be useful to avoid in their next work.

Face-to-face feedback

This, too, can take several forms, including:

- feedback to whole lecture groups on work that has already been marked and is now being returned to them
- feedback to similar groups, but at the time they have just handed in their work, while it is still fresh in their minds. This feedback of course addresses *anticipated* problems or mistakes, but can be really valuable to learners, still remembering the fine detail of their own attempts at the work

- feedback to small groups of learners, for example, in tutorials, allowing more interaction – for example, learners can probe deeper into what exactly the feedback means
- face-to-face one-to-one feedback, by appointment, or in other learning contexts such as practical classes or studio work, where tutors can often chat to individual learners in a context less formal than individual appointments.

Feedback on learners' own self-assessments

Where learners are briefed to carry out a self-assessment of their assignments at the point of handing them in for marking, tutors can then not only give learners feedback on the assignments themselves, but also on the self-assessment reflections. In practice, this can help tutors to give learners feedback which is much more focused on their real needs than just giving feedback without knowing what learners themselves already thought about their own strengths and weaknesses relating to the assessed work.

Feedback associated with peer assessment

Where groups of learners are assessing each others' work (whether written assignments, essays, reports, presentations, artefacts, exhibitions or posters), learners can get a great deal of feedback from their peer assessors. They also get what is perhaps even more useful feedback individually, directly from the processes of applying assessment criteria to other examples of work – some better than their own, and some not as good. All this helps them to place their own work in context and to work out what they may need to do next time to improve or develop their own future work.

Problems about giving feedback to learners

Most tutors and lecturers already know how important feedback is to their learners. Few, however, feel that they have really got themselves into a position where the feedback is really working.

There are further problems experienced by staff in the context of trying to link feedback to the evidence of achievement of intended learning outcomes and designing assessment tasks to align assessment and feedback appropriately.

Feedback, efficiency and learning pay-off

Ideally, we need to make informed decisions about how best to maximize the learning pay-off associated with our feedback, but at the same time to improve our own efficiency in composing and delivering the feedback. In many workshops I have asked groups of participants to write down on separate Post-it notes each different way they use to give their learners feedback (adding also *other* ways learners get feedback – for

example, from each other, from web sources, from books and handouts, and so on).
I then ask them to place the Post-its onto a chart, as shown in Figure 5.1.

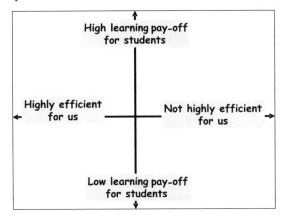

Figure 5.1 Mapping the student learning pay-off resulting from feedback to the efficiency for staff providing it

The feedback processes which people consider to have the highest learning pay-off are positioned well up the vertical axis, and so on. Those which are most efficient for us are placed towards the left of the chart. Those which are most efficient *and* have the highest learning pay-off go towards the left-hand corner of the chart.

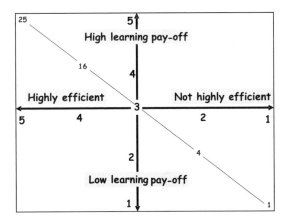

Figure 5.2 A semi-quantitative approach to learning pay-off and staff efficiency

Scales 1 to 5 can then be drawn on each axis, and the product of 'efficiency' × 'learning pay-off' worked out for the position of each of the Post-its on the chart (Figure 5.2). Table 5.1 shows a summary of the highest scoring and lowest scoring feedback processes as determined in this way at a large number of workshops. From Table 5.1, some trends can be seen, but also the fact that in different contexts workshop participants show quite a lot of variation in the extent to which they regard feedback processes as efficient or capable of delivering high learning pay-off.

Table 5.1 Learning pay-off x efficiency scores from 10 different workshops on formative feedback

High-scoring feedback methods
25 self-assessment
25 learners comparing work
25 learners self-assessing
25 individual learning
   development plan
25 learners cross-marking
25 peer marking with
   feedback
25 discussion
25 emails to group
25 peer assessment
25 computer-assisted
   assessment (adaptive)
22 adaptive computer
   feedback
20 peer assessment
20 peer feedback
20 constructive questioning
   within groups
20 self-evaluation
20 presentations by learners
20 verbal feedback
20 self-marking
20 verbal to small groups
20 small group verbal
20 verbal to whole class
20 emailing with attachments
20 e-learning with instant
   feedback
20 individual peer
   assessment
20 moderated self-
   assessment
20 group peer review
20 peer assessment feedback
20 peer critique
20 work experience
   feedback
20 opportunity for
   discussion one to one
20 peer assessment

16 returning model answers
16 email one to one
16 small group tutorials
16 supervised peer
   assessment
16 Coded grades with email
   discussion
16 model answers
16 code letters on learners
   work
16 self-evaluation
16 feedback session to a
   large group
15 assessing against learning
   outcomes
15 one-to-many email
14 criterion-based written
   feedback
14 discussion boards
12 comments on written
   work
12 peer discussion
12 target setting feed-
   forward
12 discussion – learner led
12 question and answer
   session
12 feedback during an
   activity
11 learner group feedback
10 individual written quality
   feedback
10 encouragement in the
   classroom

Low-scoring feedback methods
6 handwritten on
   assignments
6 peer assessment
6 written one to one
5 individual face to face
5 group verbal

5 signing off log sheets
5 one to one
5 giving marks only
5 single word comment
5 verbal one-to-one
   feedback
5 published marks or grades
5 one-to-one verbal
4 tick-box
4 written feedback
4 show of hands …
4 internal test with grading
   and feedback
4 written feedback that isn't
   read
4 handouts – just stuck in a
   file
4 grades with oral
   correction
4 written exams
4 exams
3 grades and comments
   written onto assignments
3 individual written
   comments on work
3 just a mark
3 grabbing comments from a
   bank
3 web conferencing
3 written assignment
   feedback sheets
2 giving a mark
2 exam
1 individual learning plans
1 grade with comment
1 learner reports
1 grades without comments
1 interim reviews
1 writing negative comments
1 just giving it a mark

The highest scoring feedback methods are frequently those involving peer assessment or peer marking, and self-assessment also attracts some high scores. This is not least because the 'efficiency for us' tends to be high, especially when large groups of learners are involved.

One-to-one feedback often attracts low scores, not least because it is inefficient for us, even when the learning pay-off is felt to be high. However, the lowest scoring feedback processes frequently include 'just a mark', in other words, most tutors know only too well that learners don't learn much from just being given a number or grade for their work.

Working through this kind of discussion about learning pay-off versus efficiency often encourages tutors to make more and better use of peer and self-assessment as tactics in a strategy to provide learners with more and better feedback using existing resources. It also helps tutors to appreciate the limitations of just giving scores or grades.

Maximizing learning pay-off through formative feedback

The following suggestions aim to give you some practical ways in which you can design feedback which helps to make learning happen with your own learners.

1 *Provide learners with a list of feedback comments given to a similar assignment or essay prior to them submitting their own.* You can then ask learners, for example, in a large-group session, to attempt to work out what kind of marks an essay with these kinds of comments might be awarded. This helps them to see the links between feedback comments and levels of achievement, and can encourage them to be more receptive to constructive but critical comments on their own future work.

2 *Give learners pre-feedback comments.* For example, send learners an email containing the comments that you have put on their assignment and ask them to give you a response. You could include in your email a set of statements to use in response to your feedback, designed so that learners could delete from the set as appropriate, or add their own responses to them, to make the task of responding to your feedback as easy as possible.

3 *Let learners have feedback comments on their assignments prior to them receiving the actual mark.* Encourage them to use the feedback comments to estimate what kind of mark they will receive. This could then be used as the basis of an individual or group dialogue on how marks or grades are worked out.

4 *Focus your comments on learners' work, not on their personalities.* Comments need therefore to be about 'your work' rather than 'you'. This is particularly important when feedback is critical.

5 *Get learners to look back positively after receiving your feedback.* For example, ask them to revisit their work and identify what were their most successful parts of

the assignment, on the basis of having now read your feedback. Sometimes learners are so busy reading and feeling depressed by the negative comments that they fail to see that there are positive aspects too.

6   *Keep a database so that you can readily refer to feedback given on the last assignment when making comments on the present one.* This relies on your feedback comments on each successive piece of work being produced and stored electronically, otherwise it would become excessively time-consuming.

7   *Ask learners to respond selectively to your feedback on their assignments.* This could, for example, include asking them to complete sentences such as:
    (a) 'The part of the feedback that puzzled me most was ... '
    (b) 'The comment that rang most true for me was ... '
    (c) 'I don't get what you mean when you say ... '
    (d) 'I would welcome some advice on ... '.

8   *Ask learners to send you, confidentially, an email after they have received your feedback, focusing on their* feelings. In particular, this might help you to understand what emotional impact your feedback is having on individual learners. It can be useful to give them a menu of words and phrases to underline or ring, perhaps including: 'exhilarated', 'very pleased', 'miserable', 'shocked', 'surprised', 'encouraged', 'disappointed', 'helped', 'daunted', 'relieved' and (other:)
    ....

9   *Ask learners to tell you what they would like you to stop doing, start doing and continue doing in relation to the feedback you give them.* This is likely to help you understand which parts of your feedback are helpful to specific learners, as well as giving them ownership of the aspects of feedback that they would like you to include next time.

10 Get learners to make a short action plan based on your feedback comments. This should then give you some confidence that they are noting what you have said and are planning to use your advice in relation to the next assignment.

11 *Cause learners to build on your feedback.* For example, ask them to include with their next assignment an indication of how they have incorporated your feedback from the last one into the present one.

12 *Don't miss out on noticing the difference.* Comment positively where you can see that learners have incorporated action resulting from your advice given on their previous assignment. This will encourage them to see the learning and assessment processes as continuous.

Risk assessment and feedback

It can be useful to think about risk assessment both for ourselves when giving feedback and for learners when receiving it. For example, if written or printed feedback should 'go wrong', the risk to tutors can be regarded as high. Suppose a given instance of feedback could be viewed as being inappropriate on grounds relating to such factors as ethnic background, gender, disability and so on, the originators of such feedback could find themselves having evidenced non-compliance with legislation such as the Special Educational Needs and Disabilities Act (2001) in the UK, and its subsequent amendments. More likely, their inappropriate feedback is likely to be picked up by institutions' quality monitoring and assurance systems or by external examiners, moderators or assessors.

However, it is probably even more important to think of risk assessment on behalf of learners themselves. One of the most effective feedback processes, at least in terms of learning pay-off, is one-to-one face-to-face feedback. If this should 'go wrong', learners can become seriously demotivated, and may discontinue their studies altogether in severe cases. Another problem is that this kind of feedback may be unwitnessed by anyone other than those directly involved, and *proving* that it was handled badly is problematic.

Feedback for high-fliers and for low-fliers

Some feedback processes are much more suitable for successful learners than struggling learners. For example, just a mark or a grade may be all that is needed by high-fliers, while a combination of written and oral feedback may be much more suitable for learners who need significant help. At the same time, learners without any problems may find it irritating to be given detailed feedback on things they have already mastered. However, learners without problems may equally feel short-changed if their less able coursemates are seen to be getting more time and attention from tutors. An appropriate balance needs to be struck, where high-fliers get useful feedback too – perhaps a combination of positive comments about their work *and* some constructive suggestions about how they can make their next piece of work even better. It is well known how desolate a learner can feel when, having consistently achieved 'A' grades, an out-of-the-blue 'B' grade hits them. This can all too often be tracked down to a lack of tutors explaining to them *why* they had been achieving 'A' grades to date. 'If you don't know how you did it, you're less likely to be able to do it again.'

Formative feedback and summative feedback

So far in this chapter, most of the discussion has been about feedback in formative assessment contexts. Another dimension which is useful to explore when reviewing the range of feedback approaches available to us is the question of which processes best lend themselves to providing formative feedback and which are more suitable for summative feedback? In some cases, the conclusions are obvious – for example, 'just a mark or grade' serves summative purposes and 'suggestions for your next assignment' serves formative purposes. However, some are much more complex, and the feedback associated with peer assessment (for example) can play a signifi-cant formative role even when it is received in contexts where the overt intention is more close to being summative. This is partly because, in some contexts, learners may actually take on board more deeply things they learn from each other, where there is no 'authoritative' agenda present, than from when they receive feedback directly from their tutors.

Formative and summative assessment processes can be regarded as two ends of a continuum. All too often, for example, what sets out to be formative feedback ends up as summative feedback. For example, when learners don't get the feedback till they have already moved on to another topic or another module, they are very unlikely to take any notice of formative feedback given on work from weeks (sometimes months) ago, and the feedback ends up as no more than summative – in other words, learners may notice the mark or grade, but not bother to read the hard-wrought comments their assessors may have added to their work. It can be argued that there is very little point providing detailed formative feedback if no notice will be taken of it, and that it would in such circumstances be just as well to limit things to marks or grades and spend the time saved on providing *real* formative feedback on ongoing work, where learners have the opportunity to make good use of the feedback in improving and developing their work accordingly.

Yorke (2002) argues that we need to spend time helping learners to make better use of formative feedback. He suggests:

> There is a case to be made for spending considerable time and resources on students undertaking their first programmes of study to help them understand the purposes of formative feedback and how their own self-beliefs can impact on the ways they receive it. Inevitably this would eat into available time for content delivery, which academic staff no doubt would be unwilling to see slimmed down, but if an institution is serious about retaining students as a key means of survival in an increasingly competitive world, then tough decisions might have to be made. (Yorke 2003: 39).

One way of helping learners to put feedback to better use is to cause them to reflect on feedback, and evidence their reflections as part of an ongoing process of becom-ing increasingly conscious of how they learn – and in this case increasing their awareness of how much they can in fact gain from feedback on their assessed work. The following reflective checklists can be used as a starting point to design your own reflection devices to allow learners to develop their approaches to planning their work and making the most of your feedback. All the better if you can persuade learners to allow *you* to see copies of their reflections, so that you too can help them further to develop their approaches to assessed work, and improve how you design feedback for them in future.

On submitting your first essay on a course

	Please tick one or more columns for each of the options below.	This is what I did.	I would have liked to do this, but didn't manage it.	I didn't think this necessary.	This just was not possible for me.	I'll do this next time.
1	I started thinking about this essay in plenty of time.					
2	I started to collect my reading materials well in advance.					
3	I discussed the ideas associated with this essay with someone, virtually or live, prior to starting writing.					
4	I had a timetable in mind for pre-reading, planning, drafting, writing, checking, doing the references.					
5	I planned out the structure of the essay logically, so my train of thought was continuous.					
6	I made reasonable efforts to clear the decks for the actual writing of the essay.					
7	I made referencing easy for myself by properly noting all of my sources as I did the reading.					
8	I showed someone a draft of my essay before I completed it.					
9	I acted on feedback I received to make my essay better.					
10	I wrote a summary/abstract that encapsulated my key points succinctly.					
11	I checked my work over carefully for obvious mistakes, and I used a spellchecker.					

Reflecting on tutor feedback on your essay

	Please tick one or more comments as appropriate.	This is what I did.	I would have liked to do this, but didn't manage it.	I didn't think this necessary.	This just was not possible for me.	I'll do this next time.	This did not apply in this case.
1	I read the tutor's comments carefully.						
2	I read my essay again to see how the tutor's comments applied.						
3	I noted things I needed to do before the next assignment.						
4	I looked back again at the assignment brief to see the extent to which my essay had complied with it.						
5	I looked forward to the next assignment to see which tutor comments might apply to my preparation for the next one.						
6	I followed up tutor advice on further reading.						
7	I used the feedback to check up on the things I did best in my essay, so I can build on my strengths in my next essay.						
8	I followed up tutor advice on my own writing practices.						
9	I shared my feedback with one or more other students to see how the commentary on my work compared with theirs.						
10	I considered aspects of my approach on which I would especially ask for feedback next time.						
11	I asked my tutor for further clarification on comments which I didn't understand.						
12	I identified any feedback comments which I felt were unjustified, so that I could find out more about them from my tutor in discussion.						

Designing feedback in response to poor work

This is the most delicate of feedback tasks. Suppose you're in a position of needing to write feedback comments to a learner whose *first* assignment you've just marked. It was a poor assignment. It would be considered a fail. Suppose, furthermore, that circumstances dictate that you've no alternative to giving this feedback in writing (or email) and you've got to put pen to paper or fingers to keyboard to compose a feedback missive to the learner concerned. Under normal circumstances, you would be wise to choose *not* to put this particular element of feedback into writing or print, and to see the learner face to face to handle this difficult situation with all the tact and sensitivity you could muster. But perhaps the learner concerned is away on a work placement, or perhaps there's just no way the two of you can get together for a face-to-face meeting in the immediate future and the feedback needs to be given sooner rather than later. Your choice of words can be critical.

At staff development workshops, I often charge participants with this difficult task, and ask them to compose a feedback letter or email dealing with the issue. I then ask them to swap letters so that they now have no idea whose they have in their hands. Next, I ask them to read aloud the letter or email they now have – but with a difference. I ask them to read it out in a sinister, threatening, menacing manner! This is to simulate how the well-intentioned language used in the document might come across to the learner concerned, who may already know the work was poor, may be having a 'bad day' and may be on the point of discontinuing their studies altogether.

It is surprising how threatening some quite ordinary words can be in this context. Words which are often followed by bad news include 'however', 'unfortunately' and even plain 'but'. There is, of course, no way that the use of these 'caution' words can be avoided, but it is worth reminding tutors that such words can cause learners' spirits to fall as they read feedback responses.

Then there's 'power language' which often creeps in. For example 'submit your next attempt' or 'resubmit your assignment after ... ' and so on. The word 'submit' puts the tutor on a pedestal, and the learner much lower down. 'Send me your next version' is so much milder somehow.

And there are the fatal phrases, possibly the worst imaginable of which is 'you've failed to grasp the basics of ... '. This position seems beyond all hope, when read out in a sufficiently sinister way!

Surprisingly, some well-intentioned ploys to soften the blow of delivering feedback on poor work can also lead to disaster. Phrases such as 'you've obviously put a lot of effort into ... ' or 'clearly you spend a lot of time on ... ' bring their own dangers. In particular, what if they hadn't? What if they rushed the assignment off at the eleventh hour, and here they find the tutor responding 'obviously you've spent a lot of time ...'? There is no quicker or more sure-fire way of losing credibility as a tutor! That learner will never trust you again.

Using feedback to make learning happen: 12 ways forward

The following suggestions are adapted from the conclusions drawn by Brown (2004) in a discussion paper on formative assessment.

1   *Help learners to* want *feedback.* Spend time and energy helping learners to under-stand the importance of feedback and the value of spending some time after receiving work back to learn from the experience. Most learners don't do this at the moment, concentrating principally on the mark.

2   *Get the timing right.* Aim to get feedback on work back to learners very quickly, while they still care and while there is still time for them to do something with it. The longer learners have to wait to get work back, especially if they have moved into another semester by the time they receive their returned scripts, the less likely it is that they will do something constructive with lecturer's hard-written comments. It could be useful to consider a policy not to give detailed written feedback to learners on work that is handed back at the end of the semester if that area of study is no longer being followed by the learner, and to concentrate on giving more incremental feedback throughout the semester.

3   *Make feedback interesting!* Learners are much more likely to study feedback prop-erly if they find it stimulating to read and feel it is personal to them, and not just routine or mundane. It takes more time to make feedback interesting, but if it makes the difference between learners making good use of it or not, it is time well spent.

4   *Give at least* some *feedback straight away.* Explore the possibilities of giving learn-ers at least *some* feedback at the time they hand in their work for marking. For example, a page or two of comments responding to 'frequently occurring prob-lems' with the assignment they are handing in, or illustrative details along the lines 'a good answer would include ... ' can give learners some useful feedback while their work on the assignment is still fresh in their minds, and can keep them going until they receive the detailed and individual feedback on their own attempts in due course. Giving 'generic' feedback at the time of submission in this way can also reduce the time it takes to mark learners' work, as there is then no need to repeat on script after script the matters that have already been addressed by the generic feedback, and tutors can concentrate their time and energy on responding to the individual learner's work, and giving specific feed-back on *their* strengths and weaknesses.

5   *Make use of the speed and power of technology.* Explore the uses of computer-assisted formative assessment. While a number of universities including Luton, Plymouth and the Open University are using computer-assisted assessment summatively, many would argue that it is currently most powerfully used to support formative feedback, often automatically generated by email. Learners seem to really like having the chance to find out how they are doing, and

attempt tests several times in an environment where no one else is watching how they do. They may be more willing to maximize the benefits of learning through mistakes when their errors can be made in the comfort of privacy, and when they can get quick feedback on these before they have built them into their work. Of course, many computer-assisted assessment systems allow you to monitor what is going on across a cohort, enabling you to concentrate your energies either on learners who are repeatedly doing badly or those who are not engaging at all in the activity.

6   *Link feedback directly to the achievement of intended learning outcomes.* Explore ways in which formative assessment can be made integral to learning. Too often assessment is bolted on, but the more we can constructively align (Biggs, 2003) assignments with planned learning outcomes and the curriculum taught, the more learners are likely to perceive them as authentic and worth bothering with. Giving learners feedback specifically on the level of their achievement of learning outcomes helps them to develop the habit of making better use of the learning outcomes as targets, as they continue to study.

7   *Provide most feedback at the beginning.* Investigate how learning can be advanced in small steps using a 'scaffolding' approach. This means providing lots of support in the early stages which can then be progressively removed as learners become more confident in their own abilities.

8   *Use feedback to let learners know what style of work is expected of them.* Devote energy to helping learners understand what is required of them in terms of writing, that is, work with them to understand the various academic discourses that are employed within the institution, and help them to understand when writing needs to be personal and based on individual experience, such as in a reflective log, and when it needs to be formal and using academic conventions like passive voice and third person, as in written reports and essays.

9   *Use feedback to help learners learn how best to use different kinds of source materials.* Help them also to understand that there are different kinds of approaches needed for reading depending on whether they are reading for pleasure, for information, for understanding or reading around a topic. Help them to become active readers with a pen and Post-its in hand, rather than passive readers, fitting the task in alongside television and other noisy distractions.

10 *Take care with the important words.* Ensure that the language you use when giving feedback to learners avoids destructive criticism of the person rather than the work being assessed. Boud (1995) talks about the disadvantages of using 'final language', that is, language that is judgemental to the point of leaving learners nowhere to go. Words like 'appalling', 'disastrous' and 'incompetent' fall into this area, but so also do words like 'incomparable' and 'unimprovable' if they don't help outstanding learners to develop ipsatively also.

11 *When possible, use feedback in rehearsal contexts.* Consider providing opportunities for re-submissions of work as part of a planned programme. Learners often feel they could do better work once they have seen the formative feedback and

would like the chance to have another go. Particularly at the early stages of a programme, consider offering them the chance to use formative feedback productively. Feedback often involves a change of orientation, not just the remediation of errors.

12 *Get learners* giving *feedback, not just receiving it.* Think about ways of getting learners to give each other formative feedback. The act of giving feedback often causes deeper thinking than just receiving feedback. Involve learners in their own and each other's assessment. Reflection is not a luxury; it is the best means available to help them really get inside the criteria and understand the often hidden 'rules of the game' of higher education. In particular, asking learners to review each other's draft material prior to submission can be really helpful for all learners, but particularly those who lack confidence about what kinds of things are expected of them.

6

Making learning happen in large groups

Learning by finding out the answers to questions

In many teaching-learning contexts, not least lectures and small-group sessions, one of the most productive ways of making learning happen is to cause learners to ask questions and provide answers to their questions. When they are working out what questions to ask, they are exploring their own *need* to learn at the time, and at the same time often working on what they *want* to find out. Asking questions is one kind of *learning by doing*. Receiving answers to their own questions is, of course, *learning through feedback*, as is hearing answers to other people's questions. Ideally, all of these processes should help them to *make sense* or *digest* the topics which are the basis of the questions.

In this chapter and the next, I am writing so as to encourage you to adopt a 'learning through answers to questions' approach. These two chapters are therefore written around a series of questions about large-group teaching and small-group teaching respectively. Another reason why I chose this approach for the present book is that I have already written a great deal about both large-group and small-group teaching. In Brown and Race (2002), we explored 'lecturing' in substantial detail, with wide-ranging references to the recent literature on the topic. I also provided practical suggestions about large-group teaching in chapter 3, and small-group teaching in chapter 4 of Race (2001). Therefore, rather than risk repeating myself here, I am using the question and answer format to extend the discussion in the particular context of this book – making learning happen.

What is a large group?

It all depends! For an increasing number of staff in post-compulsory education, classes numbering several hundreds are not unusual – especially first-year cohorts in university programmes. For others, 80 is a large group. However, many staff have hitherto worked with much smaller groups, and when numbers rise from 10 to 20, it feels like a large group. In fact, I've included much more detail on working with 20 or so learners at a time in 'Making workshops work', the final chapter in this book, and in many respects a group of 20 can be thought of as a workshop context, where the main idea is to keep them active, as participants rather than just 'an audience'.

The same applies, however, to much larger groups. Ideally, even with hundreds sitting in a lecture theatre, we want them all to be learning actively for as great a proportion of each time slot as we can manage. Each learner is still an individual, and we need to try to make learning happen in all the individual brains in the lecture theatre. It sometimes takes a bit of thought to design learning-by-doing activities which can still work with hundreds of learners at a time. Other questions and answers in this chapter address this in more detail.

How can we get learners to ask questions in large groups?

While it is relatively easy to get learners to fire their questions at us in small groups or in one-to-one contexts, it is harder to achieve this with hundreds of learners at a time. One thing that can help is to ask everyone to jot down two or three questions, and give them a couple of minutes to do so. Then ask them to compare their questions with those of their immediate neighbours. Then ask for questions. This way, you have more chance of getting the questions that are more widely owned, and more important. It is also a way of causing everyone to think about at least some questions, so that even the learners who don't get answers to their questions during the session are still able to take the questions away with them. If you'd just got learners to *think* of some questions, and call them out, many of the questions in their minds would have evaporated away very soon after the session.

However, even as discussed above, there can be another problem – dominant learners. Read on.

How can we enable learners to get answers to their questions in large-group sessions, without the sessions being monopolized by a few vociferous learners?

Following on from my response to the previous question, it remains worthwhile trying to get all the learners to write down a question or two in the first instance. When, however, you know that it will be the same learners who voice their questions, possibly because they are more confident than their coursemates, some alternative tactics can come in handy.

For example, pass out Post-its so the whole group can have one each, and ask everyone to jot down one or two questions on their Post-it. Then ask for the Post-its to be passed to you, and stick them on a flip chart, whiteboard, window or suitable wall. With really large groups, get the learners themselves to do this, it's quicker. You can then scan through the questions, picking off a Post-it at a time, and reading out the question so everyone knows what you're going to be answering. Then you can answer the question, filing the Post-it so you have an accurate record of which questions you answered.

Normally it is worth concentrating on those questions which you can readily see to be relatively common ones, so that you are satisfying the needs of a reasonable cross-section of the large group. However, it is also worth taking away with you *all* the Post-its, and looking through them in your own time, sometimes creating an 'FAQ' (frequently asked questions) sheet containing other important questions and headline answers to give out at your next meeting with the large group.

One of the advantages of Post-its is that learners still have the comfort of anonymity. It does not matter if some of the questions are banal or even silly. The point is that you find out what questions are in the minds of those who really need some answers. Those learners who would be too shy at asking a question in front of the large group are usually perfectly happy to write the question down on a Post-it. The vociferous learners have exactly the same opportunity to pose their questions, so the process can be regarded as an equal opportunities one.

How can we manage inappropriate behaviours in large groups?

This is a frequently asked question at workshops on dealing with large groups! I often use a '30-second theatre' technique with workshop participants working in threes, where one makes an 'inappropriate behaviour incident', another responds as the teacher or lecturer for no more than 30 seconds, then the third who has been observing leads a discussion on how well the exchange might have gone in a real situation, and explores alternative ploys. Some of the most frequent 'inappropriate behaviours' are discussed below.

Learners coming in late

This is increasingly common, not least because many learners have commitments which sometimes conflict with their college programmes – childcare, work-related matters and so on. It can be very infuriating, however, especially when latecomers disrupt a large group as they make their way to the remaining seats. Indeed, some latecomers seem to be only too happy to be disruptive in such circumstances.

Confronting them publicly is not the best idea. If they are indulging in attention-seeking behaviours, that would just reward them. Moreover, when latecomers have good reasons for being late, making them feel uncomfortable is not likely to increase their confidence to turn up late ever again, and they are quite likely to miss your session entirely rather than risk further embarrassment.

Probably the safest option is to ignore latecomers. Pausing while they settle them-selves in is better than trying to carry on talking but with learners being distracted by the latecomers' entry. But sometimes you can't just ignore them, and need to wait too long until they have settled down. If there are successive interruptions of this kind, it can be wearing both on yourself and on all the other learners in the group. Peer pressure under such circumstances can often come to bear on regular offenders.

Some lecturers can't resists a touch of irony. 'So glad you could join us' and so on. But this can sometimes hit hard at the odd learner who is hardly ever late. When you are able to use their names, it can be useful to say something to them by name, for example, 'There are still some seats down here, John', and this can at least have the effect that the latecomer knows that you know who he or she is.

One tactic which can reduce the incidence of latecomers is to always start as soon as reasonably possible, but with something particularly useful to learners. For example, preceding the intended learning outcomes for *this* session with five important points to carry forward from the *last* session can reward those who are punctual, particularly when these points contain useful advice relating to forthcoming assessment based on the last session.

Learners chatting to each other

This is often a sign that they are bored – or, at least, that their motivation is low. However, sometimes learners are talking to each other in more productive ways, such as:

- explaining a point to a neighbour who missed it
- clarifying what something you said actually means
- translating something into a different language for someone whose first language isn't English.

Whatever the context, however, it is unwise to continue trying to talk above a growing level of background chatter. Sometimes, going closer to the people who are chatting stops them. Alternatively, asking them 'is there a problem here?' can help you to find out what's going on.

It is more difficult to decide what to do when the problem is simply that some learners are not interested in what is going on, and are being deliberately disruptive! Asking them to leave may be an option, but if they refuse to leave it becomes a real problem.

Sometimes, a level of background chatter can be a signal to do something quite different with the large group. Options include:

- Give them a task where they are *intended* to talk to the people sitting closest to them for a few minutes – for example, put up a slide asking them to argue a case with each other, or make a decision, or think of some causes for a phenomenon. When learners are getting restless, and one of the symptoms is talking to each other, *causing* them to talk to each other for a few minutes can help them to get it out of their system.

- Make it more interesting. This is where it can be useful to inject a little humour, for example, by having a hidden action button on a PowerPoint slide which you can use to summon up an amusing picture, or something else to restore learners' concentration.
- Give them a written task to do individually first, then discuss with each other. If some learners continue chatting, you at least know that you may need to push them a little harder to get down to the task before continuing to talk to each other as intended.
- If it's near the scheduled end of the session, bring it to a close anyway, rather than press on against all the odds to cover everything you had intended to cover in that particular session.

What kinds of classrooms make large-group teaching a nightmare?

The worst environmental conditions for large-group teaching include:

- more learners than seats – aisles or steps are not comfortable
- too hot or too cold
- lack of control of the lighting, to make projected images suitably visible
- uncomfortable seats
- narrow corridors leading to and from the venue, leading to congestion when one large group needs to leave and another is waiting to enter
- poor acoustics – difficulty in being heard well at the back or sides of the room
- poor visibility – for example, in large flat rooms where learners obstruct each others' vision of yourself or of the screen or whiteboard
- 'noisy' floor surfaces, where latecomers make a lot of sound or chairs squeak as they are adjusted
- poor location of equipment, for example, a computer keyboard where you have to turn your back on the group to use the machine.

More often than not, we simply have to make the most of what we've got when it comes to large-group teaching spaces. Grumbling about the room to our learners does not solve the problems, though it can be appropriate to offer them some sympathy or encourage them to mention the problems as they see them when giving them feedback opportunities.

Some problems are within our control. Visibility, for example, can be aided by only using the top half of projection screens and whiteboards. If you're using successive bullet points on PowerPoint slides, for example, you can soon see how far down the bullet points go before learners can be seen moving their heads to see past people in front of them. Then you can aim to minimize this by designing all your slides to use the visible part of the screen.

A microphone and loudspeakers can help with audibility problems, and can save you from tiring (or even damaging) your voice by sustained attempts to speak more loudly. Some training in voice projection can also be valuable.

How can you help individuals to be heard in large-group sessions?

We've already explored some ways to get questions from individual learners, for example, using Post-its. However, it's useful to be able to respond to spontaneous questions from learners too. Always try to repeat the question back to the whole group before proceeding to answer it, as people behind the questioner may not have been able to hear the question when first posed. If the question is a long one, a complex one or an unclear one, it can be worth clarifying the question, for example, by asking 'is your question really about ... ?', or suggesting 'Let's break this question into three parts ... ' and then breaking it down into a logical sequence before continuing to answer it. Repeating the question back to the whole group also gives you a little longer to mentally rehearse how you're going to respond to it.

Sometimes, a dialogue happens between one particular learner and yourself. In such cases, if the room allows, it can improve things if you can move closer to the questioner, so that it is easier for you to interact well with this learner and so that they are better able to make sense of your responses to them. If, however, the dialogue becomes too protracted, it may be necessary to explain to the whole group that 'I think this is a matter for the two of us to explore outside this session', so that they don't feel that they are being ignored.

What do learners do that hinders learning?

We've already explored some learners actions which hinder learning – latecoming and chatting inappropriately. There are many other things they may do which get in the way of their learning. These include:

- *Taking notes rather than making notes.* At one level, this is not a problem; if they're busy copying things down from the screen or board or writing down what you are saying to them, they're unlikely to be disruptive in other ways. However, *taking* notes is usually very passive, and *making* notes is much better for learning. *Making* notes can include making their own summaries of what has been covered in the last few minutes, or annotating a handout with the main points that you have covered which are not already presented there, and so on. It is important to help learners to make notes by building in suitable time spans (for example, two minutes) to give them an opportunity to do this. It can also be useful to allow another minute or two for them to compare the notes they made with each other and add further ideas to their own notes. 'Now steal your classmates' best ideas for a minute' is irresistible to many learners.

- *Just sitting passively.* This is all too easy. Unless we *cause* learners to b large group sessions, many will just sit there waiting until they're to. something. They may look as though they're listening – even quite attent. but may have already found out that as long as though they *look* as though ι are there in spirit, they can switch off mentally! The answer is for us to continue to take control of what they do, so they have a variety of things to do and are less likely to sink into passivity. We can alternate between getting them to answer questions, discuss points with each other, make notes, solve problems, apply what they've just learned to a case study scenario, and so on.
- *Going to sleep and snoring!* This is many lecturers' worst-case scenario of things going wrong in large groups. It has to be said that for things to get this far, they must have been passive for rather too long in the first place, and we need to look to what *we* have done – or not done – to cause them to slumber. That said, it is worth remembering that at least some learners in any large group will be in *need* of sleep. Some may have worked late or early shifts, and may be already deprived of sleep. Others may have enjoyed themselves into the early hours, to the same effect. Sitting still for a long time in a relatively warm comfortable environment, especially if the lights are dimmed for slides to be seen, fulfils fairly ideal conditions for human sleep! It does not help to make anyone who has nodded off feel seriously embarrassed – that may have the effect of causing them not to bother turning up at all next time they are tired and in danger of falling asleep. The kindest thing to do is perhaps to change the activity, for example getting *everyone* to discuss a point with their nearest neighbours – even if they have to wake up the odd neighbour in the process.

What do lecturers do that hinders learning?

Learners themselves can tell us a lot about this. The worst, and all too frequent, comments that learners make about unsatisfactory experiences of large-group teaching feature one word – 'boring'. Their feedback includes:

- droning on and on
- going right over our heads
- not looking at us – or ignoring us
- going too fast – or going too slow (this is a problem in any large group, with people learning at their own speeds, of course, and we need to try to vary the pace accordingly with 'catch-up' time for the slower learners, but giving the faster ones something extra to think about so that they don't become bored)
- telling us things we already know
- not linking the topic to what *we* know about it
- doing things that seem irrelevant
- forgetting to explain *why* a particular topic will be useful
- not responding to our questions or giving us the chance to ask them

- not giving us anything to do.

Some of this feedback warns us to sharpen up our own act, to make things as inter-esting as we can, checking regularly that the large group is 'with us', and keeping each and every member of the large group as active as we can.

However, there are many well-intentioned lecturer actions which can hinder learning too. These include:

- going off on lengthy tangents to the main purpose of the session, sometimes out of a will to make a topic more interesting
- explaining things in detail when most of the group already need no further explanation
- presenting too much information without giving learners the chance to do some-thing with the information, get feedback on their attempts and make sense of the information
- sticking too closely to the agenda for the session, when all the signs are that learn-ers need a few minutes out of thinking about a difficult concept, for example
- doing *anything* for too long at a time, failing to bring some variety to learners
- being too predictable!

It is helpful to us to continuously gather feedback from our learners about what they like about our large-group sessions and what they dislike. We can't please all of them all of the time, but the more we find out about their likes and dislikes, the better we can strike a balance. It can also be really useful to sit in on colleagues' large-group sessions as often as possible. In someone else's lecture, whatever the topic, we can usually come out with two lists:

- Things that seemed to work well for them, that I can try in my own large-group sessions.
- Things I noticed which didn't work and which I'll try to avoid in my sessions.

This can all be done quite informally and, where team teaching is the norm, lec-turers find it very useful simply to learn informally from each others' approaches in this way. Many institutions nowadays have systems of peer observation, and it is then useful to have direct feedback from different colleagues about how they find our individual approaches to large-group teaching.

How can technology help to make learning happen in large groups?

The use of technology in large-group teaching has evolved rapidly in the last few decades. Until the 1960s, large-group teaching was mainly 'chalk and talk' – or, indeed, just 'talk' in some disciplines. There would occasionally be slide shows – a welcome treat for learners. But perhaps these were welcomed for two reasons – one good and one less good – some visual stimulus, but also a chance to sit back without having to write anything down!

Then came the overhead projector, making visual aids much more commonplace in large-group teaching – and in smaller-group teaching too. There was also an expectation that any good teacher in post-compulsory education should master this strange new technology, and 'educational technology' emerged as a presence in institutions. Training courses were laid on for willing – and unwilling – teachers to induct them into the mysteries of the new equipment. In the university sector, in particular, this was the first sign of moves towards training lecturers in teaching methods – it had previously been assumed that anyone who was qualified in a subject should automatically be able to teach it and assess learners' work on it. Lindsay (2004) gives a provocative and amusing account of what has happened since the 1970s in an extended review of two well-known texts now used widely in the field of educational development which emerged from these technology-based roots.

Modern lecture theatres are often very well equipped regarding technology. They are often more like cinemas than anything else, with comfortable seating, very large screens and the facilities to project images from computer consoles, with live links to the web, DVDs and cameras so that even today's newspaper can be placed on the modern equivalent of the overhead projector, and a particular article zoomed into, so that all in the theatre can read even the small print.

Overhead projection remains an option, but has been displaced to a significant extent by data projection using computer-based presentation managers, notably Microsoft PowerPoint. This is now so widely used that the word PowerPoint has itself come to be associated with most of the visual support used in large group teaching. This can easily include links to audio and video files, and is a convenient way of packaging up just about all the technological support for teaching in large-group contexts.

In Brown and Race (2002) many of the issues involved in making learning happen with such technologies are explored in the chapter on 'Lecturing tools'. The danger remains, however, that some of the very sophisticated visual images that can now be seen in lecture theatres perpetuate the danger that accompanied those early slide shows half a century ago – learners switching off and just enjoying what they see. In Anderson and Race (2002), the whole area of 'learning from screens' is explored in some detail in the context of online learning, and the arguments presented there are easily extended to the learning which happens (or doesn't happen) from the big screen in lecture theatres.

How can handouts be properly used in large groups to support learning?

Handouts have become increasingly important in the context of large-group teaching, and are important not only to learners, but as elements of the evidence used to assess the quality of post-compulsory education. I have reflected the importance of handouts by discussing their use in rather more detail than most of the other questions considered in this chapter, and linked handouts to the five factors underpinning successful learning quite overtly.

While feedback might be considered to be the lifeblood of making learning happen in post-compulsory education, handouts could be thought of as the arteries controlling the flow of information to learners' hands – but perhaps not entirely successful in getting the information processed in their brains. Returning to Einstein's idea that 'learning is experience, everything else is just information' it is easy to see that the main danger associated with handouts is that they give learners information, which does not in due course get processed by them to become their own knowledge.

Only two or three decades ago, handouts were relatively rare. Learners in lectures needed to make notes to take away from the lecture that which had been covered by the lecturer. Typically, this meant that in an hour, they could only acquire a few pages worth of information. If they had just been furiously writing out all they could capture from the lecture, this information may have been mainly unprocessed when they took it away, but at least the task of going through it again and turning it into their own knowledge was manageable. Nowadays, it is common for a great deal more information to be placed directly into learners' hands, in handout form in lectures, or made available to them in course materials, in print or electronically. They may be able to download the information upon which a lecture focuses from the intranet, even before the lecture, and then work with it, adding to it ideas they gained from the lecture itself, and build into the material their thinking after the lecture. So it is not uncommon for learners to receive one way or another 10 or 20 pages of information around a lecture – and printed pages contain many more words (numbers, pictures, graphs, diagrams, and so on) than could be written or drawn by any learner in an hour.

Similarly, where formerly learners needed to make their own notes from books in libraries, nowadays they are likely to make photocopies of the information they believe to be most relevant or important, and take the information away with them. Cue-seeking learners are probably the best at deciding which extracts are important enough for them to make their own copies, and cue-oblivious learners run the greatest risk of copying everything which *might* turn out to be relevant – this is in fact simply postponing (often indefinitely) the task of getting down to making sense of the information and turning it into their own knowledge.

How, then, can we make best use of pieces of paper with information already reproduced on them, to maximize the associated learning pay-off learners derive from them?

Handouts and wanting to learn

For a start, if handouts *look* interesting, there's more chance that they will be used and not just filed away. Making handouts look interesting can be done in several ways including:

- making the subject matter interesting to read and study
- making the information on handouts *digestible* rather than dry and forbidding
- using paper to capture diagrams, graphs, pictures and so on to bring to life the ideas concerned
- even simply paying attention to layout, choice of font, and so on.

However, the most important way of ensuring that handouts enhance learners' *want* to learn is to make sure that learners find them really *useful*. This can be partly achieved by paying attention to the content of the handouts, and helping learners to feel that at least some of the work has already been done for them in narrowing down the subject content such that everything on their handouts can already be regarded as important enough to spend some time and energy following up.

Handouts and needing to learn

Perhaps the most direct way that handout materials can help learners to take ownership of their need to learn is including (prominently) the relevant intended learning outcomes and, where necessary, translating these into language which learners can readily relate to. In other words, it is useful to give learners some guidance about what in due course they need to become able to *do* with the content of the handouts – how learners will be expected to become able to *evidence* their achievement of the intended learning outcomes.

This does not assume that all the intended outcomes can be achieved just by studying the information on a given handout. The intended outcomes can range outward, and link to what learners are expected to be able to do through their work on reference sources listed in a handout, along with guidance about how best to approach each individual source. Rather than (for example) suggest 'now read Chapter 4 of Smith and Jones', a handout is much more useful if it suggests 'consult Chapter 4, particularly sections 3 and 5, looking for answers to the following questions … ' along with a self-assessment exercise helping learners to focus their work on the source so that they do indeed get out of it the most important things. Such guidance can also include advice such as 'you don't need to bother with sections 2 or 7 unless you really want to – these are not directly relevant to your own particular intended learning outcomes relating to this source'.

Handouts and learning by doing

Throughout this book I have stressed the importance of learning by doing – particularly practice, repetition of relevant activities, and learning by trial and error. When handout materials are designed quite overtly as learning by doing devices, the chance of them just being filed away are dramatically reduced. Handouts which contain several tasks and exercises are likely to be used, not just stored. When it can be *seen* that a handout is something to do things with – for example, with boxes to be filled in, spaces for calculations to be done, and so on – at least learners know that simply leaving these boxes unfilled is not going to be sufficient. If it is made clear that the activities in a handout relate directly to the achievement of relevant aspects of the intended learning outcomes, learners are all the more likely to engage with the material. If it is also made very clear that *doing* the handout will relate well to the sorts of *doing* which will in due course be assessed (exam questions, assignments, essays, essay plans, and so on), learners become much more aware that they need to engage with the activities in a handout.

Cue-seeking learners are in their element here of course, but cue-conscious learners find this way of highlighting what is important (and what isn't) useful too, and cue-oblivious learners are still able to benefit to the extent that the things they *do* using the handout are already designed to be relevant and important, saving them perhaps from spending too much time or energy going off on tangents, or straying too far away from the intended learning outcomes which will form the basis of their assessment in due course.

Handouts and making sense of what is learned

There are several things we can do to design handouts which help learners to get their heads round ideas and concepts. As indicated above, we can design into handouts relevant learning by doing, so that learners get the chance to apply their minds to the information in the handout and process it as part of the journey towards building their own knowledge using the handout. Also as noted above, careful use of intended learning outcomes can assist learners in finding out *what exactly* they should be trying to make sense of, and alerting them to the ways in which they will need to become able to demonstrate that they have made sense of the material in the handout.

Moreover, handout materials are really useful as study guides, referencing out to a wide range of print-based and web-based sources and resources, with the handouts helping learners to see exactly which parts of these sources are most relevant to use towards their becoming increasingly able to evidence their own achievement of the intended learning outcomes.

Handouts and learning through feedback

When the primary intention of handout material is to give learners feedback on things they have already done, handouts can be particularly useful in making learning happen. For example, when learners have struggled with something, a handout showing them how best to go about it may be eagerly used. However, one of the best ways of coupling learning by doing with feedback is to include in handout materials self-assessment exercises of one kind or another, where learners can have a go at a task or problem, then find elsewhere in the handout the means to judge their own efforts, finding out to what extent they 'got it right' – and, more important, addressing the 'if not, why not?' question. Clearly there are disadvantages in making the feedback *too* easy to find – if learners can see it at the same time as seeing the tasks themselves, the temptation for eyes to stray towards the answers remains great, and only the most conscientious learners will resist looking straight at the solutions. Other learners who skip having a go at the problems may *feel* that looking immediately at the solutions is good enough, but we all know that being able to do something is not the same as *feeling* that one can do it correctly.

Some problems with handouts

Some learners take the view 'I don't need to go to the class, I can simply get a copy of the handout'. It is of course true that they can get a copy of the *information*, but with an element of good teaching just having the information is far from the equivalent of actually *being there*. Learners who miss out on the tone of voice, body language, facial expression, emphasis, clarification and, often, *inspiration* of participating in a class are seriously disadvantaged – but frequently do not realize this until too late, thinking that they've 'got' it all in their copied handout. Indeed, in many an effective face-to-face session, a handout is more of an *adjunct* to the intended learning than a summary of it.

Overlapping with this problem is 'I've already *got* the handout, therefore there's no point in me going to the class'. This happens all too often when handout materials are issued in advance or made available on an intranet before the relevant teaching session.

Perhaps even more common is the view of learners sitting in a class, with their own copy of a handout safely in their possession, taking the view 'I don't need to pay attention now, I've already got the information, I can sit back and switch off now'. True, they may already have got the *information*, but are then missing out on the best chance to turn that information into the beginnings of their own *making sense* of that information, using tone of voice and so on as cues and clues.

Another problem is that learners sometimes don't really know the answer to 'what am I expected to *do* with this handout – read it now, revise from it later, do things with it now and soon after now, just file it, collect handouts until I've got all of them and *then* do something with them ... ?' This list is endless. In fact, all such reactions to handouts could be regarded as handout-using avoidance tactics – excuses for putting off doing some *real* learning until later.

Perhaps the most significant thing about a handout is the matter of ownership. Whose handout is it? Is it simply the lecturer's? When learners have *done* a lot with a handout *during* a class, the ownership is very much more *theirs*. When there's a lot of *their* writing on the handout, they feel quite differently about it than when it was exactly the same as everyone else's copy of the handout. In fact, they're then much less likely to loan it to a friend who missed the session, to copy – they might lose *their* thoughts in the process – or, indeed, they may feel 'why should so-and-so benefit from the work *I've* done on these pages?'

I have included below an example of a self-assessment checklist which learners could be given, aiming to get them thinking exactly how they are making use of handout materials. The example I chose for the checklist refers to a handout accompanying a particular lecture, but the idea of making such a checklist can easily be extended to help learners to self-evaluate how they are making use of *any* handout – any collection of information, exercises, subject matter and so on.

How can we help learners to make meaningful records of learning in large groups?

I've already referred to the differences between *making* notes and just *taking* notes. It can be useful to help learners themselves to take ownership of the need to capture much more than just the information which is covered in large-group sessions. Remind them that even just an hour or two after a lecture, especially if they have already been in two or three other lectures, much of the fine detail will have evaporated away.

Suggest that learners consciously try to capture questions which go through their minds all the way through large-group sessions, and jot these questions down in their notes (perhaps in a different colour). These questions can include things they would have asked but didn't, questions other learners asked, questions about things not yet understood, and so on. Even when questions are jotted down only to be followed by the answers becoming clear, it is valuable to have written down the question, and then perhaps ticked it or drawn an arrow to where the answer is now written down.

How can we ensure that learning in large groups is inclusive?

In any large group, we need to be responding as best as we can to the fact that the group is likely to be diverse in several ways, perhaps ethnic background, age range, experience levels and ability range. We also need to do whatever we reasonably can to make ourselves heard more easily by those who find it difficult to hear us, and make both ourselves and our visual aids more visible to those with restricted eyesight. Everything we do to make a large-group session more satisfactory for those with special needs should automatically improve things for everyone else at the same time. There is further discussion of inclusive teaching in Chapter 8 of this book.

Checklist on using a handout during and after a lecture

	Please tick one or more columns as appropriate for each choice below.	This is what I did.	I would have liked to do this, but didn't manage it.	I didn't think this necessary.	This just was not possible for me.	I'll do this next time.	This was not possible for this handout.
1	I filed the handout together with other handouts from this course, but haven't yet *done* anything with the handout itself.						
2	I read through this handout within three days of getting it.						
3	I marked up the handout with my own ideas during the lecture.						
4	I marked up the handout with my own ideas within a few days of the lecture.						
5	I wrote on the handout my own questions about the topic, so that I would not forget these questions.						
6	I compared *my* questions and notes on the handout with at least one other learner's thoughts.						
7	I have tried the tasks and exercises in the handout now, and learned useful things through doing this.						
8	I have followed up the handout by reading suggested reference materials.						
9	I have used the handout as a framework to add further notes from other sources I have consulted.						
10	I found that the intended learning outcomes gave me a useful frame of reference, helping me to structure my work on the handout effectively.						
11	I missed the lecture concerned, but have now got a copy of the handout.						
12	I feel that I have mastered the handout, and that there is nothing further I now need to do with this bit of subject matter to be ready for any aspect of it that will come up in assessments.						

What's the difference between the kind of learning in a large group, and that which goes on in tutorials, seminars or problem classes?

In some subject disciplines, subject coverage is split carefully between large-group sessions and various kinds of small-group sessions. Probably the most important features of the learning which we should strive to engender in large groups are:

- helping learners to see the big picture – including exactly where tutorials, seminars and other teaching-learning elements contribute to the overall context
- giving the whole group shared experiences – for example, developing attitudes and feelings towards the subject matter and the various sources and resources available to deepen the learning experience
- providing the overall information map – for example, using handouts, downloadable files from the intranet, reading lists, specific references and so on
- helping learners to set their sights regarding the real meaning of the intended learning outcomes, and the ways in which learners' achievement of these outcomes will be assessed in due course
- sharing expectations about what learners are required to do on their own, so all members of the whole group are aware of the expected scope of reading around the subject they are intended to do
- providing an opportunity for clarification, so that collectively learners can have their questions answered
- helping learners to gain a real sense of identity in the cohort and to see the links between the different subject areas they are studying.

Tutorials, seminars and other small-group learning contexts are necessarily not identical learning experiences for different sub-groups of the whole cohort, so large group sessions need to address all the things that *all* members of the whole group need to share.

What are the drivers of genuinely interactive learning in large groups?

Ideally, each large-group session should be a learning by doing occasion for all members of the group. However, it is much easier – given the chance – for learners to simply sit there watching someone else do all the work! Lecturers often complain of learners wishing to be spoon-fed. It is therefore often an uphill struggle to *cause* learners to remain active during large-group sessions, and many lecturers find it easier just to lecture.

Once learners *realize* that they are doing important elements of learning during large-group sessions, attendance levels improve – in both senses of the word 'attendance'. We can get learners on-side to a significant extent by suggesting that our rationale for keeping them busy during large-group sessions is to make best use of their precious time, so that their learning is well-started during each session, rather than them having to go back to their notes and handouts and start learning when assessment deadlines are looming up.

What kinds of briefing do learners need to help them understand how best to learn in large-group contexts?

In particular, learners need guidance on what to do in lectures. Especially in first-year courses, they may feel strangely lonely even in a packed lecture theatre, with no idea what they are expected to do – write it all down? Sit there and think about it? Try to look as intelligent as possible? Be quiet and 'good' and not interrupt by asking questions?

Some guidance on the differences between note-taking and note-making can be very welcome. It is best that this kind of guidance is regarded as everyone's business, and not just the remit of a specialist in learning support services. When we all share our suggestions about how to make the most of large-group sessions, learners pick up a much more balanced picture of the possibilities open to them and the different ways their lecturers themselves found successful when studying.

In particular, learners need to be well briefed on the importance of intended learning outcomes as a framework for their learning, and as the basis of a specifications framework laying down the standards of the evidence that they themselves need to become able to provide for their learning in the different kinds of assessment which will follow.

What kind of ground rules should be established for large-group learning?

It is best if our approach to setting ground rules is a mutual affair. We can specify what *we* will try to do with a large group, for example:

- Start and finish each session punctually.
- Be helpful by providing clear details of the intended learning outcomes near the beginning of each session.
- Help learners to understand exactly what standards we will be expecting them to reach as to the evidence we will seek from them regarding their achievement of the intended learning outcomes in due course.
- Answer their questions – either as they come, or at intervals every now and then during the sessions.
- Be available at specified times and places for individual or groups to come and discuss particular problems or difficulties with us.

In turn, we can suggest some ground rules for members of the large group, along the lines of:

- We expect you to arrive punctually, as a courtesy to each other and to me.
- When not punctual for unavoidable reasons, enter with as little disturbance as possible.
- Do not distract other learners by inappropriate chatter.
- Be ready to participate by answering questions, working in buzz groups, and so on.
- Come suitably prepared by doing suggested pre-session work.
- Respect all fellow learners and avoid being offensive to anyone present.

Whose responsibility is it to make learning happen in large groups?

It can be argued that it is our responsibility to facilitate learning in large groups, rather than just attempt to transmit information to the learners. However, this only works when the responsibility is shared and we succeed in persuading learners that they, too, need to play their part to gain optimum learning pay-off from their participation in each session.

Why do we have large groups anyway?

There are many reasons why large-group teaching is increasingly important in post-compulsory education. Not least, with policies to widen participation, there are many more learners in our systems, and it is clearly cost-effective to try to work with them in large groups for at least some of the time. But perhaps the most significant reasons for making good use of large-group teaching is to give whole cohorts of learners shared experiences, so that each learner feels part of the group and knows what is expected of them.

What can we do to enhance the want to learn in large groups?

Ideally, each large-group session should result in as many as possible of the group members going away fired up to continue their learning. Different lecturers achieve this in completely different ways. Probably the most important common factor is enthusiasm. If we seem bored with a subject, there's not much chance we will inspire others to go and learn more about it. But it's not just enthusiasm for the subject that matters. Learners are quick to pick up the vibrations of our enthusiasm for *themselves*. Lecturers who come across as really *liking* learners – and respecting them and treating them accordingly – do much to inspire learners to learn.

How can we clarify the need to learn in large groups – shared standards, putting outcomes to work?

Large group teaching contexts are our best shot to clarify the need to learn. This is not least as this is the *fairest* context to give learners information about exactly what we expect of them. This is the context where it is fair to tell everyone at once about the assessment standards which underpin the achievement of the intended learning outcomes. Large-group sessions are occasions when we can give cues and clues about the sorts of exam questions which would be reasonable ways to measure learners' achievement of the intended outcomes – much better than giving such clues to only *some* of the learners in particular small-group tutorials or in response to individual questions privately. We can collect learners' individual enquiries about the standards expected of them from all sorts of contexts, but the best chance to clarify our expectations is when *all* the learners in a cohort are present. Indeed, if we make a habit of using large-group contexts to let learners into the fine detail of our expectations, large-group session attendance is improved.

What can we get learners to do in large groups?

In Brown and Race (2002) we listed things learners actually do in lectures, and added some further things their lecturers *hope* that they may be doing. I have combined the two lists in Table 6.1, which shows that just about all of human life goes on in large-group sessions, including at least some actions which can be linked in straightforward ways to wanting to learn, taking ownership of the need to learn, learning by doing, learning through feedback and making sense of what is being learned. You might find it useful to mark up the activities in Table 6.1 with the following codes:

W = wanting to learn
N = taking ownership of the need to learn
D = learning by doing
F = learning through feedback
M = making sense of what is being learned

and then concentrating in your own large-group sessions on facilitating those learner actions which have the highest learning pay-off. Some of the learner actions 'hit' more than one of W, N, D, F and M, and these are all the more worthwhile to make space for in large group teaching. 'Understanding the subject' is not included in the list, as it takes a combination of several of the most productive actions to make this a reality. I should also point out that Table 6.1 shows only *some* of the things learners do in large group teaching sessions!

Table 6.1 Some things learners do in large group teaching sessions

Adding important points to the handouts

Admiring the cool, calm way the lecturer handles awkward questions

Answering each other's questions

Answering the lecturer's questions

Asking each other questions

Asking the lecturer questions

Being bored

Being impressed by the way the lecturer makes the technology work

Catching up with the report that's due in at 11 o'clock

Challenging their assumptions

Chatting to the next learner

Coming down from illegal substances

Considering dropping out of the course

Copying down important things from the screen

Copying things down from the board

Copying things down from the screen

Copying things down (or trying to) that the lecturer says

Discussing things with each other

Doing calculations, but then missing other things that are being said

Feeling desperate for a cigarette

Feeling embarrassed for the lecturer, standing there struggling away

Feeling embarrassed that they couldn't answer the question

Feeling faint

Feeling put-down by the lecturer's response to their answer

Feeling that they've heard all this before

Feeling the light dawning – and trying to capture it

Feeling they are only capturing some of the points

Feeling too hot

Finding out what others think

Fretting about their relationships

Getting annoyed at the learner in front busy texting on a mobile

Getting excited and wanting to find out more and more about the topic

Getting hungrier

Getting really tired

Having complex ideas clarified

Having misconceptions debunked

Hearing a range of opinions

Highlighting things in the handouts

Hoping that the cheque has come in the post

Itching to get to their books to get into the topic deeper

Jotting down their own answers to the lecturer's questions

Jotting their notes onto the handout materials

Learning things

Listening and thinking, but most of their thoughts being gone again two hours later – or two minutes later sometimes

Listening to the cricket scores

Looking at the visual images on screen and comparing them with works of art seen in exhibitions

Looking for cues about how to tackle the assignment

Lusting after that learner two rows in front

Making additional notes to the handout materials

Making links with things they had learned previously

Making mistakes in buzz group tasks and learning from them

Making notes

Missing things – while writing down one point, two others have been made that they couldn't get down

Never getting down as much as they're trying to

Nodding off

Picking up cues about what's important

Practising things

Sharing ideas

Still thinking about a previous lecture on a different topic

Summarizing what's being discussed

Taking down notes

Thinking about concepts

Thinking about the cheque which didn't arrive this morning

Trying not to cough

Trying out short problems and getting feedback on how they undertook the task

Trying to make connections between theory and practice

Trying to sort out what's important and what's just background

Trying to stay awake

Waiting for the minutes to go by

Waiting, and waiting for some of the class to get things down and for the whole thing to move on

Wanting to leave, but not daring to

Wanting to talk to their neighbour to check out whether they are the only one who can't see the point

Watching the lecturer

Watching the on-screen presentation

Wishing they hadn't said such-and-such to so-and-so

Wishing they'd looked at the last two sets of notes, and wondering whether this would have made the present lecture make sense to them

Wondering how on earth this person got to be a lecturer

Wondering if they will dare ask so-and-so out

Wondering what the lecturer's partner is like

Working out what seems likely to be coming up in the exam

Working out where to try to live next

Worrying about an unwanted pregnancy

Worrying about the assignment on another module

Worrying about the credit card demand

Worrying about whether they will be chucked off the course

Writing down their own questions for later study

Writing down their own questions so that they can check them out later.

What can we do in large groups?

Probably the most important thing to say at the outset is that there is no one best way of running a successful large-group teaching session – different people do it well in quite different ways. Asking workshop participants to identify the most important large-group teaching behaviours gives a wide range of responses, all of which have their place. But each works best for different people in different ways. Table 6.2 shows a list of such behaviours.

All these processes can be regarded as contributing to making learning happen in large groups. Note how many of these actions go well beyond just 'lecturing' or 'telling learners things'. The more different things we can include in any large-group session, the less likely it is that it will be found to be boring by learners.

How best can we make use of large groups as a feedback-rich environment?

Too often, the value of lectures as feedback-receiving opportunities is underused. We can give each and every learner in even the largest group feedback, but only if we have got them to do something – decision-making, problem-solving and so on. But we can get much more feedback to each member of a large group if we include buzz-group episodes, and get them arguing, debating, speculating, practising, explaining things to each other and so on *during* the large-group session. It is worth remembering how valuable it is for each learner not just receiving feedback, but giving it to fellow learners. Both processes link strongly to making sense of what is being covered.

Table 6.2 Some things teachers can do to make learning happen in large-group teaching sessions

Adapting the session to the actual needs of the group at that time	Initiating discussion
Asking learners questions	Inspiring learners
Asking learners to identify issues	Listening to the learners
Being accessible and approachable	Making it relevant to learners – personalizing it
Being enthusiastic	Managing the time well
Being flexible	Orientating and guiding
Causing learners to revise	Providing notes
Challenging learners' thinking	Questioning
Developing learners' study skills	Quizzing learners
Doing a variety of things	Relating their work to the forthcoming or ongoing assignment
Encouraging them to ask questions	
Encouraging feedback	Reviewing material they have previously learned
Encouraging participation	
Entertaining	Setting learners challenges
Explaining concepts	Setting the scene – placing the present bit into context
Explaining outcomes/objectives	
Facilitating learners working in groups	Setting the scene about how learning should happen
Facilitating processing of material	
Getting feedback from learners	Signposting the intended learning
Getting learners to do things with handouts	Stimulating interest
Getting learners to make individual learning plans	Storytelling
	Testing learners
Giving learners feedback on their work	Using humour where appropriate
Giving learners practical examples	Using mixed methods
Giving value-added to person who bothers to turn up	Using real examples
	Using their experience
Having prepared properly	Using visually attractive material

We can pave the way towards making optimum use of the feedback-rich environment of large groups by taking away the perceived pressure we often feel, that *we* must use the precious time to cover as much as possible of the syllabus content prescribed. We can make time to use in feedback by using handouts to provide learners with the information they need, rather than allowing them to simply gather it from us in a one-way process. We can then get learners working individually or collectively *processing* the information in their handout materials, making sense of it as they proceed.

How can we help learners to make sense of things in large-group contexts?

Ideally, we need to make learning happen *in* large groups, not just some time later when learners revise the contents of a session for exams or assignments. Helping learners to get their heads round ideas and concepts *during* large-group sessions is best done by making sure that there are plenty of learning-by-doing episodes during the session, each followed by feedback (from fellow learners and from us) so that each learner has the opportunity to find out how much making sense has so far occurred. Our best chance to help learners to make sense of things is when they have us with them, with all the extra dimensions of tone of voice, body language, eye contact, repetition, emphasis and so on. Few of these dimensions can be taken away from the large-group session itself, unless learners have distilled these into their notes and handouts.

We can, however, cause further making sense to occur, by setting tasks for learners to do between one session and the next, so that they engage in further learning by doing, practice, trial and error, and so on. This is made all the better if we can arrange that they get feedback as quickly as possible – for example, by encouraging them to do some of the tasks in small groups with discussion. Alternatively, we can, for example, issue a problems sheet at the end of the session, with a marking scheme and model answers in a sealed envelope. Few learners fall into the temptation of opening the envelope before they have had a go at the problems. The feedback they get when they do their self-marking and compare their work to the model answers is much more rapid than if they had to wait until the next teaching session. We can put some pressure, where necessary, on learners to make sure that they actually *do* the between-sessions work by quizzing the whole group about the work in the opening minutes of the forthcoming session, choosing names at random to shame any learners who have not got round to the task.

Why does large-group learning always have to take place on campus? Courtrooms, exhibitions, sports arenas, Trafalgar square ...

Not least because of the demand for suitable teaching spaces, large-group teaching tends to be timetabled into lecture theatres and large classrooms. The best of these are often heavily booked, and staff are reluctant to give up such bookings. That said, there are often alternative venues where at least some aspects of large-group teaching can be arranged from time to time. One advantage of arranging the occasional session somewhere completely different from the lecture theatre is the power of memory by association. If a particular topic happens to be the *only* part of the syllabus that was experienced in the sports hall or local theatre, it will probably be better remembered by most of those present. Outdoor venues can be a welcome relief when the weather is suitable. Courtesy demands, however, that any substitution of venue is treated systematically, so that if, for example, the best-equipped lecture theatre is relinquished for a session, the theatre can be used by another group, giving that extra bit of variety to that group's learning experience. Nothing makes a member of staff so unpopular than when colleagues find out that they had not actually used a 'booked' room.

How can we help learners to follow up their learning from lectures?

Left to themselves, learners often simply add their notes and handouts to piles of similar information-bearing papers. Sometimes, it's only when revising for exams or tests that they return to these original materials and, unsurprisingly, it is then often not at all easy to make sense of the materials. All the *extra* impact of tone of voice, emphasis, body language, repetition, clarification and so on has evaporated away from the information in the notes and handouts. Learners often ask themselves 'Was I actually *there* for this session? Did I copy the notes from someone who was there?', and sometimes: 'Is this really my handwriting?'

We can advise learners how useful it is to follow up each large-group session within two or three days, to edit and improve the notes and handouts while the memory of the session itself is still present. One way of helping learners to realize for themselves the importance of not losing the experience of large-group teaching is to get them reflecting on what they do after the average lecture. The self-assessment checklist shown opposite is one way of alerting learners to what we hope they will be doing after each lecture. Furthermore, if we can persuade learners to give us copies of filled-in self-assessment questionnaires of this kind, we too can find out a lot more about what they are actually doing after each large-group session; this may make our expectations rather more realistic.

Summing up: making lectures unmissable!

This chapter has been about making learning happen in large-group contexts – usually called 'lectures' on timetables. We've already seen that the act of *lecturing* is rarely the best way of making learning happen, and that we need to be thinking carefully about what learners are doing while sitting in lecture theatres or large classrooms. In this final section of the chapter, I would like to condense some of my main suggestions, linking them particularly to the context of starting off a lecture series – there's no second chance to make that vital first impression.

Every new lecturer's nightmare is getting a lecture series off to a bad start, and learner attendance falling off as the series goes on – or worse, lots of learners later failing the related exam, and the blame coming back to the lecturer. But this isn't confined to new lecturers.

A wise and experienced colleague told me how a couple of years ago he fell in with his institution's policies, and put all his lecture handouts on the intranet, and also all his PowerPoint slides. He did this a couple of weeks ahead of each lecture, for the sake of any learners with special needs. But two things happened. Attendance fell off at his lectures and exam performance in due course worsened dramatically. He analysed this. The learners who didn't come to his lectures only gave him back in exam answers that which he'd given them in the handouts and Power-

Self-assessment checklist to use after a lecture

	Please tick one or more columns for each of the options below.	This is what I did.	I would have liked to do this, but didn't manage it.	I didn't think this necessary.	This just was not possible for me.	I'll do this next time.
1	I've looked through my notes to check I understood everything.					
2	I've reread the handout, and made extra notes on it to help me to remember what seemed clear at the time.					
3	I've jotted down questions where I don't yet understand something, on my notes and handouts for me to follow up later.					
4	I've filed my notes carefully where I can find them easily later.					
5	I've followed up reading suggestions made by the lecturer.					
6	I've noted down for revision purposes the three most important things from the lecture.					
7	I've looked back at the course outline to see how this lecture fits into the programme as a whole.					
8	I've looked forward on the course outline to see what will be coming up in the next lecture.					
9	I've made sure that the intended learning outcomes for the lecture are included in or with my notes.					
10	I've checked how well I reckon I've already achieved each of the intended learning outcomes, and marked these decisions against the outcomes for future reference.					

continues overleaf

Please tick one or more columns for each of the options below.	This is what I did.	I would have liked to do this, but didn't manage it.	I didn't think this necessary.	This just was not possible for me.	I'll do this next time.
11 I've asked my fellow learners for their reactions to what we learned in the lecture.					
12 I've compared my notes with those of at least one fellow learner, and added in things I missed.					
13 I've self-tested myself on what I remember from the lecture, and to find those parts that are in danger of slipping away again.					

Point slides, nothing more. The learners who did attend his lectures gave back more, from the thinking which he got them to do *during* his lectures, and the reading around the subject that he inspired them to do *after* his lectures. Yet many colleagues continue to put up all of the information for learners in similar ways, and it is often now institutional policy to do so. We need to make sure that our best efforts to respond to learners with special needs do not end up disadvantaging many more learners.

Therefore, giving learners information is only part of the business of designing a lecture, so we've got to make sure that lectures are learning experiences, not just information distribution events, and particularly that *first* lecture in any series – a make or break occasion for many a learner. In other words, we've got to try to make lectures unmissable! It's got to be worth *being* there.

Twenty suggestions for making learning happen in large groups

1   *Start reasonably punctually*. When most of the group is there, get started. Remind learners of some of the things they should already know, about which you're going to go into in more depth. Ask those present a few questions to find out more about what they already know. Don't be unkind to people drifting in late – that won't encourage them to come in to your next lecture if late again. Don't punish the people who are punctual by making them wait too long for their less punctual colleagues. Gently allow the people who are coming in late to feel that they may have missed something useful.

2   *Make good use of intended learning outcomes*. Near the start of the lecture, let learn-

ers in on what *they* should be able to do by the end of that particular lecture. And at the end of the lecture, show the intended outcomes again, and check to what extent learners now feel that they have cracked the learning outcomes. Let them *feel* the added value of having been there. Bring each lecture to a close – don't just stop.

3 *Always link lectures to assessment.* Give learners cues and clues about how this particular lecture 'counts' in due course. Whenever you say 'You'll need today's material for exam questions like so-and-so' you'll notice learners jotting something down!

4 *Lecturers should be seen and heard.* Use a mike if it helps. Don't just say 'can you hear me at the back?' Ask someone in the back row a question and find out. And don't dim the lights to show your slides at the expense of learners no longer being able to see *you*. Remind yourself that low lighting for too long at a time is one of the components of the natural conditions to induce human sleep!

5 *Don't keep slides up too long.* Learners will keep looking at the screen, even when that screenful is quite finished with. Get them to look at *you* now and then. For example, when using PowerPoint, on most systems pressing 'B' on the keyboard makes the screen go black. Pressing 'B' again brings it back.

6 *Avoid death by bullet point.* Make different slides *look* different – include some charts or pictures, where possible. If you're confident with technology, put in some optional very short video clips now and then – but nothing which would matter if it didn't work straight away.

7 *Try to cause the learners to* like *you*. Smile. Be human. Look at them. Respond to them. If they like you, they're more likely to come to your *next* lecture too.

8 *Think of what learners will be* doing *during the lecture*. Don't worry too much about what *you* will be doing, plan to get your learners' brains engaged. Get them making decisions, guessing causes of phenomena, trying out applying ideas, solving problems and so on. They'll learn more from what they *do* than from what you tell them.

9 *Get learners note-making, not just note-taking.* For example, try to get learners to put down *their* views and ideas, not just write out yours. You can give them *your* ideas on a handout or on the intranet. Note-making is unmissable, note-taking isn't. And mere note-taking can be a very low learning pay-off activity.

10 *Don't put too much into that first lecture.* It's better to get learners thinking deeply about a couple of important things, than to tell them about half-a-dozen things and lose their attention.

11 *Be kind to learners' brains.* Concentration spans are measured in minutes, not hours. Break up each lecture into at least three parts, with something lighter in between the tougher bits.

12 *Bring in some appropriate humour.* The odd funny slide, amusing anecdote or play on words can work wonders at restoring learners' concentration levels. Then follow something funny up with an important point, while you've still got their full attention.

13 *But don't use humour if it's not working!* Watch their faces, and respond accordingly. If they're liking the funny bits, keep putting them in, but if they're not, don't!

14 *Give learners something to take away.* But not just a printed handout – learners who miss the lecture will easily get copies of these. And that's just information – not knowledge. Make handouts something that learners will give *thought to.* For example, use a 'gapped' handout, where learners themselves add in the most important points from time to time, in their own words. And give them time in the lecture to do this. Something that they have *made* is seen as much more important than something everyone was simply given.

15 *Flag up related sessions.* For example, if you're lecturing to a large group, and learners will be going later into tutorial sessions to follow-up the content of the lecture, show learners some of the questions which will be covered in the tutorials, to get them started on thinking about them.

16 *Think twice about giving out handout copies of your PowerPoint slides.* When this is done, learners can switch off their brains, thinking 'I've already got what's on the screen, I don't need to think about it now'. And if you give out copies of 24 slides, and only get through 16 in your lecture, learners will get the wrong impression. Leave yourself the luxury of being able to choose *which* slides you will show. When time is running out, miss out some less important ones to make space for that important closure.

17 *Keep yourself tuned into WIIFM.* 'What's in it for me?' is a perfectly intelligent question for any learner to have in mind. Always make time to remind learners about *why* a topic is included, and *how* it will help them in due course.

18 *Don't be unkind to learners who missed your* last *lecture.* They're here now, giving them a bad time won't encourage them to come again. And at least *some* learners will have very good reasons for not having been able to be there last time – illness, crises, whatever. The more unmissable your lectures are, the more they will try not to miss them whatever else is happening in their lives.

19 *Don't overrun.* At least some of your learners are likely to have something else to go to after your lecture, and perhaps with not much of a margin for error. If you come to a good stopping place and there are 15 minutes left, do your closing bit and stop. Learners actually *like* lectures which finish early now and then.

20 *Pave the way towards your next lecture.* After reviewing what learners should have got out of the present lecture, show (for example) a slide with three questions which will be covered in next week's instalment.

7

Making learning happen in small groups

As with the previous chapter, I aim here to give some short responses to a number of frequently asked questions about small-group teaching, building in now and then discussion about how small-group teaching can link productively to wanting to learn, establishing ownership of the need to learn, learning by doing, learning through feedback and making sense of what is being learned. However, the final chapter of this book, 'Making workshops work' returns to the whole area of small-group teaching and learning, and also uses small-group contexts to bring together a number of themes from different parts of the book, so I will leave quite a lot of the discussion of small-group teaching until that chapter. I suggest that you may usefully use the present chapter as a prelude to 'Making workshops work'.

What sorts of small-group teaching are there?

There are many contexts which can be thought of as small-group teaching. *Tutorials* in some institutions are scheduled meetings between a tutor and a few learners, often used to follow up the content of lectures and to get learners applying what they are meant to do with theories and concepts. One problem is that learners don't necessarily know what is expected of them in tutorials. Sally Brown says of her first experiences of tutorials as a learner, 'I tried to be good, and sit quietly and listen to what the tutor had to say'. Tutorials are ideal occasions for learners to bring their own individual questions and problems and to seek help from the tutor. In some institutions, the word tutorial is used to describe face-to-face meetings between a tutor and one learner at a time. With increasing class sizes, however, it is not uncommon to find the term 'tutorial' used for groups of as many as 20 learners.

Seminars are often confused with tutorials. Learners often don't know what they're supposed to do in these sessions. The essential difference between a seminar and a tutorial in many tutors' minds is that in seminars, learners themselves contribute most of the content, for example, by preparing to talk as individuals or small groups about pre-allocated topics, then open the topics up for discussion.

Other kinds of small-group teaching include laboratory work, studio work, problems classes, and practical work of various kinds where learners work independently or in twos and threes, with individual support from time to time from tutors.

How can we shut the teacher up in small groups?

Probably the most significant danger in most small-group learning contexts is that teachers just continue to teach, and learners are not involved as much as they should be. Sometimes the blame goes to the teacher, but often teachers continue to talk to fill the silence caused by learners *not* being ready, willing or able to contribute.

It takes a little nerve for a teacher to pose a question to a small group of learners and wait for them to answer it. Silence is threatening, and it's all too easy for teachers to go for the comfort of filling the silence. It can be better to wait a while, and if the silence is still continuing, to clarify the question, putting it into other words or breaking it down into more manageable sub-questions.

One of the best ways to cause learners to participate is to give them a little time, individually or in twos or threes, to jot down notes in response to a question, *then* ask them to give their answers orally. Armed with some jottings, most learners feel more confident to speak.

We also need to encourage learners to participate, particularly by not ridiculing their contributions when they are wrong, and always trying to find something positive to say in response to their efforts.

What tutor behaviours are least likely to make learning happen in small groups?

I've already mentioned that just continuing to teach (or lecture!) can damage the learning pay-off which might have resulted from small-group work. However, the most damaging tutor behaviour is not taking small-group teaching as seriously as large-group teaching. For example, it is relatively rare for a large-class session to be cancelled or postponed, but much more common for small-group sessions to be cancelled at short notice. This infuriates part-time learners who may have travelled to the institution just for the cancelled tutorial. Learners are quick to get the message that if small-group sessions are not valued by their tutors, the sessions can't be very important.

Another tutor behaviour which can easily damage small-group teaching is to put learners down. If they arrive late, for example (perhaps for unavoidable reasons), a sharp retort from a tutor can make them feel really bad about being there at all, and sometimes they don't return to small-group sessions again. More often, however, tutors demotivate learners by responding inappropriately to their comments and questions. This is likely to make learners less likely to participate and undermines the whole rationale of the less formal communication between tutors and learners which small-group teaching should allow.

Table 7.1 which follows shows a long list of 'teacher behaviours which can damage or destroy group work' gathered from participants at several different workshops on small-group teaching. It can be useful to give this list to learners, and ask them to underline or circle any they feel are spoiling their group work!

What tutor behaviours really make learning happen in small groups?

The obvious answer is avoiding as many as possible of the long list of damaging behaviours given in Table 7.1. However, the short list of characteristics of tutors who successfully facilitate small-group work (Table 7.2) can also be considered.

How big is a small group?

It all depends. In some subjects, a small group is no more than about four learners. However, seminar groups are often much bigger, for example a cohort of 300 learners may be broken into seminar groups of around 20. Problems classes in maths, science and engineering may be as large as 40 – bringing the danger that they become a continuation of large-group teaching unless tutors take care to keep the focus on learner activity, for example, by dividing the group up into fours or fives, so that every learner has an opportunity to discuss things and gain feedback from peers. With group sizes of three to six or so, there is less chance of passenger or bystander behaviours, and it is fairly straightforward to cause everyone to contribute. With larger groups, however, it becomes more difficult to keep everyone engaged.

Where can small-group learning happen?

Small-group sessions can occur just about anywhere. Small teaching rooms are often heavily timetabled in institutions, and it is all too common for a tutor and small group to be seen wandering the corridors looking for a suitable venue, particularly if a tutorial or seminar has had to be rescheduled. Small-group sessions often spill over into other areas, including lounges, dining areas and, even, the nearest comfortable pub (but we need to remember that if the group contains members whose religion prohibits alcohol that this venue would be entirely inappropriate).

By common consent, small-group sessions on (for example) late Friday afternoons or early Monday mornings are often rescheduled, but this can add to the difficulties of finding suitable space. In most institutions, staff are urged only to book rooms for sessions that definitely will take place, rather than make block bookings

Table 7.1 Teacher behaviours which can damage or destroy group work

Allowing bad group dynamics
by poor selection of the
group structure.
Allowing domineers
Allowing passengers
Allowing personality clashes
Aloofness
Autocratic leadership
Being biased
Being boring
Being disrespectful to
learners
Being egotistical
Being insensitive to learners
needs and personalities
Being partisan – e.g. just
putting one point of view
Being too critical
Belittling
Critical of individuals
Criticizing
Dividing groups up badly
Dominating
Expectations of learner
knowledge being too high
Failing to nurture
Favouring clones
Focusing on individuals
Group favouritism
Having favourites and
enemies
Ignoring slower/shyer
learners
Ignoring some learners
Imposing own views
Inadequate planning
Inappropriate group
selection
Inconsistency
Indifference
Interfering in group process
Interrupting
Isolating strong learners
Lack of chairpersonship
Lack of feedback to/from
learners

Lack of focus
Lack of imagination
Lack of knowledge
Lack of monitoring
Lack of preparation
Laziness
Leaving the room at the
wrong time
Making instructions too
complex
Managing time poorly
Negative and angry criticism
Negative attitude to group
Negative remarks to
learners
Not allowing sufficient time
Not appreciating group
dynamics
Not being aware of group
members' interests
Not being consistent
Not bringing quieter
learners out
Not checking progress
Not controlling learners
who talk too much
Not defining the outcomes
and assessment criteria of
the group session
Not encouraging focus on
discussion
Not ensuring equal
contribution – quantity
and quality
Not establishing clear
expectations
Not following up
Not giving clear directions of
the task and its intended
outcome
Not giving feedback to
learners
Not having a clear purpose
Not having a clear rationale
for doing the task through
group work

Not listening to learners
Not prompting
Not setting proper focus
Not stating/meeting aims
and objectives
Not valuing people
Over-prompting
Poor classroom management
Poor communication
Poor facilitating skills
Poor feedback
Poor geographical
arrangement
Poor group/time
management
Poor management/timing/not
allowing everyone to
participate
Poor materials
Poor observation
Poor planning of content and
time
Poor preparation
Poor presentation
Poor task allocation –
unequal sharing
Poor task design
Poor time allocation
Poor timekeeping
Putting learners down
Restricting creative thinking
Sarcasm
Selecting groups badly
Setting self up as expert.
Setting tasks in unclear ways
Showing favouritism
Taking over
Talking about self
Tendency to lecture
Tending to retain control
Tutor domination
Unclear brief
Unclear objectives
Unclear or changing brief
Unclear presentation of
outcomes

Table 7.2 Characteristics of tutors who successfully facilitate small-group work

Challenging appropriately	Giving clear instructions	Nurturing
Designing tasks well	Giving feedback	Praising
Discussing	Involving learners	Questioning
Empathizing	Listening well	Rewarding
Enabling learner participation	Managing groups well	Sharing
Encouraging	Monitoring	Varying methods
Enthusing	Motivating	

for a whole semester, even when some of the small-group sessions are going to happen in alternative places such as computer suites, laboratories or field visits.

How can we ensure in small groups that learners don't feel marginalized, alienated and ignored?

Using learners' names can help. The simplest and most effective way of getting to know their names in small groups is to give learners self-adhesive labels, ask them to write down what they prefer to be called, and stick the labels to their clothing. This has the advantage of revealing what they *really* want to be called – at least some of their chosen names will be different to what might be printed on a class list. Addressing learners by name makes a surprisingly big difference, especially when asking questions or giving feedback. When learners spend much of their contact time in very large groups, where they can easily feel just one of a crowd, small-group teaching can compensate.

It is up to tutors to ensure that learners don't feel alienated in a small group. Where there is just one female learner in a group, or one male learner, care needs to be taken not to allow this to cause them to feel exposed in any way. Similarly, ethnic background differences need to be handled sensitively. The best way of checking that all is going well in small-group sessions is to have a sufficiently relaxed and informal atmosphere so that it is easy to keep asking 'How are you finding these sessions?' and 'Is there anything we can do to improve these sessions for you?' and so on.

Under what circumstances does deep learning happen in small groups?

Deep learning is most likely to happen in small-group contexts when all five factors underpinning successful learning are involved. In other words, when students are motivated to the extent that they *want* to learn from the small-group setting and have clear targets so they know what they *need* to be getting out of the session, conditions are optimized for high learning pay-off to occur. When tutors ensure that there is plenty of opportunity for learning by doing, practice, trial and error and participation, deep learning is all the more likely to occur. When the small group is facilitated so that learners gain useful feedback from each other as well as from the tutor, conditions are further improved. Deep learning is then known by learners to be occurring, to the extent that they realize that they are making sense of the subject matter being addressed in the session.

What kinds of imperatives mitigate against effective small-group learning?

The principal factors getting in the way of effective small-group teaching include:

- learners not turning up, perhaps because they don't feel small-group contexts are as important as large-group sessions
- tutors not taking small-group teaching as seriously as they take large-group teaching, and arriving for small-group sessions relatively unprepared
- small-group teaching being viewed in institutions as not very cost-effective compared to large-group teaching
- insufficient attention being paid by tutors to what is *best* covered by small-group work, compared with what should be covered by large-group teaching
- learners not doing their part in preparing for small-group sessions
- failure to adjust group membership and composition when particular groups fail to work well together
- failure to clarify the intended learning outcomes for small-group sessions
- tutors continuing to teach in a non-participative way
- difficulties in finding suitable spaces and environments for small-group teaching
- dominant learners being allowed too much air time in discussions
- passive learners being allowed to remain passive
- difficulties in achieving equity of the learning experience when a large group is divided into several small groups, and particularly when different group sessions are facilitated by different tutors.

Most of these factors can be addressed directly by tutors, provided they themselves are indeed convinced of the benefits for learners of small-group teaching contexts.

What duration is ideal for small-group sessions?

In practice, the duration of small-group sessions is less important than how well the time is spent. A well facilitated small group can achieve in as little as half an hour much more than a poorly facilitated group achieves in a couple of hours. The problem with short duration sessions is that the time can all too easily be eroded if it takes some minutes to get everyone there. Where small-group sessions last for an hour or two, it is important to build in a variety of processes and get learners involved in different tasks and activities. When small-group learning is working well, learners often comment that the time has flown by, even when the session lasts a day or half-day as in the sort of workshops discussed in the final chapter of this book.

Why can't learners lead small-group learning sessions?

They *can*. Learners are helped to lead small-group sessions (seminars in particular) if they have clear, manageable briefings about what exactly is expected of them, sufficient time to prepare to take the lead and are not interrupted too often by tutors! It remains important that the task of leading sessions is not made too daunting for any shy or retiring learners, nor just given to the vociferous ones. Tutor interventions need to be restricted to when the learner leading a session really needs to be rescued or helped out – but even then it can be better to facilitate other learners coming to their aid.

What institutional factors make small-group learning really difficult?

Some institutional factors which get in the way of small-group learning include:

- difficulties finding sufficient suitable small-group learning venues when very large groups are split up into a lot of small ones
- timetabling difficulties finding sufficient tutors to facilitate parallel small-group sessions
- tutors who lack the experience or expertise in the subject matter, especially when other parallel sessions are being facilitated by the lecturer responsible for the associated large-group sessions
- tensions between research and teaching getting in the way of researchers putting enough time and effort into preparing for their small-group teaching work
- the institutional ethos regarding small-group teaching, if it is regarded as not very important or 'a bit of a luxury' or 'just the icing on the cake'
- lack of feedback from learners on their experience of small-group teaching when, as often happens, monitoring and evaluation tends to focus on large-group teaching.

What can we do to help learners *want* to learn in small groups?

The best we can do is to make small-group sessions so enjoyable that learners can't wait to come along to them! However, this is perhaps rather harder to achieve if the session is a problems class on applications of the second law of thermodynamics.

It is a measure of the success of small-group teaching sessions if learners always feel that it is worth coming along and joining in, and that they leave with things they simply wouldn't have got if they'd missed the session – handouts, explana-

tions, answers to their own questions, ideas and, particularly, the feeling that during the session they had made sense of parts of the subject matter. If they feel
they've not got anything more than some extra information, the want to learn is
hardly likely to be enhanced. We can easily gather feedback from learners, for example, asking them to rate small-group sessions in terms of how much they feel them
'time well spent'. When learners feel that they have progressed their own learning
faster as a result of participating in a small-group session than they would have
done simply studying the topic on their own, they are likely to come to the sessions
with greater expectations and increased willingness to take part actively.

How best can we use small-group contexts to clarify the learning *need*?

Small-group sessions are ideal occasions to spend extra time clarifying the intended
learning outcomes so that learners gain a greater awareness regarding what exactly
we are, in due course, going to expect them to do to evidence their achievement of
the outcomes. While we should be doing this in large-group contexts too, small-
group sessions can allow us to let learners *see* examples of the kind of evidence we're
looking for, for example, portfolios, dissertations, past essays or assignments, and
subject-specific artefacts such as drawings, photos, posters and so on.

Small-group contexts are also an opportunity to answer learners' questions about
how exactly assessment works. We can use small-group sessions to get learners
themselves applying assessment criteria to past work or their own work, and we can
clarify for them how the criteria are used in practice.

What actions do learners learn most from in small groups?

Table 7.3 reflects the views of actions we can help learners to do in small groups, to
maximize their learning pay-off.

There are, of course, countless other subject-specific things we can get learners
doing in small groups, but it is useful to ask learners from time to time exactly what
they are finding works well for them in terms of learning pay-off.

Table 7.3 What we can help learners to do in small groups, to maximize their learning pay-off

Agreeing solutions	Engaging	Reviewing
Analysing	Explaining	Selecting
Arguing	Guessing	Sharing
Assessing	Helping	Sketching
Connecting	Listening	Solving problems
Debating	Note-making	Succeeding
Demonstrating	Participating	Summarizing
Designing	Questioning	Talking
Discussing	Remembering	Watching others

How best can we maximize the feedback learners get from each other in small groups?

Feedback is most useful when it is about something learners have just done. We can therefore give them tasks to do in small groups (and before the sessions), then get them reviewing each others' efforts and explaining what they think about them.

It is useful to discuss with learners how best to receive feedback from each other (and, indeed, from ourselves). For example, learners often need to be encouraged not just to shrug off positive comments or praise, but to allow themselves to *accept* such feedback, swell with pride about it and take on board exactly what they have done well, not least so that they can continue to build on their achievements. They also need to be helped to receive critical feedback well, not become defensive and try to justify their actions, but listen carefully to the feedback and see what they can learn from it so that mistakes or deficiencies can be useful learning experiences for them.

What kinds of challenges can we offer learners in small-group teaching?

In many subjects, small-group contexts are very suitable for engaging learners in problem-solving activities, particularly those where we need to start them practising on relatively straightforward problems, then increase the complexity and difficulty a little at a time so that they learn by repetition while still being suitably stretched.

We can also use small-group sessions to develop their group skills. For example, we can show learners how to contribute to a brainstorm of ideas about a problem scenario or case study, then how to prioritize which of the ideas might be the most profitable to develop, and so on.

It is always useful for us to have some prepared questions or scenarios available for each small-group session, particularly those which help learners to make sense of things they will need in later formal assessments, so that whenever there is time available we can help learners to have a useful learning experience together, aided by them being able to see the relevance of what they are doing to what they need to become able to do by themselves without help in due course.

Why do we persist in pretending that small-group teaching is as good or better than other methods?

This sort of question tends to be asked by those who don't like small-group teaching – or are not very good at doing it. However, when small-group teaching is done badly, it might be better if it had been abandoned. Sadly, too many learners report unsatisfactory experiences of learning in small-group contexts. One answer to the question is that a great deal of normal human learning takes place in what can be regarded as small-group contexts – families. Therefore, it should be a natural part of any wider learning environment.

What do learners do to ensure they learn nothing in small groups?

Human nature being what it is, it is easier to be passive in small-group learning situations than to take the risk of being active but wrong. The words 'passenger' and 'bystander' are often used to describe the behaviours that can lead learners to get nothing out of small-group work.

Some learners are shy and embarrassed about being expected to join in to discussions in small groups. However, as tutors we need to help them to gain the confidence to contribute actively, and it is important that they don't feel 'put down' if they get things wrong or don't communicate their ideas effectively at first.

One of the most common ways in which learners get nothing out of small-group work is not turning up! This is often because learners think that all the important material will be linked to large-group sessions such as lectures, and we need to make it very clear to them all that, although most of the *information* may be given out in large-group sessions, the *making sense* of the information by applying it and practising with it is often best done in small groups, where there can be quick and individual feedback to all present, helping them to turn the information into their own knowledge.

Where is the real learning pay-off in small-group teaching?

The real learning pay-off from small-group teaching is linked to the following factors:

- increased opportunity for learners to ask us questions
- more time for us to spend answering specific questions
- the opportunity for us to make ourselves approachable to learners and get to know them as individuals
- the chance to give high-quality feedback to individuals in the group, where eye contact, tone of voice, body language and emphasis can all clarify our feedback – much more than just written, printed or emailed comments can
- the chance for learners to learn from the feedback *others* are receiving
- the opportunity for learners to find out how their learning is going by comparing the level to which they are making sense of concepts and ideas with each other
- the opportunity for us to gain feedback about how their learning is progressing,

allowing us to make adjustments where necessary to other teaching contexts, including large-group sessions.

What exactly are we trying to do in small groups?

Ideally we should be using small-group teaching to achieve as many as possible of the things we wish to do to help learners to succeed, but which can't be directly incorporated into large-group teaching or resource-based learning. This is why it can be so wasteful if small-group sessions just degenerate into a continuation of what we're doing in large-group contexts.

Among the additional outcomes of successful small-group work are the following:

- the opportunity for learners to develop their confidence in speaking, presenting, arguing, discussing, debating and so on
- the opportunity for learners to practise and develop their oral communications skills, such as those they will need for job interviews or oral exams
- the chance for learners to develop and practise their interpersonal skills, learning how best to work collaboratively with different people
- the chance for learners to reflect together on how their learning is going and to find out more about how they stand compared to their peers
- the opportunity to get learners deepening their own learning by explaining difficult ideas and concepts to each other.

Why use small-group teaching at all?

When small-group teaching is really working well, there are many additional learning outcomes which are achieved through such contexts, many of which have already been described in the preceding sections. Further light is thrown on the value of small-group work from cases where class sizes have increased to such an extent that small-group work (particularly tutorials and seminars) has had to be discontinued, and manifestations such as the following develop:

- increased drop-out and failure statistics, because learners don't have enough opportunity to have help with their difficulties
- more time being taken trying to help those learners who make appointments for one-to-one help with particular problems – often the same problem many times over
- more interruptions to the flow of large-group teaching, when it is no longer possible in a lecture to reply to a question 'this is just the right sort of question to discuss in detail in your next tutorial – bring it along then and make sure that it is sorted out to your satisfaction'

- increased risk of learners succeeding satisfactorily in written assessment scenarios, but not having gained the level of mastery of the subject matter that comes from discussing it, arguing about it and explaining it to other people
- increased risk of lecturers remaining unaware of significant problems which learners were experiencing until too late – when the problems turned into assessment failures.

Perhaps the most significant reasons for using small-group teaching are the benefits learners acquire which lie beyond the curriculum as expressed through intended learning outcomes; the *emergent* learning outcomes associated with small-group work help learners to equip themselves with skills and attitudes they will need for the next stages of their careers – and lives.

8

Responding to diversity and widening participation

Colleagues in post-compulsory education are only too aware of the ways in which the student communities in educational institutions are changing, as a greater proportion of the population continues its education beyond school. Somehow, however, it is quite difficult for college teachers to pin down what they should be doing to try to respond to the increasing diversity resulting from widening participation, and the greater awareness of the importance of addressing special educational needs, resulting from legislation such as the Special Educational Needs and Disabilities Act in the UK, effective from 2002.

This chapter opens with a discussion of the changing nature of the learner population in post-compulsory education, and some suggestions about how we may try to achieve 'differentiation' in groups where the ability range is consequently expanded. The remaining part of the chapter discusses some dimensions of how special needs and disabilities can be addressed by considering how exactly some particular needs can be linked to the factors underpinning successful learning discussed throughout this book.

Differentiation

In the further education sector in the UK, there is now significantly increased emphasis on catering for the greater mix of abilities within any classroom or cohort, and the term 'differentiation' is used to describe the process of ensuring that high-fliers are catered for alongside low-fliers. In the quality assurance inspection processes operating in further education, it is now recognized that differentiation is on the agenda, and how staff approach achieving differentiation is being monitored by those observing teaching and learning in action.

Extending the discussion to higher education is more problematic. The situation in many respects reflects the further education picture, with greater mix of ability in cohorts, but there is sometimes significant concern about any tendency towards 'dumbing down' the higher education curriculum to respond to the changes experienced in the learner population, and more emphasis on defining and establishing suitable benchmarks for acceptable levels of achievement and standards relating to assessment of learners.

Achieving differentiation – addressing how higher-fliers and lower-fliers learn

One way of gaining insight into how best to achieve differentiation in practice is to link it to how we can choose to address differently the five factors underpinning successful learning as discussed throughout this book. Table 8.1 presents some starters for this discussion.

How students are changing

In a wide range of higher and further education institutions, I have asked workshop participants whether they feel that the student population is changing as a result of widening participation and changes in society in general – they almost always respond affirmatively. Asking them to go further and report *how* students are changing is very revealing. I ask participants to jot down, then prioritize, completions of the starter 'students nowadays are becoming more ... '. Table 8.2 shows the most common responses, accrued from a dozen or so different places in the UK and Australia (with surprisingly little difference in responses in these countries). I have arranged the overall table in alphabetical order of contributions. Some entries, for example, 'assertive', 'aware of their rights', 'demanding' and so on were repeated many times in the responses, but I have deleted the repetitions here.

It can be inferred from data like those in Table 8.2 that:

- students are indeed changing
- widening participation is being evidenced by a range of different behaviours, approaches and attitudes among learners in post-compulsory education
- staff are well aware of these changes, which is a reassuring sign that they are already addressing the changing student population in teaching, learning and assessment contexts.

In the remaining sections of this chapter, I would like to continue the theme of responding to diverse learners, but extending the discussion to some of the 'special needs' which are found more often in our learning contexts as widening participation causes the learner population within post-compulsory education to mirror more closely the population at large.

Table 8.1 Achieving differentiation through addressing the factors underpinning successful learning

Factor underpinning successful learning	Low-ability learners	High-ability learners
Wanting to learn	These learners may need considerably more encouragement than average, to help them to maintain their efforts to achieve.	It can be important to ensure that these learners do not become bored by a pace which is too slow for them, causing them to lose motivation and momentum in their learning.
Taking ownership of the need to learn	It can be important to try to minimize the extent to which these learners may feel intimidated by the nature and depth of intended learning outcomes. It may be necessary to break down such outcomes into 'chunks' which can be seen as being achievable by these learners, so that they approach their work on them with sufficient confidence and determination.	High-ability learners may find the intended learning outcomes too simple for them, and may resent having to work slowly towards demonstrating their achievement of them. Allowing them to fast-track to such achievement can help. Also, it can be useful to think about how best suitable extensions to the intended learning outcomes may be designed, allowing high-ability learners the opportunity to feel that they are stretching themselves and going beyond the original outcomes, but ensuring that they don't feel threatened by extra expectations placed upon them.
Learning by doing – practice, repetition, trial and error, and experience	Probably the best way to address the particular needs of lower-ability learners is to break the learning by doing into smaller, more manageable elements, and to allow for more repetition where needed, and for a slower overall pace. They will need a greater degree of supervision, so that they can be helped directly to make the most of learning by trial and error.	High-ability learners may need less repetition, and may be able to work on larger 'chunks' of learning by doing without much supervision.
Feedback	Feedback is particularly important to low-fliers, particularly the forms of feedback which can celebrate their step-by-step successes and help them to build their confidence as they proceed. The feedback may need to be focused on face-to-face contexts, where tone of voice, body language, emphasis, facial expression and so on can enrich the feedback messages, and reassure these learners when necessary.	We need to be careful to ensure that high-ability learners do not feel disadvantaged by the greater time and energy which must necessarily go into giving feedback to their lower-ability fellow learners. At the same time, we need to check that high-ability learners feel good about their achievements being celebrated in our feedback, and not just allow ticks or high scores to tell the story. They, too, need to gain reinforcement about exactly what they have got right along the way.
Making sense – digesting	For lower-ability learners, these processes necessarily take longer, and we need to try to make sure that they feel that it is acceptable to learn slowly when appropriate. Furthermore, the number of times it may take for the 'light to dawn – then fade away again' is higher, and we need to make sure that these learners feel that it is understandable for some things to have to be learned and re-learned a number of times before the learning becomes more secure.	High-ability learners can have their own problems regarding making sense of concepts and ideas. Because they may be more readily able to demonstrate achievement of learning outcomes quite quickly, there is the risk that they do so without properly deepening their learning, and thus lose their grasp of concepts and ideas, possibly coming as an unwelcome surprise for them if this is found to have happened in assessment contexts.

Table 8.2 How students are felt to be changing. Workshop participants completions of 'nowadays students are becoming more … '

Addicted to their mobile phones	spoon-feeding	Likely to have an educational need	general population
Affluent	Female	Likely to have	Reliant
Anxious	Flexible	childcare issues	Respected
Assertive	Focused on grades	Likely to have mental	Result focused
Assessment focused	Focused on money	health needs	Rich (some)
Aware of their rights	(or lack of it)	Likely to receive text	Richer
Aware of themselves as consumers	Foreign	messages	Savvy
Bad legacy from A level	From different socio-economic strata	Litigious	Selective
Bigger gender balance inequalities	Goal-oriented	Local	Self-aware
Career orientated, less academic	Greater ability range – particularly lower	Mark-driven	Serious
Challenging	Harassed in terms of time and money	Materialistic	Smelly
Comfortable with technology	High maintenance	Mature	Some may be paying much more for being here
Computer literate	Higher expectations	Militant	Spoon-fed
Confused	Impoverished	Minimalist	Strategic
Consumer oriented	Inclined to see themselves as consumers	Mobile	Streetwise
Critical	Instant gratification oriented	More variety of background knowledge	Stressed
Culturally diverse	Instrumental	Not willing to take risks	Struggle with language
Demanding	Intellectually challenged	Numerous	Technically competent – IT
Dependent	Interested in certainties	Numerous but not numerate	Technologically competent
Dependent on spoon-feeding	Internationally diverse	Only prepared to work towards assessments	Time-short
Depressed	IT literate	Outspoken	Travelled
Deskilled in some areas	Label-conscious	Overseas	Unconcerned about exams
Differing in ability	Lazy	Part-time	Under financial pressure
Difficult to categorize	Less aware of responsibilities	Passive	Under pressure
Disengaged	Less committed	Politically correct	Unprepared
Disrespectful	Less linguistically competent	Poor (some)	Unrealistic
Distracted	Less professional	Prepared to challenge us in the lecture room	Varied in academic ability
Diverse	Like customers	Pressurized	Visual
Diverse age	Like to be spoon-fed	Questioning about why	Visual learners rather than readers
Easily bored	Likely to be at risk regarding dropout	Reacting to fragmented education	Vocationally oriented
Elderly	Likely to be working	Ready to blame others	Wider socio-economic background
Employed	Likely to come in with qualifications which don't fit	Reflective of the	Work focused (part-time)
Expectant of everything being done for them			Working 20 hours
Expecting a greater return			Worldly
Expecting more			

Responding to special needs

'Making learning happen' is essentially about responding to the needs of *all* learners, and in various ways this is addressed throughout the book. This section, however, is focused on responding to learners' *special* needs, in other words the particular needs of various categories of learner present in differing proportions among the wider populations of learners in further and higher education.

What's changed regarding special needs?

People with 'special' needs have been amongst our learners throughout the evolution of post-compulsory education, but in recent years a number of trends and developments have highlighted the problems which some of them face, and the need for us to respond appropriately to their various needs. In addition, over the last 20 years in particular, significant advances have been made regarding detecting and identifying many special needs, and how best to make adjustments to teaching, learning environments and assessment instruments and processes so as to minimize any disadvantages which can arise for at least some of the manifestations of special need. For example, a great deal more is now known about detecting and responding to dyslexia.

Widening participation policies are gradually transforming the spectrum of learners in post-compulsory education. It now seems a distant past where only about 5 per cent of the population entered post-compulsory education; nowadays in the UK, for example, the talk is about no less than 50 per cent of the population having at least some experience of higher education. This means that a different 'slice' of the overall population is now present on post-compulsory education programmes and courses. That in turn means that the population in any large lecture group, for example, now contains a proportion of learners who previously would not have been there. At least some of these learners have special needs of a wide range of types. For example, any large group of learners is likely to have at least some who are affected by some degree of dyslexia. Also, post-compulsory education has become much more accessible to learners with visual impairments, hearing impairments, limited mobility and other sources of special need. There are significant proportions of any population affected by such conditions as diabetes and epilepsy, and these too are often represented in educational contexts. Alongside this picture, there is now much more known about how best to respond to identified special needs in the context of programmes which are designed for all learners, rather than isolate those with special needs into separate programmes designed specifically for them.

In addition, however, a wide range of what could be considered as mental health needs are now represented amid any large group of learners. These don't just relate to conditions which are directly associated with cognitive processing, but also include short-term or long-term manifestations of stress, anxiety, depression and the various conditions resulting from exposure to mind-altering agents, not least alcohol, but also other drugs and medicines.

Learner attitudes have also changed significantly in recent years, reflecting the tendency for society as a whole to be more aware of rights and more likely to resort to law if injustice is felt to have happened. Learners are more litigious. This greater sensitivity to customer rights is reflected in learners' expectations of teaching and learning environments and processes. Furthermore, should lack of appropriate attention to any identified special need end up by disadvantaging particular learners when they come to be assessed, appeals and even legal action can come as no surprise.

A further dimension of change is the increased attention paid to feedback from all learners, and the ways that quality assurance processes and systems make use of this feedback. External accountability links firmly now to funding provision in one way or another in most post-compulsory education systems and contexts. Within all the feedback from learners which is collected, collated and analysed, is at least some feedback which reflects how those learners with special needs have fared alongside those without such needs. We need to be ready to interpret all feedback as yet one more source of information about such needs.

Meanwhile the relevant legislation has evolved. In 2002 in the UK, the provisions of the Special Educational Needs and Disabilities Act (SENDA) came into effect. This legislation repealed the education exemption which had previously applied to post-compulsory educational provision, bringing the full impact of the 1995 Disabilities Discrimination Act to bear on teaching, learning and assessment in further and higher education. SENDA requires that no learners should be disadvantaged because of any special needs they may have, and that provision (and assessment) should include 'reasonable adjustments' so that such learners have every opportunity to demonstrate their achievement alongside those without special needs. Moreover, provision is required to make such adjustments in an anticipatory manner. In other words, since it may reasonably be expected that a significant number of learners in any large lecture group may be affected by some degree of dyslexia, provision needs to be adjusted so that these learners are disadvantaged as little as is reasonably practicable.

We need also to be aware that not all special needs have anything to do with something which is 'wrong'. For example, anyone learning in a second language in which they are not reasonably fluent, can be regarded as working under conditions of a special need. We may make every effort to help them to improve their fluency in the language concerned, but this often does not allow them to develop their language skills fast enough to keep pace with the growing complexity of language which may arise in the subject matter, or in the wording and design of assessment tasks and activities.

We need to remember not to ignore or undervalue the most significant source of expertise in how best special needs can be addressed – namely, the owners of the needs. Learners themselves usually know a great deal about any special need they have lived with over the years. They know what works for them, and what doesn't. We need to keep asking them 'how best can I help you' in as many contexts as possible – lectures, group work, individual work, practical work and preparation for assessment. Very often their answers can not only help us to make adjustments which are really effective for them, but can spare us wasting time and energy making changes which we *imagine* are going to be useful but which are often of limited value in practice.

When special needs remain undiagnosed, the problems are more profound. Some special needs evolve quite gradually, not least some of those of the mental health variety. When a learner has a physical accident and ends up for example with mobility problems, at least the problems are apparent, and it is relatively clear what sorts of help may be needed. It is however the invisible onset of special needs which poses the greatest problems for learners and tutors alike. Sometimes learners may begin a programme of study with no knowledge of having any special needs, and then it gradually emerges that problems exist. The most frequent triggers are to do with assessment of one kind or another. When learners underperform in assessment contexts, the possible causes include the effects of one or more special needs.

While there is already a wealth of experience relating to how best to accommodate the most commonly identified special needs, it remains an uphill struggle for subject-based teachers in post-compulsory education to respond to the considerable spectrum of such needs which may be present simultaneously in a given group of learners. It is also important to ensure that learners *without* any special needs are not themselves significantly disadvantaged by the steps which are taken to respond to special needs. The phrase 'inclusive practice' is increasingly used to describe attempts to design teaching, learning and assessment for the whole range of learners in a group. In fact, it can be argued that in many cases, whatever helps learners with identified special needs can indeed be of help to *all* learners, as will be shown further in the analysis of particular contexts which follows in this chapter.

Expert help with special needs

Most institutions of post-compulsory education have expert help available both to learners with special needs and to those teaching them, responding to them and supporting their learning. Large institutions are often able to provide or arrange quite elaborate levels of support when needed, ranging all the way to 24-hour assistance when really needed. The 'disabilities unit' or 'equality unit' in a large institution will usually contain personnel trained in identifying and responding to specific learning needs, and such people can provide a great deal of help to tutors and lecturers regarding how best to approach handling particular teaching contexts when special needs are known to be present. It is important that the dimension of special needs is addressed in staff development and induction programmes, so that, at the very least, staff become aware of where to find expert help when needed and, at best, become able to make reasonable adjustments to all their teaching approaches to anticipate the presence of the more common special needs.

Special needs and 'wanting', 'needing', 'doing', 'feedback' and 'making sense'

My argument here is that it is useful to think about various special needs in terms of how these five factors underpinning successful learning are affected in each individual context. In other words, some or all of these factors could be considered to be 'damaged' or 'limited' by particular special needs. If, then, we can identify which factors are impeded in a given context, we are in a better position to explore how best we may be able to compensate for the 'damage', and respond directly to each factor underpinning successful learning.

The following is intended just to be a starting point on our journey towards being able to make adjustments to teaching, learning and assessment to respond to learners with selected special needs. Not least, we need to continue to ask learners themselves how best we can respond – almost invariably they know more about their own special needs than anyone else. That said, I believe it is particularly useful to look at which one or more of the five underpinning factors could be damaged, as a way of fine-tuning our own thinking about how we may start to go about compensating for the damage.

Responding to special needs by compensating for the 'damage' to the factors underpinning successful learning

Dyslexia

A great deal is now known about dyslexia, both in terms of how to detect its effects, and how to respond. In short, however, dyslexia can be regarded as making it harder for learners to process information and turn it into their own knowledge, particularly when the information they are working with is in written or printed form, or where they need to be capturing information into written form from lectures, libraries or the web.

Which factors underpinning successful learning may be damaged, and how?

Making sense: words and sentences can be regarded as 'getting in the way' of making sense, particularly when the language level is complex, or the amount of printed and/or written information to be handled is great.

Learning through feedback: it may be more difficult for learners to make sense of written feedback.

Needing to learn: it can be harder for dyslexic learners to take on board ownership of targets when these are printed on handouts or in course handbooks. For example, they may find it harder to interpret exactly what is meant by intended learning outcomes and information about assessment processes, instruments and criteria.

Wanting to learn: possibly the most significant way that dyslexic learners may have the 'want' damaged is the increased fear of failure which they may be bringing forward from their past educational experience, for example, when they may have underachieved due to their special needs.

Learning by doing: practice, trial and error, repetition and so on are less likely to be problematic for learners with dyslexia, so long as the 'doing' is not overly based on materials which are linguistically challenging. Indeed, learners with dyslexia tend to have found already the increased value of learning by doing, and are usually ready to invest in it.

What adjustments may we be able to make to compensate?

Making sense: Using shorter sentences in our teaching can help. Using shorter rather than longer words can help. In particular, in task briefings and exam questions, we can avoid learners misinterpreting tasks and wasting time and energy going off on tangents to them.

We need also to make as much use as possible of the non-textual aspects of learning, for example making full use of the power of communication available in face-to-face teaching and learning contexts, where tone of voice, body language, facial expression and so on can all contribute strongly to learners making sense of what they are thinking about. Similarly, group work can help learners affected by dyslexia to make the most of the opportunity to share the ways in which other learners around them are making sense of the subject matter being learned.

As always, it is useful to ask learners 'how best can I help you to make sense of this bit?'

Learning through feedback: Face-to-face feedback can compensate for this, again making the most of tone of voice, emphasis, repetition where necessary. Where everyone is being given written feedback (whether handwritten, printed or emailed) it can be particularly necessary for us to find ways of debriefing learners affected by dyslexia on what exactly we are intending them to get out of each element of feedback, and using face-to-face communication to ensure that they are interpreting our feedback appropriately.

Group learning contexts can also be helpful, where dyslexic learners can also learn from feedback from their peers, and from the feedback we give their peers.

Needing to learn: Using face-to-face opportunities to explain intended learning outcomes can help, adding tone of voice, emphasis, and the opportunity for learners to seek clarification when they are not yet sure exactly what they are intended to become able to do or how exactly the evidence of achievement they produce will be assessed in due course. Explaining the intended learning outcomes all along the learning pathway is of course very useful for *all* learners, not just those affected by dyslexia – just one element of best inclusive practice.

Wanting to learn: One of the best things we can do is to try to help learners to develop their confidence as early as possible, for example, by building in the opportunity for some 'early success' so that dyslexic learners feel that they are up to the tasks which will follow.

Learning by doing: We can sometimes help by ensuring that we keep tasks based on reading and information retrieval to manageable proportions. Helping *all* learners to gain an idea about which are the really important sources, and which are for background reading can pave the way for dyslexic learners to ensure that they don't dissipate unreasonable amounts of time and energy on the less relevant materials.

Visual impairment

As with dyslexia, visual impairment ranges from a mild effect on learning to a very significant one. Where the effects are really significant, learners have usually a lot of knowledge about how best they can be assisted in day-do-day learning contexts. Turning information into knowledge is clearly harder when much of the information concerned is visual. Depending on the extent of the impairment, some sources can be much easier to handle than others – for example, material in electronic formats which can be turned into sound by computer software can be much more accessible than material only available in print.

Which factors underpinning successful learning may be damaged, and how?

Learning through feedback: this is mainly impaired by any lack of being able to see facial expression and body language accompanying face-to-face feedback from tutors, and also from fellow learners. Also, where written or printed feedback is issued to learners, those with visual impairments cannot revisit it as easily as those who can just glance at it again. Even though the feedback may be able to be turned into audio, it is still more time-consuming to return to a particular point when required.

Needing to learn: it is easy to forget how easy it is for students *without* any visual impairments to look at intended learning outcomes at any time – on the screen in lectures, in handouts, in course or module handbooks, and so on. Indeed, we *intend* the learning outcomes to be a frame of reference to help learners set their targets and take ownership of what they are preparing to be able to do to demonstrate their achievement. Students with visual impairments can all too easily miss out on the essentially *visual* nature of the ways we usually communicate learning outcomes to learners. Similar considerations arise in coursework task briefings and so on.

Wanting to learn: this unsurprisingly can be reduced when there is considerable enjoyment in the visual side of learning. Similarly, when visual means are used to help learners make sense of things – for example, mind-maps, flow charts and so on, the motivation of visually impaired learners can be significantly reduced when they find it more difficult to make sense of the subject matter concerned.

Learning by doing: some tasks may simply not be possible for learners with particular levels of visual impairment. When dealing with practical work, there may also be safety implications.

Making sense: it is often surprising to people without visual impairment just how much *making sense* happens by a combination of thinking about information and stimuli gathered visually. For example, all sorts of handouts, screen-based learning materials and, indeed, learners' own notes are often improved by the inclusion of pictures, flow charts, mind-maps and so on. For visually impaired learners, there may be difficulty in compensating for the roles that these illustrations play in making sense of the subject matter concerned. Also, in face-to-face sessions, learners without visual impairment gain a great deal quite subconsciously from our facial expression, body language and so on.

What adjustments may we be able to make to compensate?

Learning through feedback: Sound can again compensate to at least some extent for difficulties in receiving feedback visually. It can be useful to check with learners that they really have received the feedback we intend to give them, elaborate where necessary on points they had not quite understood in our feedback, and compensate for aspects where they need more detail.

Needing to learn: It can help to make the intended learning outcomes and coursework task briefings available in sound, so that visually impaired learners can hear them at will. It can, in fact, help *all* learners to make full use of the clues and cues which we can build into intended learning outcomes through tone of voice, emphasis and so on. It is important that all learners know what we really mean by each intended learning outcome, and it is much more satisfactory to communicate these using both sound and vision when possible.

Wanting to learn: Since the extent of, and effects of, visual impairment vary so widely, probably the wisest way to set about compensating for damaged 'want to learn' is simply to keep asking visually impaired learners straightforward open-ended questions such as 'how can I make this topic better for you?' As always, learners with disabilities are likely to know very well what will be of particular help in their own individual contexts.

Learning by doing: We need here to concentrate on designing *other* tasks whereby visually impaired learners can achieve the relevant intended learning outcomes, and other means whereby they can demonstrate their achievement of the outcomes. This is directly what legislation such as SENDA in the UK requires, making 'reasonable adjustments' in an anticipatory manner, so that we don't have to stop and think for too long before being able to provide suitable alternative tasks for visually impaired learners.

Making sense: It can be useful to seek expert advice on the most appropriate design of illustrations and flow charts in handouts and screen-based materials. 'Techdis' in the UK is a source of such advice. Visual impairment can range widely in scope and severity, and most visually impaired learners already know a great deal about what works best for them in compensating for their difficulties, and it is useful to ask them directly how best we can make adjustments to our learning materials to minimize their problems.

Auditory impairment

There are several ways in which hearing difficulties can impede learning. Turning information into knowledge becomes harder when significant dimensions of the information come from tone of voice, emphasis and so on. In lectures, even though induction loops may help learners to hear the lecturer, hearing-impaired learners may find it particularly difficult to hear other learners' questions. Many common-sense approaches can reduce the problems for most hearing-impaired learners, for example, making sure that the lecturer's face is well lit (particularly when dimming lights to show slides) and clearly visible to them, to help with lip-reading. A simple desk lamp placed at an appropriate position on the lecture bench or podium can make a big difference in this respect.

Which factors underpinning successful learning may be damaged, and how?

Making sense: hearing-impaired learners are in danger of missing out on some or all of the clarification which other learners gain from explanations where tone of voice, emphasis and so on convey much of the meaning.

Learning through feedback: when learners are restricted in gaining feedback auditorily, for example, in face-to-face contexts, there is the danger that they may place too much emphasis on written, printed or online feedback without having the same opportunity to probe what it *really means*, as is available to learners who can ask about it and hear the responses. Hearing-impaired learners may also miss out on the informal feedback which comes through discussions with fellow learners, and may not themselves realize how much this can be disadvantaging them.

Needing to learn: hearing-impaired learners may miss out on much of the informal face-to-face explanation of – and clarification of – intended learning outcomes in lectures and other face-to-face contexts. They therefore may be less well informed about the targets they are heading towards, and less clear about the kinds of evidence of achievement that in due course will be expected of them.

Wanting to learn: this can be damaged and undermined by embarrassment associated with hearing impairments. This is at least partly caused by what seems to be an all to common reaction to people who don't latch on to what we say to them – that they are 'slower' or 'more challenged' by the subject matter. As any hearing-impaired learner will confirm to you, slowing down your speech or shouting is not the best way forward.

Learning by doing: some aspects of learning by doing may not be available to learners with hearing impairment, for example, due to safety requirements. Also, when they are engaged in practical work, they may not be able to attend to instructions at the same time as performing operations, as they may need to watch the person giving the instructions to lip-read.

What adjustments may we be able to make to compensate?

Making sense: Since there are so many contexts where loss of auditorily received information can affect learners' ability to make sense of concepts and ideas as they turn information into their own knowledge, the most satisfactory way of compensating remains to keep helping them to find out how well (or not) they are making sense of important elements of subject matter, and asking them 'how can I help you to make sense of this?'

Learning through feedback: It remains worth checking that hearing-impaired learners are really understanding the feedback that we give them. When we find that a particular point has not yet got across in print or on-screen, at least we are able to try to use other ways of addressing that point or clarifying it.

To compensate for peer-group informal feedback, it can be worth finding out more about who *can* be heard more easily among the peer-learner group, and making best use of those who have a natural ability to 'be heard' more readily than others. This is not, of course, to be confused with mere *loudness*. Some people are much easier to lip-read than others, and so on.

Needing to learn: It can help to make intended learning outcomes, evidence descriptors and assessment criteria really speak for themselves in print, whether in course handbooks, on-screen or in handout materials. This of course helps *all* learners, but can be particularly valuable to those who may be missing out on the tone-of-voice clarifications which arise in face-to-face teaching-learning contexts and group-work contexts.

Wanting to learn: The most significant way of helping to avoid damaging hearing-impaired learners' 'want' to learn is to educate both teachers and fellow learners to respond sensitively and successfully to the real needs associated with auditory difficulties. Perhaps everyone should from time to time sit through a colleague's lecture with ear plugs in place, just to remind them of the effects of hearing impairments, and to clarify which aspects of presentation can compensate for at least some parts of the problem.

Learning by doing: In most cases, it is possible with some forethought to design tasks and briefings which allow learners with hearing impairments to achieve the same learning outcomes, perhaps by slightly different routes.

Mental health needs

This general heading in fact covers a very wide range of needs and conditions, ranging from depression, anxiety, Asperger's syndrome and mania to schizophrenia – any of which can have significant or even profound effects on learners' ability to handle various teaching-learning situations. Also, there are the much more common effects which can be regarded as affecting in one way or another learners' 'state of mind', including fatigue (often due to working shifts at night to support study) and conditions related to consuming alcohol or other mind-altering agents. Furthermore, most learners at some time (and some learners for most of the time) are affected by various levels of stress, attributable to a wide range of sources – financial, emotional, self-esteem related, and so on.

Some mental health conditions can be slow-onset, and grow in intensity so gradually that they are not noticed for some time – including by their owners. Other conditions can be precipitated very rapidly by life-changing events or crises.

As with other special needs, mental health needs of most kinds lie on a continuum, ranging from what we would regard as 'normal' (including occasional stress or anxiety) to 'abnormal' requiring expert help and support. Borderlines are very difficult to define.

Perhaps the most important difference between mental health needs and physical ones is that learners affected by mental health conditions are *not* necessarily able to give realistic responses to our question 'how can I best help you with this?' Some learners may have a firm grasp on exactly how their special needs can best be addressed, but others may be quite wrong in their view of what is likely to be best for them. That is why it is so important for anyone whose job is about making learning happen in post-compulsory education at least knows the nearest sources of expert help in addressing the more significant mental health problems – counsellors and other appropriately trained personnel, who invariably have their own links to the specialists who may be needed on occasion.

While it can be safely assumed that in a lecture theatre full of students, some will at any given time be impeded by one or more mental health needs or conditions, it is quite impossible for a lecturer to know exactly which conditions may need to be addressed. One can't really ask the students to respond to 'hands up those of you who have mental health problems today please'!

Which factors underpinning successful learning may be damaged, and how?

Making sense: the effects here can range very widely. In some cases, learners may be able to make sense of some things perfectly well – even exceptionally well – while other topics or subject areas may come to be distinct blocks.

Learning through feedback: some learners may be unreceptive to feedback, both from tutors and peers. Others may take feedback too seriously, and get it entirely out of proportion, especially when it happens to be critical.

Learning by doing: some learners may be unable to sustain effort for as long as their fellow learners. Some may find it particularly difficult to focus properly on a given task.

Wanting to learn: this can become seriously undermined, when learners with mental needs tend to retreat into a world of their own problems and difficulties. Conversely, sometimes learners with particular mental health needs can be found to be setting their own self-expectations unrealistically high, causing problems when they fail to live up to their own demands on themselves.

Needing to learn: the most general risk is that learners with mental health needs are in danger of not taking ownership of the standards as intended. They may make their own interpretations of what is meant by the intended learning outcomes, evidence descriptors and assessment criteria, only to find in due course that they've made incorrect judgements about them.

What adjustments may we be able to make to compensate?

With such a wide spectrum of mental health needs, and such differences in the possible levels, extent, or timescale of such needs, it is not possible to offer point-by-point advice on how to respond to the 'damage' to each of the five factors underpinning successful learning in the same way as in the preceding analyses of special needs.

However, there are some general ways to respond to the possibility – indeed, probability – that in any group of learners there will be some mental health needs at any time.

An obvious, but nonetheless important, aim is to avoid conflict, temper, distress or highly charged emotional exchanges for all learners at all times. For example, it is worth refraining from overreacting to challenging or unexpected behaviours from any learners, however irritating they may be to us – and, indeed to the rest of the learners in a group. While 'normal' learners may weather such minor storms perfectly adequately, those with particular mental health needs may get them quite out of proportion.

It is worth aiming to be as approachable as possible, so that learners with mental health problems – transient or developing – feel able to come and seek help and advice.

In any case, it is really useful to get to know the support systems and mechanisms of your own institution really well, so that you know exactly where to go to find expert help when needed by your learners. Getting to know the people providing such support is really useful, and allows you to seek their advice informally before deciding whether a particular learner's problem is one which would take you out of your own depth.

Hidden and visible disabilities

In the foregoing analysis, the ways in which particular physical and mental health needs can be thought about in terms of which of the factors underpinning successful learning may be 'damaged' were used as a starting point towards allowing us to think about how we may be able to compensate in the various specific contexts. In some ways, our task is more straightforward when the disability is visible to us. When a learner arrives in a wheelchair, or with a guide dog, we are immediately prompted into thinking 'how best can I help this person?' in the context of our own teaching material, learning environment and so on. It is all the more helpful when the owner of the disability is already an expert in how best we can respond to their situation. Other disabilities, however, are hidden. We've already thought about this in the context of at least some of the mental health problems, but there are physical disabilities which can also be quite hidden.

Diabetes, for example, is likely to be represented in any lecture theatre full of students. While it is rare for a diabetic learner to collapse into a coma in a lecture, it is far from rare for a diabetic to lose concentration during a lecture (or practical class, or seminar, or whatever) at a time when blood sugars may be running low – before lunch, for example. Despite the notices on the doors of many teaching rooms in post-compulsory education about 'no eating or drinking in this room', the most satisfactory solution for a diabetic's problem in a pre-lunchbreak teaching session may well be to eat a banana or have a suitable drink. Indeed, confident diabetics may well come up to you and explain that they may need to take such action from time to time. It is worth making sure that our response to any such unexpected behaviours is restrained. We need to be similarly open-minded to the possible reasons why learners, who could be suffering from back pain, hypertension, heart conditions, epilepsy and all sorts of other physical conditions including common colds and doses of influenza, might behave in an unexpected manner in our teaching-learning environments – including leaving altogether unexpectedly. If someone walks out, it is not necessarily the case that we have been boring the person concerned!

The most important common factor throughout this chapter has been that responding well to learners with identifiable 'special needs' is usually good for everyone else too. When we improve our task briefings by using clearer sentences and shorter words to help dyslexic learners, it also helps everyone else. When we make best use of tone of voice to help learners with visibility impairments, it helps well-sighted learners too. When we make good use of visual aids to help learners with hearing impairments, it also helps well-hearing learners. In short, inclusive practice is good for everyone. Moreover, I suggest that the approach of looking analytically at how to respond to the factors underpinning successful learning in each scenario of physical or mental health need is a productive way of helping us to address the factors for everyone, not just for those with such needs.

Conclusions

This chapter as a whole has ranged widely around the consequences of widening participation, particularly the greater spread of ability within cohorts of learners, and the increased presence of various special needs. In former times when post-compulsory education was designed for a relatively elite proportion of the population at large, cohorts of learners were much more homogeneous than nowadays. There are two distinct approaches to coping with the changed situation:

- to try to help all learners to fit in to the educational contexts they encounter
- to try to adjust the educational environment to be more suitable to all the learners whose needs it is intended to address.

The latter approach is, I would argue, all the more achievable by continuing to think of how best to design our learning environments to address the five factors underpinning successful learning. In other words, inclusive teaching could be defined along the lines of responding as follows:

- doing everything we can to enhance the *want* to learn of all participants in post-compulsory education
- clarifying as well as we can the *need* to learn, as spelled out by the intended learning outcomes we formulate to define our curriculum
- adjusting the *learning by doing* tasks and activities we design for learners, to allow all learners to have suitable opportunities to practice, learn through mistakes, and learn from their individual experiences
- maximize the *feedback* that all learners gain both from us and from each other, and adjust the feedback processes towards those that are most effective for learners as individuals
- help all learners to *make sense* or *digest* the information they encounter, and respond to their different ways of doing this.

To achieve these aims, we need to continue to seek feedback from all our learners, not just on their experience of our teaching, but also in their individual experience of learning in the context of their own particular needs. Learning, after all, is done by individuals. Each learner learns in a particular way. Inclusive teaching is about helping all learners to optimize their own individual learning.

9

Addressing employability

Part of the purpose of post-compulsory education in the grand scheme of things is to help learners become ready for what is likely to be one of the main features of the rest of their lives – getting a job and staying in employment. For the last two decades and more, there has been a lot of discussion about the balance we need to strike in our educational provision between deepening learners' knowledge and understanding of the subjects they are studying, and developing the skills they will need for their careers. Many aspects of becoming more employable can be developed alongside the subject-related knowledge and skills which are the basis of the main intended learning outcomes of our provision. Indeed, it is perfectly possible to formulate intended learning outcomes for the whole field of 'becoming more employable', and to assess learners' evidence of achievement of these outcomes alongside the subject-based curriculum.

What do we mean by employability?

It is useful to try to establish exactly how wide the field of employability might range. This list illustrates how different people think of different things when asked to explain what they mean by employability:

- Being able to participate in a group in a way that makes both you and the rest of the group believe that you are doing something worthwhile.
- Doing something that someone else assigns a value to, measured by a wage.
- (A person who has) demonstrable intellectual curiosity, generosity of spirit, understanding of purpose, and adaptability.
- Being positive, responsive, thoughtful, well informed, organized, sociable and, above all, able to listen and try to fit in while also contributing to the workplace.
- The ability to reflect, be flexible and adaptable and responsive within limits set by you.
- Having the skills which make you attractive to employers in your chosen field, or having the skills to set up a practice within your chosen field.

- The ability to say 'yes'!
- High-level ability to learn in as many modes as possible, individual and shared, and ability to make evidence-based judgements.
- To work in an environment which allows you to fully utilize and explore the skills you gained during your studies.
- Someone who can work with a team, in a profession, having acquired the relevant skills.
- Having some things or some qualities that you can sell, or that someone will pay for.
- Having the skills and qualities that enable someone to maintain being employed.
- The ability to be of some use to someone, somewhere, someday.
- The ability to interpret appropriately your role within an organization.
- The freedom and mobility to fulfil personal growth, which is valued financially.

What else is 'employability'?

Do we need to think of it as 'earnability'? Many, perhaps most, learners in post-compulsory education already have some measure of this, through various part-time jobs they engage in to afford to continue with their education. To what extent, we may ask, is employability 'hold down a job' ability? Some learners are perfectly satisfactory at getting a job every now and then, but are not so good at keeping it. Sometimes boredom sets in. Perhaps a more fundamental aspect of employability is along the lines of 'have a satisfying life' ability? This is more about making wise choices in the first place regarding what sort of employment suits individual learners. Perhaps the wisest learners see employability in terms of 'fulfil your potential through work' ability?

How can we help learners to *show* that they are employable?

There are many good reasons for building into our curriculum opportunities for learners to evidence their employability. Employers themselves know better than to rely simply on academic results when choosing the right candidate for a post. They seek evidence of employability from letters of application, CVs and, above all, from interviews with job applicants.

Evidence of employability needs to arise from purposefully designed learning by doing activities, including plenty of opportunity to learn by trial and error in safe environments – mock interview panels, CV selection panels and so on. Therefore, it is useful to think when designing learning by doing towards the achievement of subject-based intended learning outcomes, to what extent the same activities can embrace the skills and attributes associated with employability. This gives learners practice at evidencing their employability, and in contexts where it is not just seen as an add-on, but as a process directly linked to the mainstream curriculum.

How can we help learners to *feel* that they are employable?

As always, feelings are developed most quickly by feedback. In particular, when learners engage in activities where they are evidencing aspects of their own development relating to employability, they can gain a great deal of feedback from each other, often informally, but also purposefully, for instance, in the context of peer assessment. For example, getting learners to role-play interviewers and candidates in interview simulations, and capturing the process on video, can help learners to see themselves as future employers might see them, and learn by trial and error in a safe context.

We can get learners to put together applications for fictional posts, and allow them to learn by judging each others' applications as 'shortlisting committees', prior to using these applications as part of the basis for the interview simulations. They then learn a great deal about which aspects of an application may lead to good (or difficult) interview questions. The whole process develops their written and oral communication skills by practice, and trial and error, in a safe environment and can do a lot to help them to feel that they can succeed in making a good job of preparing to be seen to be employable.

Should we also be preparing learners for 'unemployability'?

In many people's lives nowadays there are episodes *between* employment of one kind or another. It is a valuable life skill to be prepared to survive without employment for a while, and not just sink into a morass of despair and gloom. For many learners, the time *before* the first significant employment opportunity can seem like an age. We need to equip learners to work constructively at not just filling their time when out of employment, but at heading purposefully towards the next employment opportunity, and continuing to build up their employability.

Should we also equip learners regarding 'sackability'?

Perhaps this is just as important as many aspects of employability, in a world where very significant numbers of people lose their jobs through no direct fault of their own, through redundancy, restructuring of organizations, mergers and takeovers, fixed-term contracts coming to an end, expected renewal of contracts not happening, and so on. Few education programmes really prepare learners for the trauma associated with losing a job – something they are quite likely to experience at least sometime in their lives.

Developing employability by building on learners' own experiences

Many learners in post-compulsory education already know a lot about employability. It is far from unusual for learners themselves to have had more varied experience at being employed than their tutors in post-compulsory education, many of whom have had a relatively stable and trouble-free pathway through only a limited number of posts during their careers. It is important that we don't fail to recognize the breadth and diversity of the experience of at least some of our learners, and help them to value it, share it with their less-experienced colleagues and build on it.

Mapping aspects of employability

Knight and Yorke (2003: 151–2) comment on a range of 'aspects of employability' drawn from the 'Skills *plus*' project which ran in four varied universities in the North-West of England between 2000 and 2002, and sought to bring fresh thinking into the incorporation of skills in curricula in higher education.

Knight and Yorke note that in the table of 'aspects of employability' they present, the acquisition of disciplinary understanding of skills is assumed, and that the *application* of these skills is included as '30' of the 39 listed in their table, which is reproduced below.

A: Personal Qualities
1 **Malleable self-theory:** belief that attributes (e.g. intelligence) are not fixed and can be developed.
2 **Self-awareness:** awareness of own strengths and weaknesses, aims and values.
3 **Self-confidence:** confidence in dealing with the challenges that employment and life throw up.
4 **Independence:** ability to work without supervision.
5 **Emotional intelligence:** sensitivity to others' emotions and the effects that they can have.
6 **Adaptability:** ability to respond positively to changing circumstances and new challenges.
7 **Stress tolerance:** ability to retain effectiveness under pressure.
8 **Initiative:** ability to take action unprompted.
9 **Willingness to learn:** commitment to ongoing learning to meet the needs of employment and life.

10 **Reflectiveness:** the disposition to reflect evaluatively on the performance of oneself and others.

B: Core Skills

11 **Reading effectiveness:** the recognition and retention of key points.
12 **Numeracy:** ability to use numbers at an appropriate level of accuracy.
13 **Information retrieval:** ability to access different sources.
14 **Language skills:** possession of more than one language.
15 **Self-management:** ability to work in an efficient and structured manner.
16 **Critical analysis:** ability to 'deconstruct' a problem or situation.
17 **Creativity:** ability to be original or inventive and to apply lateral thinking.
18 **Listening:** focused attention in which key points are recognized.
19 **Written communication:** clear reports, letters, etc., written specifically for the reader.
20 **Oral presentations:** clear and confident presentation of information to a group.
21 **Explaining:** orally and in writing.
22 **Global awareness:** in terms both of cultures and of economics.

C: Process Skills

23 **Computer literacy:** ability to use a range of software.
24 **Commercial awareness:** understanding of business issues and priorities.
25 **Political sensitivity:** appreciates how organisations work and acts accordingly.
26 **Ability to work cross-culturally:** both within and beyond the UK.
27 **Ethical sensitivity:** appreciates ethical aspects of employment and acts accordingly.
28 **Prioritizing:** ability to rank tasks according to importance.
29 **Planning:** setting of achievable goals and structuring action.
30 **Applying subject understanding:** use of disciplinary understanding from the higher education programme.
31 **Acting morally:** has a moral code and acts accordingly.
32 **Coping with ambiguity and complexity:** ability to handle ambiguous and complex situations.
33 **Problem-solving:** selection and use of appropriate methods to find solutions.
34 **Influencing:** convincing others of the validity of one's point of view.
35 **Arguing for and/or justifying a point of view of a course of action.**
36 **Resolving conflict:** both intrapersonally and in relationships with others.
37 **Decision-making:** choice of the best option from a range of alternatives.
38 **Negotiating:** discussion to achieve mutually satisfactory resolution of contentious issues.
39 **Teamwork:** can work constructively with others on a common task.

Knight and Yorke (2003: 203) concluded from the 'Skills *plus*' project that 'if progress was to be made in encouraging employability throughout a programme, then, especially in highly modularized programmes, it is necessary to look away from summative assessment practices with their own often unrealistic demands for reliability, and towards other ways of providing developmental feedback and helping students to make claims to achievements.'

Striking the balance between independence, collaboration and followership

There is much discussion of the importance of using post-compulsory education to develop learner autonomy and independence, but the ways that learning is driven by assessment often pushes us in the reverse direction towards conformity and uniformity. One aspect of employability which attracts a lot of attention is the development of leadership. However, particularly in the early stages of employment, perhaps an even more important set of skills and attributes can be identified linked to the concept of 'followership' – at any time there need to be more followers around than leaders, even when some perfectly capable leaders are present. Looking back at Knight and Yorke's 'aspects of employability', it is interesting to note how many of the factors link to decision-making, communication and leadership attributes. Perhaps we also need to think about some attributes which could be thought of as more conformist, perhaps including the following:

- recognizing when *not* to air one's own views, in the interests of getting things done, and promoting teamwork
- listening without giving one's disagreement away by body language, facial expression and so on, when disagreement is not important – or, indeed, needs to be shelved for the purposes of the task in hand
- accepting action plans that are not quite as good as that in one's mind, so that others continue with the increased momentum which comes from their sense of ownership of the action plan
- allowing others to do things which one could have done better, to aid everyone's contribution to a task.

Conclusions: five factors underpinning successful employability?

All five of the factors underpinning successful learning discussed throughout this book can be considered to link strongly to developing learners' employability.

- *Wanting to learn*: this links closely to the sort of motivation employers value. Getting learners to think consciously about their want to learn during their studies at college paves the way to them being conscious of their own driving forces in general, and helps them to remain more aware of what they want in employment. This, in turn, helps them quickly to communicate their ambitions both to prospective employers at interview – helping to secure a job in the first place – and to their actual employers when in post – helping them perhaps to justify some training or development they would like, or indeed to secure promotion as 'someone who knows their own mind'.

- *Taking ownership of the need to learn*: working towards targets is necessary in the day-to-day life of being employed. Working towards other people's targets, in particular, is very important in the early stages of any post. Skills gained working out what intended learning outcomes actually boil down to in practice, are usefully extended to breaking overall targets in post into achievable manageable steps.
- *Learning by doing*: any job can be regarded as an extension of practice, repetition, learning through mistakes, and so on. If we can help learners to be more conscious of their learning by doing while in post-compulsory education, they are likely to remain so as they move into employment, and continue to be more willing and able to 'have a go' at new problems, even when some trial and error will be involved.
- *Learning through feedback*: this is perhaps the most important of the factors underpinning successful learning, when we consider the links to employability. Employers value highly the skills of good listeners. However, *receptive* listeners are those who take feedback on board rapidly and easily, and adjust their actions accordingly. Similarly, the skills of *giving* feedback constructively are very important in work-based contexts, and employees who experience least difficulty supervising other employees are all the more valued by employers. Helping learners to become really conscious about how they respond to feedback, and how best to give feedback to others, are useful aspects of the overall purposes of post-compulsory education.
- *Making sense – 'digesting'*: helping learners become aware of how best they achieve this paves the way for them to continue to become better at it during employment. The more conscious we help them to be about what works best for them in getting their heads round new scenarios and concepts, the better they can take charge of understanding the employment contexts they find themselves in, and the less likely they are to rush into things having only thought through the consequences at a superficial level.

Moreover, learners who become skilled at learning, and consciously reflecting about their own learning, are in a strong position to continue to develop as learners long after leaving post-compulsory education. Equipping learners to be able to get the most from their brains paves their way towards lifelong learning – employers value 'a good learner' possibly more than anything else. Therefore, when the primary purpose of post-compulsory education is to equip learners for their future careers, there is nothing better we can do for them than help them to take conscious control of how they learn best.

10

Putting the learning into e-learning

What's wrong with e-learning?

Long before the age of electronic communication and information technologies, Einstein said 'knowledge is experience – everything else is just information'. In a nutshell, the hub of the problem we currently face with e-learning is that most of it is presently just e-information, not yet e-learning.

The greatest danger in e-learning is well known to be mouse-clicking onwards without reflecting. It is all too possible for vast quantities of information to appear before e-learners' eyes – and then disappear into the mists of time – without them being caused to process any of that information and turn it into their own knowledge. We need to find ways of causing e-learners to turn information into knowledge more systematically, more effectively and more efficiently. In short, for e-learning to be fit-for-purpose there has to be learning pay-off.

Another way of looking at the problem is that too often e-learners only engage in 'surface' learning, rather than the 'deep' learning we would like them to achieve. Often this is because of the speed with which they are bombarded with transient information. We need to cause them to slow down. Getting e-learners involved in self-assessment, or peer assessment, or group assessment can slow them down and allow them to deepen their learning. The very act of assessing causes deep learning. Assessing involves making judgements and decisions about one's own work, or other people's work. Assessing involves applying criteria and determining standards. One learns much more from assessing one's own work than from simply having one's work assessed by someone else.

Looking at e-learning materials at the time of writing this book, I feel that around 5 per cent of those I see are really, really excellent. These materials use the new technologies for what they're really good at, for example, giving learners interesting things to do, then providing quick and responsive feedback about what they've just done, helping them to make sense of what they did, and deepening their learning continuously. But around 50 per cent of the materials I see remain quite primitive in the learning side of the equation, even when the technology-side is fine. The other 45 per cent are somewhere between these two positions.

I expect that within another 10 or 20 years, most of the things that presently go wrong with e-learning will be so well known to us that we will avoid them. Most of the things that presently make the very best materials work well will have been adopted as benchmarks for learning design. The main purpose of this chapter is to try to accelerate these processes, by helping you to interrogate e-learning in terms of 'what works?' and 'what goes wrong?'.

What's so special about e-learning?

This, perhaps is the whole problem with e-learning at the time of writing this book! It's regarded as 'special', 'different', 'something else'. There are people whose whole job description is to do with e-learning. They tend to be the people who are expert with the technologies used to design and implement e-learning. But the danger is that the technologies tend to take over, and too little thought goes into what is happening in learners' minds when they're doing e-learning. The situation reminds me of the observations of Lindsay (2004) writing about the evolution of educational development some decades ago, from the position where 'special' training used to be provided in the use of the then new overhead projector.

Learners themselves are well into the new technologies, often some way ahead of their tutors. 'When stuck, ask a student' has been my own motto for years! Most learners use the new technologies in sophisticated ways for play, and the design of graphics and interaction in computer-based and online games is often far more sophisticated than the equivalent design of e-learning materials. The level of investment in the most popular games would be the envy of any educational e-learning developers. One consequence of this is that learners' expectations are raised, and when they encounter e-learning materials which look quite basic by comparison, their trust in the content of the e-learning is undermined – the *want* to learn being damaged.

Looking around the staff development provision for tutors in post-compulsory education, there is a lot of emphasis on e-learning, virtual learning environments, particular software packages and so on. Many institutions seem to be busy turning the curriculum into e-learning alternatives. There seems to be the notion that this will save money, increase flexibility of provision and solve all manner of problems. In 10 or 20 years time, I suggest, we will be much more careful about *which* elements of the curriculum we select for e-learning development. At present we seem to think that *anything* can be converted to e-learning. But soon, I hope that we will use e-learning for what e-learning is really good at – and won't touch e-learning with a bargepole for those things where it just doesn't work well.

Amidst all the discussion of the merits of competing platforms for virtual learning environments, and all the rhetoric about the design of 'learning objects', I think it is timely to remind ourselves of what we actually *mean* by a learning environment. Most of us, when purposefully learning nowadays, are likely to use computers and the Internet. But we still find ourselves with pens in hand, books, articles and pieces of paper beside us, making notes as we go – or typing our thoughts through a keyboard into the machine. We still need to talk to other people as we go – virtually or face-to-face. In other words, we still need feedback as we're learning, and still continue to learn by doing – the same sorts of practice, trial and error and repetition as we've always done, except nowadays computers and keyboards are involved. But our learning environments are seldom *just* computer, keyboard and screen. We still use the paper-based information sources, even when we download long documents then print them out because they're easier to use than when just seen a screenful at a time – and because we can use our pens and highlighters on the paper as we proceed into making sense of the information itself.

In an article from the US persuading managers to make more of e-learning in 'blended learning' contexts, Pratt (2002) refers back to the comparative advantages of traditional learning environments as follows:

> More traditional forms of learning, such as instructor led sessions in a class-room, also have some advantages:
> - The enthusiasm of the facilitator (instructor) for the content is contagious and encourages learning.
> - People prefer to learn in a social situation.
> - There is accountability in a classroom that is missing in e-learning.
> - Learning occurs casually and indirectly when individuals interact.
> - Instructor-led sessions remove people from their daily work responsibilities, so participants can focus on learning. There is no such protection when using e-learning methods.
> - The questions and comments of class members help raise and address important issues and make it comfortable for others to talk.
> - The pattern of learning in a group environment is established in almost everyone's school experience and connects us with our past.
> - The facilitator speeds the process of knowledge acquisition.
> - Classroom experiences provide opportunities for learners to practice and rehearse skills and receive feedback from others. (Pratt, 2002: 76).

In short, when e-learning is mature and fits easily into the 'blend', it will be just another tool in the overall toolkit from which we select fit-for-purpose tools in our mission towards making learning happen. But at present e-learning could be regarded as being far from mature. I believe that when we look back at the present time with the hindsight to be gained in the next couple of decades, we will judge our present stage of development of e-learning as being the first faltering steps in its development, with a few very promising examples lurking here and there.

Learning from e-learning experience

There is already a massive literature on e-learning. To do justice to the title 'putting the learning into e-learning' really needs a whole book, not just a chapter!

At the time of writing, one of the most thorough discussions of the pedagogy of e-learning comes from the Joint Information Systems Committee (JISC), 2004, where the update to the pedagogy strand starts by reminding readers of its core aims:

- to provide the post-16 and higher education (HE) community with accurate, up-to-date, evidence- and research-based information about effective practice in the use of e-learning tools
- to promote the application and development of e-learning tools and standards to better support effective practice.

Laurillard (2001) provides a thought provoking and informed overview of the status of the new technologies in higher education. Salmon (2002; 2004) has focused strongly on the necessity to get learning by doing happening in e-learning contexts, and has developed a pedagogy for online learning accordingly. There is also a great deal of practical experience available, for example, McAndrew (2003) and Thorpe (2003) in working papers downloadable from the website of the Higher Education Academy in the UK. Sources such as these radiate out to a wealth of other writing about online learning and computer-based assessment, and the whole area seems to be dominating the content of many of the leading scholarly journals in education.

However, in the context of the present book, I do not believe a scholarly discussion of authoritative work is either possible or appropriate, but rather that what is needed in the context of making learning happen using e-learning is an increased awareness of some of the problems which presently beset so much e-learning, and a sharing of the experience that is already widely available in the post-compulsory education sector where many people are struggling at the electronic equivalent of the chalkface, trying to help learners using the new technologies. Therefore, the approach I am using in this chapter is to share this experience, then try to seek out the questions we need to have in mind to interrogate e-learning, so that we can work purposefully towards solutions to the various problems we are finding. As with any other kind of learning, the more we know about the questions, the more likely we are to be able to find the answers in due course.

Learning from screens

E-learning in post-compulsory education includes computer-based learning packages, and online learning through intranets and the Internet. In all these contexts, we need to explore how effectively 'learning from screens' is likely to take place. We are relatively accustomed to interrogating 'learning from paper' in the contexts of handouts, books, articles and so on, even when it is well known that, unless there is substantial learning by doing and feedback, the learning pay-off from paper can be all too minimal. The next section of this chapter looks critically at 'learning from screens', and particularly at some of the questions which can be in learners' minds as they confront any particular screenful of a computer-based learning package or online sequence.

Perhaps the most important indicator that learning from screens is *not* happening successfully is if the learner at the keyboard looks for the 'print' command. In short, if someone learning from a computer-based package needs to print something, it is a signal that it was not possible to do everything that may have been intended with it on-screen.

The following comparisons between screen-based learning and paper-based learning are adapted and extended from some I did earlier in chapter 5 of Race (2001).

Some advantages of screen-based learning over paper-based learning

- *Wanting to learn may be enhanced.* For many learners, the whole business of sitting at a computer is more attractive than working through books and handouts, and can make them more receptive.
- *Learning by doing can be addressed directly.* With screen-based learning, moving on can be made conditional upon learners making choices, picking options, entering text and so on, so that they can't just scan through the material in the same way that they could with paper-based resources.
- *There can be instant feedback on-screen to pre-planned decision-making.* For example, choosing an option in a screen-based multiple-choice question can lead to immediate feedback on whether it was the best option to select and (more importantly) 'if not, *why* not?'.
- *Feedback can be withheld on-screen until some learning by doing has happened.* For example, the feedback to a selection in a multiple-choice question can be withheld in computer-based learning until learners have made their selections. In print-based materials it can be all too tempting to check out the feedback responses *before* having made a firm choice.
- *Computers can add sound to on-screen feedback.* Where learners can use headphones, for example, the benefits of tone of voice can be exploited in feedback responses to learners' keyboard choices.
- *Computers can route learners on to what they need next.* For example, if learners have succeeded in several on-screen questions, they can be moved on to something which may be more challenging to them (some harder questions) or, if they are struggling with the on-screen tasks, they can be moved back to some further practice questions.
- *Computer screens are less likely to cause information overload.* Paper, whether in books, articles or even handouts, tends to get filled up with print. The limit of screen size causes at least some economy of information presentation. However, this advantage can all too easily be thrown away by congested screens of information, especially when what is designed to appear on-screen is too closely linked to what might have otherwise been presented on paper. And things are made much worse, of course, if screen after screen contains information with no *doing* or *feedback*.

Some disadvantages of screens compared to paper

- *'Now you see it, now it's gone!'* Visual memory tends to be relatively transient. If something important is on-screen, there is every chance it will evaporate from learners' minds after a few more screens of information. This is probably the most serious of all the problems with e-learning at the time of writing this book.
- *It is too tempting simply to move on to the next screen when the present one doesn't make sense.* The next part may be more understandable, but learners lose track of what they have *not* made sense of – out of sight, out of mind. With paper-based resources it is easier to go back at any time to those pages which didn't make sense.
- *It can be harder to get the overall* feel *of screen-based resources.* This is the other side of one of the advantages from the previous list. With print-based resources, it is relatively easy to scan through the materials to see the 'big picture', which can be a helpful prelude to working through the materials in more detail.
- *Screens can't be used anywhere.* Learning from screens is dependent upon being beside a computer and monitor, or laptop.
- *Screens can't be spread out around a teaching room or learning space as easily as paper.* This means that learners can't move around as freely as they could with print-based learning resources. It also tends to mean that learners in a computer-based teaching space are working as individuals, and too often missing out on the feedback they may have got from each other if they had been working with paper-based materials.
- *Computer-based learning resources are often less easy to navigate than paper-based learning resources.* With a book, handout or article, it is easy to flick backwards and forwards to consolidate what has already been learned, and to spy out the landscape of what is to come. With computer-based learning, this is not always nearly so easy.

Is this screenful actually working?

Imagine a learner looking at a single tiny element of a computer-based learning programme, or a single screen of information online on an intranet or the Internet. Any, or all, of the following questions could go through the learner's mind while looking at a single screen of information. In Table 10.1, I've linked these questions to the five principal processes underpinning effective learning, as outlined in this book:

- wanting to learn
- taking ownership of the need to learn – the intended learning outcomes
- learning by doing, practice, repetition, trial and error
- learning through feedback
- digesting, making sense of what is being learned.

Table 10.1 Linking e-learning to the five factors underpinning successful learning

Some questions which could be going through a learner's mind	Some links to the factors underpinning successful learning
Why am I seeing this particular screenful? Why is it there? Can I just skip it? Is it just padding? Can I move straight on from here?	*Wanting* to learn could be damaged if there is not a good reason for the screenful being there. *Needing* to learn: the rationale for the screenful's existence should at least confirm what the learner needs to get from its presence. *Making sense* is much less likely to happen when learners aren't sufficiently aware of the part that particular screenful plays in the bigger picture.
What are the intended learning outcomes associated with this particular screenful? If there aren't any, why is it there at all?	*Wanting* to learn could be undermined if the purpose of the screenful is not self-evident. *Needing* to learn: if what is on the screen is not linked to intended learning outcomes, the message could be that it's not needed and not important enough to think about. *Making sense* is less likely to occur, if there doesn't seem to be a need to do something with what is on the screen.
What exactly am I supposed to do with this bit? How am I supposed to handle it? Am I intended to be jotting down my thoughts? Are there on-screen tasks for me to do such as picking options, entering text, entering numbers, clicking boxes, moving objects around and so on?	*Learning by doing*: this is addressed when the screenful is an *interactive* one, in one way or another. The *doing* could be practice, learning by mistakes, or more sophisticated, for example, requiring quite a bit of thought *before* action. If there isn't anything to do with what's on the screen, it is all too easy to think that it's *just* background information.
Will I be able to get back to this bit if I want to, or need to? How important is this particular bit? If it's important, will I have another chance to think about it, without having to go backwards to find it?	*Digesting – making sense*: putting the screenful into perspective is an important part of making sense of it. If it's not clear from the screenful whether it will be important or not, the learner may assume it is not important. The *repetition* side of learning by doing may be missed out. With paper-based learning, learners may return often to a tricky page; in e-learning materials they may not find it easy to get back to 'difficult' screenfuls.
Where does this bit fit into the big picture? Where does it fit in to the overall intended learning outcomes? How much will it count for in forthcoming assessments?	*Wanting* to learn, *needing* to learn, *digesting*: if the screenful does not clearly link to the overall learning programme, the learner may decide it's just there 'in passing' and learn very little from it.
How will I tell whether, and when, I've succeeded with this bit? Will I get feedback from the computer itself? Will I have to write down, or key in, something that will lead to later feedback from a tutor? Will I be given something to compare with what I'm asked to do with the screenful?	Learning through *feedback*: the availability of feedback to the learner, after doing something with what's on the screen, gives the message that the screenful is important enough to be taken seriously. One of the most significant advantages of e-learning is the chance to give learners very rapid feedback on what they've just done. However, that feedback needs to be very well designed, so that it *responds* to what they did and doesn't just tell them what the 'right' answer should have been.

Some questions which could be going through a learner's mind	Some links to the factors underpinning successful learning
Where is this bit leading me? Where is it taking me from? Can I tell where I'm heading? Am I supposed to remember where I'm coming from, and what I learned from previous screenfuls?	*Digesting – making sense*: it is easy to get lost in computer-based scenarios. It is perfectly possible to ensure that each screenful has enough context-setting included, so that this danger is minimized. It is also possible to have visual 'maps' so that learners always know where they are in the grand scheme of things. Unfortunately, this 'navigational' agenda is often not addressed well enough.
Who else is involved? Will someone be assessing what I've got out of this bit? Am I supposed to be doing this on my own or am I expected to talk to other learners about it? Is anyone watching me? Would I treat it differently if they were?	These questions can link to *all* the factors underpinning successful learning. *Feedback* can be forthcoming on-screen or from a tutor. *Learning by doing* can be coupled to discussing the screenful with fellow learners. The additional interaction and feedback can enhance *wanting* to learn and consolidate the *needing* to learn agenda, and aid the *making sense* process.
What else should I be thinking about while this bit is on-screen? Should I be looking at printed resources as I go? Should I be looking at notes I'm making as I go?	These questions can link to *all* the factors underpinning successful learning, particularly *digesting – making sense*. This is about integrating the screenful with other important parts of the learning environment.
What else am I learning from this bit? What am I learning over and above what's on screen at the moment? How important are these other things I'm thinking about? Will they be assessed in some way and, if so, when, how and by whom? Will I get feedback on these other things I'm thinking about?	These questions can link to all the processes underpinning successful learning, particularly *feedback* and *digesting*. If the further agendas associated with the screenful are interesting and seen as important, the *wanting* and *needing* to learn aspects are also enhanced.
What am I learning about myself? How is this bit helping me to develop as someone who can learn effectively and independently from a computer-based resource? How am I developing skills at managing my own learning?	Questions like these involve the *digesting – making sense* aspect of learning, as well as developing receptivity to *feedback*, and the ability to develop one's own motivation. This can be about the difference between deep and surface learning.
So what? If there have not been any good reasons for looking at the screenful after thinking through all of the questions above, is there any reason at all for it being there?	Cut! Or present the information in another way, such as on a handout or in an accompanying manual. If the screenful is not addressing at least some of the questions listed above, it may as well be deleted from the on-screen agenda of the learning package.

The questions and comments in Table 10.1 are just a start, and are presented in a random order. The next sections of this chapter continue the process of interrogating e-learning, and linking the interrogation to a wide range of experience of people working at developing e-learning with learners in post-compulsory education.

Interrogating e-learning: a checklist

The checklist which follows is adapted from a more comprehensive one I published as Appendix 1 in '500 Tips on open and online learning' in 2004 (Race, 2004). The checklist is particularly intended to help you make decisions about the strengths and weaknesses of e-learning materials and media. It can be used as a 'yes/no' interrogation device as it stands, but can also be used as a qualitative measure if you prefer to think of your responses to each question in terms of 'always', 'usually', 'often', 'sometimes', 'rarely' and 'never' or possibly rating materials against each question using a five-point scale (for example, 4, 3, 2, 1, 0 respectively). In each case, the principal question is in bold print, and supplementary or explanatory sub-questions follow, sometimes with a sentence or two of rationale, or suggestions about what may need to be done if the material does not already match up to the questions.

1 **Are the intended learning outcomes stated clearly and unambiguously?** This is where you may wish to 'translate' the stated intended outcomes of particular e-learning packages, making them more directly relevant to the learners who will use them. This can often be done by adding 'for example, ... ' illustrations showing how and when the intended outcomes will be relevant to their own situations.

2 **Is it really *learning* material?** In other words, is it avoiding just being information? Especially in the case of e-learning, the danger of just presenting screen after screen of information needs to be avoided. The most common – and most severe – criticism of many online learning materials is that 'it's just an online book!'

3 **Do the various components provide a complete and effective learning environment?** For example, in e-learning situations, are there paper-based materials to work with alongside the on-screen components? Are there suitable opportunities for communication with other learners and with tutors, face to face or virtually? Are there opportunities for learners to receive ongoing feedback on their progress?

4 **Is there plenty of activity?** Learners need to be able to practise, try things out, make mistakes and get feedback from the materials. Their learning is much more linked to what they *do* while working through the materials than merely to what they see on-screen.

5 **Is it easy for learners to find their way backwards and forwards?** Can they navigate their way through the materials? This is sometimes called 'signposting' and includes good use of menus in on-screen materials and e-learning delivered through virtual learning environments. Well-signposted materials allow learners to get quickly to anything they want to consolidate (or 'digest') as well as helping them to scan ahead to get the feel of what's to come.

6 **Can learners bookmark things and return to them at will later?** With print-based materials this is easy enough – many learners use highlighter pens to

remind them of important or tricky bits, or stick Post-its to pages so they can find them again quickly. Equivalent processes are perfectly possible to arrange in electronic packages.

7 **Is the material broken into manageable chunks?** Learners' concentration spans are finite. We all know how fickle concentration is at face-to-face training sessions. The same applies when learners are learning from resource materials. If an important topic goes on for screen after screen, we should not be surprised if concentration is lost.

8 **Does the material avoid any sudden jumps in level?** A sudden jump can cause 'log off from the machine' cues to learners working on their own. It is just about impossible for authors of learning materials to tell when they have gone one step too far too fast. The first people to discover such sudden jumps are always the learners who can't understand why the material has suddenly left them floundering. In well-piloted materials, such difficulties will have been ironed out long before the packages reach their published forms, but too many materials have not allowed for this vital process to happen.

9 **Are there plenty of things for learners to *do*?** For example I suggest that there should be something to do on most screens in e-learning materials. If we accept that learning mostly happens by practising, making decisions or having a go at exercises, it is only natural that effective interactive learning materials are essentially packaged-up learning by doing.

10 **Is the material encouraging deep learning rather than surface learning?** The key to this is the extent to which learners are helped to make sense of what they are doing when they try tasks or answer questions. It is therefore important that they are helped to stop and reflect on their attempts rather than simply press on with further learning by doing, except where the activity is primarily designed for practice and repetition.

11 **Is good use made of self-assessment opportunities?** It is important that much of the learning by doing leads on to feedback, allowing learners to self-assess how well they have answered the questions or attempted the various tasks as they learn. This means that in the best learning materials, the tasks, questions and exercises need to be structured, so that feedback *can* be given to whatever learners are likely to do with them.

12 **Are the tasks clear and unambiguous?** With e-learning resources, it is crucial to make sure that people working on their own do not have to waste time and energy working out exactly what the instructions mean every time they come to some learning by doing. Shortening the sentence length of questions and activities can often make a huge difference to how well learners get their heads around the meanings of the tasks.

13 **Are the questions and tasks inviting?** Is it clear to learners that it's valuable for them to have a go rather than skip the tasks or activities? It is sometimes an art to make tasks so interesting that no one is tempted to give them a miss, especially if they are quite difficult ones. However, it helps if you can make the tasks

as relevant as possible to learners' own backgrounds and experiences.

14 **Are the tasks sufficiently important?** Learning by doing should not be there simply for its own sake. There should be at least some useful learning pay-off associated with each task learners attempt. An exception can be when the odd task is included for entertainment rather than for learning – which can be useful when done appropriately.

15 **Is the comfort of privacy used well?** One of the strongest advantages of e-learning is that people can be free to learn by trial and error, without the embarrassment of someone like a tutor seeing their mistakes. Self-assessment tasks can allow learners to find out whether or not they have mastered something, and gain feedback about how their learning is progressing.

16 **What about learners who know they can already do the tasks easily?** If such learners are forced to work through tasks they can already achieve perfectly well, they can get bored and frustrated. In print-based materials learners will choose to skip these tasks, but in some computer-based materials they can't move on till they have done each task and they can find this tedious. It is, of course, possible to avoid this situation by having diagnostic exercises which allow learners who have already mastered something to move further on into the materials without going through all the tasks designed for their counterparts who need them.

17 **Will learners be caused to put fingers to keyboard, or use the mouse?** It is important to ensure that learners continue to make decisions, for example, by choosing an option in a multiple-choice exercise, so that they can then receive feedback directly relating to what they have just done. Online learning by doing can also make good use of drag-and-drop, text entry, number entry and a wide range of activities with much higher learning pay-off than simply moving on to the next screen.

18 **Cumulatively, does the learning by doing test learners' achievement of the intended outcomes?** Perhaps one of the most significant dangers of resource-based learning materials is that it is often easier to design tasks and exercises on unimportant topics than it is to ensure that learners' activities focus on the things that are involved in them achieving the intended learning outcomes. To eliminate this danger, it is useful to check that each and every intended learning outcome is cross-linked to one or more self-assessment questions or activities, so that learners get practice in everything that is important.

19 **Does the e-learning prepare learners for future assessment?** When learners have worked diligently through a package, the learning by doing they have engaged in should collectively prepare them for any assessments that they are heading towards – whether it be tutor-marked assignments, exams, practical tests and so on.

20 **Is feedback immediate?** One of the advantages of e-learning is that immediate on-screen feedback can appear every time learners make a decision, or select an option, or enter a number and so on.

21 **Does feedback really *respond* to what learners have done?** For example, when they have had a go at a self-assessment question, does the feedback they receive give them more than just the correct answer to the questions? If learners don't give the correct answer to a question, telling them the right answer is of very limited value; learners need feedback on what was wrong with their own attempt at answering the question.

22 **Does the feedback remind learners about exactly what they actually did?** Ideally, the original task, question or activity should still be in sight while learners view the feedback to what they did with it. With on-screen materials it is best that the task or question – and the choice or decision learners made – remains visible on screen when the feedback responses appear.

23 **Do the feedback responses meet each learner's need to find out: 'Was I *right?*' 'If not, why not?'** When learners get a self-assessment question or activity right, it is quite straightforward to provide them with appropriate feedback. It's when they get them wrong that they need all the help we can give them. In particular, they need not only to know what the correct answer should have been, but also what was wrong with their own answers. Multiple-choice question formats are particularly useful here, as they allow different learners making different mistakes each to receive individual feedback on their own attempts at such questions.

24 **Do feedback responses provide appropriate praise without patronizing learners?** It's easy enough to start a response on-screen with words such as 'well done'. However, there are many different ways of affirming, and saying 'splendid' may be fine if the task was difficult and we really want to praise learners who got it right, but the same 'splendid' can come across as patronizing if learners felt that it was an easy question. In such cases 'yes indeed' or 'correct' may be more appropriate starting points for confirmatory feedback.

25 **Do feedback responses include something that will help learners who got things wrong *not* to feel like complete idiots?** One of the problems of working alone with resource-based learning materials is that people who get things wrong may feel they are the only people ever to have made such mistakes! When a difficult question or task is likely to cause learners to make mistakes or to pick incorrect options, it helps them a lot if there are some words of comfort, such as 'this was a tough one!' or 'most people get this wrong at first'.

26 **Is each part introduced in an interesting, stimulating way?** The first screen or two of on-screen materials are critical. There's no second chance to make a good first impression! If learners are put off a topic by the way it starts, they may never recover that vital 'want' to learn it.

27 **Do introductions inspire confidence?** Attitudes are set early in any learning experience. Confidence is perhaps the single most important predeterminant of success. When learners start something feeling that they can indeed succeed, they are much more likely to continue to be motivated even when the material becomes more testing.

28 **Are there clear and useful summaries or reviews?** Do these help learners to make sense of and consolidate what they have learned? In any good face-to-face session, tutors or trainers take care to cover the main points more than once, and to remind learners towards the end of the session about the most important things they should remember. When designing e-learning materials, authors sometimes think that it's enough to put across the main points well – and only once! Summaries and reviews are every bit as essential in good learning materials as they are in live sessions.

29 **Can summaries provide a fast-track function for high-fliers?** Those learners who already have achieved particular intended learning outcomes may only need to remind themselves of those elements of knowledge, rather than work through tasks and exercises they can already achieve. Summaries can be particularly useful to them to check out what they can already do, and move on quickly to parts of the material which will deliver further learning pay-off to them.

30 **Is each non-text component as self-explanatory as possible?** In face-to-face sessions, learners gain all sorts of clues as to what any illustrations (for example, overheads or slides) actually mean. Lecturers' tone of voice and facial expressions add much to the explanation, as well as the words they use when explaining directly. With learning packages, it is important that such explanation is provided when necessary in print or on-screen.

31 **Will most learners be able to work through the material in a reasonable time?** Some things take longer working under one's own steam – others are quicker that way. It is useful to have a good idea how long it will take on average for learners to work through each element of a learning sequence, but to recognize and accept that some will take much longer, and some much less time.

32 **Will the average learner *enjoy* using the material?** In some ways this is the ultimate question. When learners 'can't bring themselves to log off from the programme on the computer because it is so interesting to work through it' there's not usually much wrong with the learning materials.

Making e-learning happen: institutional contexts

The following ideas and suggestions were gathered from a planning meeting in which I participated at Leeds Metropolitan University in January 2005, where staff concerned with developing e-learning talked with representatives from the Higher Education Academy responsible for e-learning development, and with colleagues from other universities with significant track records in getting e-learning going. The discussion included the benefits of moving towards 'blended learning', where face-to-face teaching and e-learning provision should be designed to mix seamlessly and enhance each other's contributions to the learning experience.

How can we go about implementing e-learning in institutions?

If there is already an ethos of working in teams – for example, as is the case in the Open University (OU) in the UK, that is regarded as being the best way to develop e-learning provision, as indeed the OU has already got e-learning going for around 60,000 of its 200,000 students, particularly in the context of supporting their learning. But in many institutions, teamworking is less well developed, and numbers of students are fewer.

Transatlantic experience shows that US institutions develop online materials quite differently. Staff are appointed not as subject teachers, but as material developers, and the ethos is to make such development profitable, sometimes by subcontracting aspects of the development, for example, to developers in India, where highly qualified (including by American universities) staff are available to design online materials at a much lower cost than can be arranged locally.

What causes e-learning implementation to fail?

Some failures have occurred because of poor surveying of the market, and unanticipated problems in causing institutions to work together collaboratively in educational climates such as that of the UK where institutional leaders feel that they are in competition. For example, the UK e-University (UKeU) initiative is thought to have failed mainly because it didn't engage successfully with conventional universities, and failed to make real partnerships as universities did not find it to be an enabling organization. Other difficulties were associated with the UKe-U's attempt to design a new e-learning platform, which institutions investing in their own systems did not find attractive, preferring to retain ownership of the platforms they were using. At the same time, however, the success of the UKe-U was to put blended learning on the map in the UK.

Ignoring learners' wishes for at least some face-to-face opportunities can cause e-learning implementation to fail. For example, it has been found that e-learners really want at least some residential face-to-face tutoring, and induction elements of provision in addition to the e-learning itself. Even the younger generation of e-learners, while being very quick to learn to use the technology side of e-learning, tend to associate 'real' learning with the presence of a teacher, and the assessment dimension which has already accompanied most of their learning.

It is difficult to provide really good online support for e-learners working at a distance. Although even in the UK Open University, rather less than half of all students attend face-to-face tutorials, students really value online support, but the most difficult thing to achieve remains getting them into good online discussions, and it has been found necessary to build such participation into summative assessment to cause them to engage well – assessment continues to drive learning even in e-learning contexts.

Other problems have been attributed to lack of support from senior management in some institutions, especially when their view was that e-learning would simply make staff more efficient and save money. Also, the committee structures and institutional infrastructures of traditional universities are built around the provision of face-to-face teaching and learning, and can be unwieldy and slow to respond to the changes of ethos which need to accompany good e-learning provision.

What works in helping traditional institutions to develop e-learning?

One UK institution provided funding to be spent on further developing e-learning when specific targets were met. It is said that this approach evolved into responding to the situation where individual staff were prepared to convert a module into e-learning in return for the provision of a laptop computer.

Other institutions have rewarded staff by reducing their teaching load by, for example, 50 hours in an academic year, as recognition for the time spent converting a module to e-learning.

Some institutions have encouraged staff by appointing 'Professors in e-learning' on the basis of successful development of e-learning.

Recommendations for implementing e-learning

- Before you try to do it, be an e-learner yourself.
- Make sure e-learning courses don't fail students – word-of-mouth comments spread quickly, and in funding systems such as those operating in the UK, with the spotlight firmly on retention and achievement, failing students is seen to be a costly process.
- Recruit staff specifically on their ability to develop e-learning rather than to provide (for example) 18 hours a week face-to-face provision. Different sorts of contracts are needed, as typical academic contracts are not written to support any other form of academic delivery than the traditional way. Different sorts of post advertisements are needed, for example, 'lecturer in e-learning'.
- Make sure that the staff who develop e-learning don't end up in the situation where someone else picks up the rewards for their investment of time and energy.
- Change the academic structure to make it easier for learners to drop in and out of educational provision. For example, in New Zealand it is much easier for learners to drop out of higher education, and then at any point work further towards their degrees simply by adding some further modules, with e-learning as one of the ways they can do this. In the US, the average time to get a 'four-year degree' is around six years.
- Staff workloads should be related to student learning hours, but there should be some way of calculating this in different ways of facilitating student learning

hours other than contact hours.

- Recognize that the income stream associated with e-learning comes from having satisfied students at the end of the day.
- Appoint project directors whose full-time job is to direct e-learning as projects, supported by part-time staff in faculties and schools, rather than hoping that part-time work will be enough on its own.
- Make better use of learners who have already been successful e-learners, in the development of new e-learning – they know what worked for them and what wasn't worth spending time on.

Towards a strategy for designing the learning into e-learning

The most difficult stage in starting out to design e-learning resources can be working out a logical and efficient order in which to approach the separate tasks involved. Figure 10.1 shows a diagrammatical way of thinking about how the factors underpinning successful learning can be addressed when designing e-learning materials. The strategy suggested below should help you to avoid wasting too much time, and particularly ensure that the work you do is directly related to composing e-learning material rather than ending up only with yet more e-information.

1 *Think again!* Before really getting started on designing e-learning material, it's worth looking back and asking yourself a few basic questions:
   (a) Am I the best person to create this material?
   (b) Have I sufficient experience of being an e-learner myself?
   (c) Are there any experienced e-learning editors there whose expertise I can depend upon?
   If after asking these questions, you decide to press ahead with designing your own e-learning material, the following steps should save you some time and energy.
2 *Don't just start writing subject material.* An e-learning resource is much more than just the subject matter it contains and, in particular, needs to be something for learners to *do* rather than just something for them to read on-screen.
3 *Start with your intended learning outcomes.* It is worth making a skeleton of the topics that your material will cover in the form of learning outcomes, at least in draft form, before writing anything else. Having established the intended learning outcomes, you are in a much better position to ensure that the content of your e-learning material will be developed in a coherent and logical order.
4 *Adjust the wording of the intended learning outcomes.* For example, see what you can do to make the outcomes as they will appear on-screen to help learners to *want* to achieve them. Make sure that learners are able to relate to why they *need*

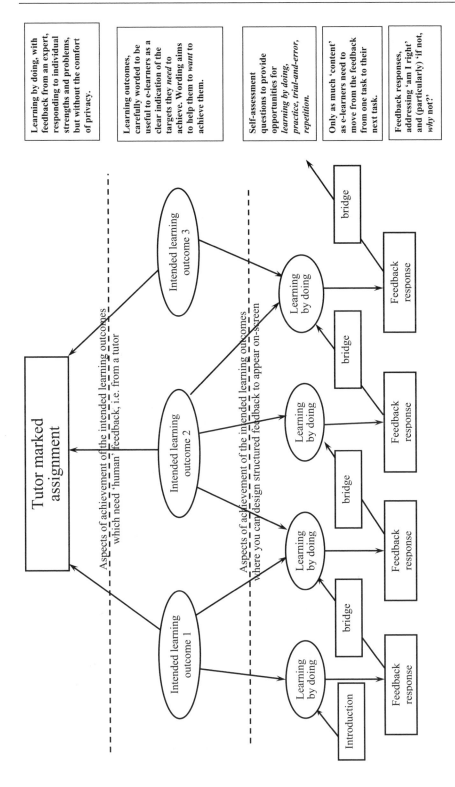

Learning by doing, with feedback from an expert, responding to individual strengths and problems, but without the comfort of privacy.

Learning outcomes, carefully worded to be useful to e-learners as a clear indication of the targets they *need* to achieve. Wording aims to help them to *want* to achieve them.

Self-assessment questions to provide opportunities for *learning by doing, practice, trial-and-error, repetition.*

Only as much 'content' as e-learners need to move from the feedback from one task to their next task.

Feedback responses, addressing 'am I right' and (particularly) 'if not, *why* not?'

Tutor marked assignment

Intended learning outcome 1

Intended learning outcome 2

Intended learning outcome 3

Aspects of achievement of the intended learning outcomes which need 'human' feedback; i.e. from a tutor

Aspects of achievement of the intended learning outcomes where you can design structured feedback to appear on-screen

Introduction

Learning by doing

Learning by doing

Learning by doing

Learning by doing

Learning by doing

bridge

bridge

bridge

bridge

Feedback response

Feedback response

Feedback response

Feedback response

Feedback response

Figure 10.1 Designing e-learning: A diagrammatical representation of a strategy for developing an element of e-learning adapted from Anderson and Race (2002)

to become able to achieve them, so that they gain a sense of ownership of the intended outcomes.

5 *Design your learning-by-doing elements.* These should be questions, tasks and activities, firmly based on aspects of achievement of your intended learning outcomes. Some of the outcomes may require several tasks and activities to cover them. It is also useful to plan in draft form activities that will span two or three learning outcomes simultaneously, to help pave the way towards integrating your e-learning material and linking the outcomes to each other.

6 *Work out where the learning by doing needs a 'human' response.* These aspects will end up in tutor-marked assignments, where individual feedback can be given to learners on their own strengths and weaknesses.

7 *Work out where you already know how to respond to learners and can design feedback responses to structured questions.* These will become the in-built tasks, questions and activities in the e-learning material, where learners can get immediate and self-sufficient feedback on-screen as they work through the material.

8 *Test your draft questions, tasks and activities.* It is extremely useful to test these questions and tasks first, with anyone you can get to try them out, particularly learners who may be close to your anticipated target audience. Finding out their most common mistakes and difficulties paves the way towards the design of useful feedback responses, and helps you adjust the wording of the tasks to avoid ambiguity or confusion.

9 *Plan your feedback responses.* Decide how best you will let your learners know how well, or how badly, they have done in their attempts at each of your tasks, activities and questions. Make sure that each feedback response addresses the questions 'was I right?' and, particularly, 'if not, why not?'.

10 *Map out your questions, tasks and activities into a logical sequence.* Along with the matching learning outcomes, this provides you with a strong skeleton on which to proceed to flesh out the content of your open learning material.

11 *Design 'bridges'.* Most of these will lead from the feedback response you have written for one question, task or activity, into the next activity that your learners will meet. Sometimes these bridges will need to provide new information to set the scene for the next activity. It is important to ensure that these bridges are as short and relevant as you can make them, and that they don't run off at tangents to the main agenda provided by the skeleton you have already made. This also ensures that you make your writing really efficient, and saves your valuable time.

12 *Write the introduction last.* The best time to write any introduction is when you know exactly what you're introducing. It is much easier to lead in to the first question, task or activity when you know how it (and the feedback associated with it) fits in to the material as a whole, and when you already know how and why you have arranged the sequence of activities in the way you have chosen. Although you may need to write draft introductions when first putting together your e-learning material for piloting, it is really useful to revisit these after test-

ing out how learners get on with the activities and feedback responses, and to include in the final version of each introduction suggestions to learners about how to approach the material that follows, based on what was learned from piloting.

13 *Keep the big picture in sight.* Figure 10.1 shows a diagrammatical illustration of the links between intended learning outcomes, tutor-marked assignments, learning by doing, 'bridges' and feedback responses. It can be useful to 'story-board' the e-learning material in a similar way, so that you don't lose sight of exactly what purpose is being served by each component as you design it.

14 *Start planning other 'layers'.* For example, if some learners have difficulty with the learning-by-doing elements, you may need to add another layer of activity and feedback to take them more slowly through those areas, with more repetition and practice. For those learners who are sailing through the material, you may need to fast-track them towards later elements in the material, without them becoming bored by doing too many things that don't stretch them appropriately.

Conclusions

There is no doubt that an irreversible change has already taken place regarding information retrieval and communication, and that electronic technologies are here to stay in daily life, including the whole gamut of teaching, learning and assessment. While the benefits of information being cheaper, more easily accessible and more rapidly communicated are profound, human learning evolves slowly, and we are not automatically equipped to make best use of the revolution in information. We need to continue to work towards gaining a better understanding of what works best in helping people to make learning happen with all this information. The questions and concerns shared in this chapter could help us to appreciate the size of the gap between information provision using the new technologies and the quest to make learning happen with all these technologies and information formats.

11

Making workshops work

Rationale for this chapter

I have chosen to end this book with a chapter on designing *training* workshops for several reasons:

- Designing self-contained, discrete workshops brings into play most of the ideas I have been advocating throughout the book, not least the emphasis on learning by doing, feedback and responding to learners during and after an element of teaching and learning.
- Getting the paperwork right is critical in designing and running effective training workshops, not least adjusting the wording of the intended learning outcomes, planning learners' activities and working out sensible timescales for the overall event and for each of its components.
- Many of the things which add up to make a good workshop also apply to all the other teaching-learning contexts discussed in the book as a whole, not least lectures, small-group sessions, and so on.
- In many respects, training workshops are at the cutting edge of making learning happen, with wider-ranging and different audiences than simply students in educational institutions.

Training workshops are at the very heart of 'making learning happen', in that when designing workshops we need to think first and foremost about what exactly participants are going to be *doing* during the workshop, and how they will get quick and useful *feedback* on what they have done, so that they *make sense* of what they are learning. Moreover, we need to plan the intended learning outcomes carefully to maximize the extent to which these will help participants to *want* to engage with the workshop activities. We also need to make workshop programmes sufficiently relevant to participants' training needs, so that they take ownership of the *need* to engage fully during the workshop.

Therefore, this chapter sums up just about all the philosophy I have been putting forward in the book as a whole, in the context of relatively short, specific teaching-learning events. I hope that you will be able to put the ideas and suggestions in this chapter to work for you not just in any work you yourself do which falls into the category of training workshops, but throughout your teaching and learning support activities. In no small way, it can be worth thinking of each element of teaching in the same way as a training workshop – where you focus on some intentional learning you wish your learners to undertake within a given time span in a particular location, and work at helping them to leave the session having achieved well-thought-out learning outcomes.

In this chapter, I offer some detailed suggestions relating to designing intended learning outcomes, and fine-tuning these to the experience participants may already bring to a workshop. I have also included some discussion of various ways of arranging seats and tables in small-group learning contexts, to maximize the interaction between participants themselves, as well as that with the facilitator. Furthermore, I have included suggestions about refining task briefings, to maximize the learning by doing which participants can achieve through the activities around which workshops are designed. Towards the end of the chapter, various ways of getting feedback from workshop participants are explored, so that workshop designs can continue to improve based on participants' experiences.

The wider picture of 'making learning happen'

Making learning happen in post-compulsory education is not just confined to lectures, tutorials, seminars and other 'taught' contexts. Increasingly, there are elements that are closer to the world of training, where learners are workshop participants on relatively short but intense training elements, often for time spans of a half-day or whole day. The word 'workshop' is in wide use for such elements.

Sometimes, participants at training workshops may be normal college-based learners, for instance, attending sessions with sharply defined intended outcomes. For example, many institutions provide training sessions for learners on aspects of computing, library usage, website development and so on. Also, most institutions provide training workshops for teaching staff on a wide range of topics including effective lecturing, facilitating small-group work with students, marking and feedback, and responding to student diversity (to name but a few of many topics).

In addition, workshops are often provided to meet the needs of participants from outside the institution, for example, employees or managers from commerce, industry and public-sector bodies. The learning design of such training workshops is very important, not least as many institutions are in a competitive environment regarding the marketing and provision of such programmes.

Because of the high levels of learner activity in well-designed training workshops, the language used in this chapter changes slightly, and the term 'participants' is used for learners. However, as I hinted at near the start of this chapter, it is a good idea to regard your learners as participants in all learning contexts and environments.

Specifically, in the context of training workshops, this chapter aims to help you to:

- identify key process aspects of effective training workshops
- devise intended training outcomes for workshops
- explore a range of techniques for gathering and analysing feedback from your workshop participants
- reflect during and after each workshop, and adjust future provision on the basis of this reflection.

Effective training is about effective learning

It is widely accepted that for training to be effective, workshop participants need to be actively engaged rather than simply 'receiving'. In other words, there is little place in a good training workshop for extended lecturing by the presenter, or even for significant episodes of direct presentation. Short elements of presentation, however, can play useful parts in a training workshop, for example:

- to set the scene before launching participants into an activity
- for raising awareness of the context relating to a forthcoming activity
- to help participants to get the 'big picture' and map out in their minds the various components of handout materials and other resources in their workshop pack
- to debrief in plenary the outcomes of an activity which participants have engaged in.

So how does effective training work? Effective training responds to the five factors underpinning successful learning discussed throughout this book as follows. Characteristics of successful training workshops include:

- *The 'want' to learn is addressed directly.* Participants know that they're in the right place at the right time. They know that they've chosen the right training workshop, because the outline programme was just what they needed (or wanted). They know that their time will be well spent. They know that they're not just going to be sitting listening to things they already know, or things they don't need to know. They're going to be learning – and enjoying learning.
- *The need to learn is identified carefully and responded to.* Participants know where they're going. They're clear about what they're intending to learn during the session, and why they *need* to learn this. They can see how what they will take away from the training workshop will be useful in their day-to-day job. They're also getting the chance to express what they *want* to learn, over and above what they may need to learn. They are confident that, as far as is reasonably practicable, the training workshop will address what they want to learn alongside what they need to achieve.

- *There is abundant opportunity to learn by doing.* Participants are busy for substantial parts of the workshop duration. They're learning by doing. They're learning by practising. They're learning by having a go at things. They're learning by making mistakes and finding out why (in a supportive, encouraging learning environment of course). They're learning by repeating things till they become good at doing them.
- *Plenty of feedback is built in.* Participants get a lot of feedback on their 'doing' as above. They get feedback from each other. They get feedback from the trainer or facilitator. They get feedback from the handouts, on-screen resources and so on used during the training session.
- *Participants have the chance to make sense of what they're doing.* They don't just follow instructions blindly, or follow a recipe. They think *why* they try things, *why* things work, *what exactly* happened when they tried something, what *else* happened, and so on. In other words, they digest what they're doing, and digest the continuous feedback they receive on what they're doing.

This chapter on designing training workshops aims to help you to ensure that each and every step along the way of planning, designing, facilitating and reviewing your training workshops will be fine-tuned to ensuring that participants' experience of the event will be as described above – active, focused, productive, relevant and enjoyable.

Planning training to make learning happen

The 'syllabus' for a training workshop needs to be self-contained, clear, concise and understandable to people deciding whether or not a given workshop will meet their needs and expectations. A workshop outline should ideally set the scene, so that intending participants are enabled to:

- see what the workshop is about
- find out what the workshop is intended to do for them
- work out what sorts of activities they are likely to be engaged in during the workshop
- establish the timescale of the workshop
- decide, on an informed basis, whether or not to enrol for the workshop.

Perhaps the most serious dimension of critical feedback about training workshops relates to participants who feel that the workshop did not achieve what had been advertised. Therefore, whatever else a training workshop addresses, it remains important that everything that was on the advertised agenda is covered, and done so quite demonstrably and overtly. This means that it is better to ensure that the published agenda is entirely realistic and achievable, rather than being too aspirational and ambitious.

To achieve these aims, a workshop outline usually needs the following elements:

- *title of the overall workshop*
- *rationale* – setting the scene or context
- *intended workshop outcomes* – establishing what the participants should be able to achieve by the end of the workshop – the workshop equivalent to intended learning outcomes discussed in many parts of this book
- *workshop outline programme* – setting out the approximate timescale of each phase of the workshop
- *'about the facilitator'* – a brief biographical note where necessary.

Example of a workshop outline

The following example is meant simply to indicate the format and structure of a one-page workshop outline or 'flier', and is based on a typical half-day workshop which could be used to train trainers in some fundamental principles of training workshop design.

Workshops that work

Half-day workshop led by Fred Smith.

Thursday 17 April 2005: 0915–1300

Conference Room 2: McArthur Suite, Lovell's Hotel, Station Road, Norchester, NC1 2AB

Rationale

Training workshops need to cause participants to become better able to do things which are relevant to their own needs or ambitions. This workshop will help you to explore how best to design your own training workshops, based on sound principles of effective learning in group contexts.

Intended workshop outcomes

After participating in this workshop, you should be better able to:

- design training workshops to be interactive and productive learning experiences for your participants
- express intended learning outcomes for your workshops so that participants can clearly see what they may gain from such workshops
- produce a workshop outline, which will be a useful yet flexible framework around which to fine-tune the workshop on the day.

Workshop outline programme

0915 Coffee and registration

0930 Introductory Post-it exercise: 'designing training workshops would be much better for me if only I could ... '

0950 Five factors underpinning successful learning in training workshops: presentation and discussion

1020 Exercise in pairs: drafting intended learning outcomes for a training workshop

1040 Report back: discussion of intended learning outcomes design

1100 Coffee/tea

1120 Exercise in small groups: designing activities for participants to do in workshops

1140 Crossover: producing a workshop outline for a training workshop

1200 Exhibition: posters showing workshop outlines produced by groups

1215 Revisiting the intended learning outcomes of this workshop, and adjusting them

1220 Workshop feedback from participants

1225 Action planning round

1230 Close of workshop; buffet lunch.

About Fred Smith

Fred is an experienced trainer, working in commercial and industrial organizations as well as with various educational and local government institutions. He has published widely on the design of training workshops, and is known for keeping workshop participants busy and engaged.

Getting the title right

For obvious reasons, it is best to keep the overall title short. An example of a title which would be far too long is: 'The implications of the Special Educational Needs and Disabilities Act on the delivery of online learning in Construction and related disciplines'.

The roles to be played by a well-chosen title are often best achieved by having a short main title, with a slightly longer sub-title, giving useful extra detail about the 'slant' of the event. For example: 'Construction Education: online learning – implications of SENDA'.

Sometimes it's worth putting a twist in the wording of a workshop title, to draw more attention to a particular aspect which will be addressed by the training event, for example: 'Construction Education and SENDA: keeping it legal!

Designing your workshop rationale

Essentially, this should explain *why* the topic of the workshop is likely to be important to the target audience for the training. The 'Rationale' as set out on the workshop publicity material should set the scene, but very briefly – it can be expanded upon at the start of the training event if necessary. If the Rationale is too long on the publicity material, the effect can be to 'dilute' the impact of the event, or even to put people off booking up for it. In practice, it is best to compose the Rationale *after* designing the intended learning outcomes and *after* planning the rest of the event programme. This is because it is only after doing these things that there is likely to be a clear picture of exactly how this particular event actually fits in to the overall picture being addressed by the workshop.

Designing your intended learning outcomes

These may equally be called 'intended training outcomes'. In effect, they are the same thing – statements of what workshop participants are intended to become able to achieve by participating in the workshop. In commercial, organizational and industrial contexts, the use of the phrase 'intended training outcomes' is commonplace, but in some educational organizations (not least universities, colleges, distance learning providers, and so on) there is some reluctance to accept the word 'training' in this context, and 'intended learning outcomes' may be found more acceptable to these particular target audiences. These outcomes are in effect the 'objectives' of the training event, but the term 'intended outcomes' has latterly become preferred in general – perhaps because 'objectives' were sometimes perceived as being too restricted or narrow.

As with all other aspects of making learning happen in post-compulsory education, it is vitally important to get the intended learning outcomes right! This means that they should not be composed quickly or lightly, but should be reworded and re-formulated several times during the planning of a training workshop, until they have become a clear and unambiguous way of describing exactly what those participating in the event can realistically be expected to achieve within the particular timescale applying to the event.

Intended learning outcomes should be

- Specific – in other words they should spell out exactly what workshop participants will be able to do after taking part.
- Measurable – participants' learning gain should not just be 'in their minds' but should be reflected in their actions after the training event, in ways that can be seen and (if necessary) quantified.
- Achievable – in other words the intended learning outcomes should not be 'noble aspirations' but practicable targets, realistically possible within the

timescale and scope of the training event.

- Realistic – the intended learning outcomes should not be overambitious for the context and timescale of the training event, nor the participants' levels of competence and experience.
- Time-specified – it should be possible to specify which of the intended learning outcomes will have been achieved during the training event itself, and which will remain to be developed as workshop participants continue to develop in their own work the learning that they take from the training event.

(These five characteristics of well formulated intended learning outcomes are sometimes summarized by the acronym 'SMART' for 'specific, measurable, achievable, realistic and time-specified.)

Suggestions on formulating intended learning outcomes

The suggestions below don't just apply to training workshops, but can easily be extended to the design of intended learning outcomes for all aspects of post-compulsory education.

1 *Avoid words such as 'understand' or 'know' or 'appreciate'.* Such language is too vague. Rather than specify that 'by the end of the training workshop participants should understand so and so' it is much better to focus on what they should have become able to *do* with the learning which they have gained during the event. In other words, peoples' 'understanding' can only be quantified in terms of their actions, and a good training event should be designed to impact on participants' practice, not just their thinking or knowledge.

2 *Make it clear that the outcomes relate to the participants themselves.* While it is perfectly possible to state intended outcomes as those of the event itself (in other words, for example, 'the objectives of this workshop are to explain the relevance of SENDA to computer-based learning design') it is better practice to address the intended learning outcomes directly to the participants (for example, 'after participating in this workshop, you will be able to take into account a range of special educational needs in screen design aspects of computer-based learning').

3 *Design intended learning outcomes partly on a 'need to know' basis.* For example, work out for yourself what your workshop participants *need* to achieve through your workshop. Check out their training needs, not least with typical members of the target group for your training event. When a training event clearly addresses what participants need to become able to do, its success is assured.

4 *Adjust learning outcomes to include what participants may also 'want to achieve'.* Often, the 'need to know' agenda and the 'want to learn' agenda coincide. However, there are usually additional aspects which participants *want* to learn, whether or not they actually need to achieve them. Wherever possible, represent both in your intended outcomes. 'Wanting' to learn something is a much

more powerful driver than merely 'needing to learn it', so it is worth doing whatever you can to ensure that at least some of your intended learning outcomes will address participants' 'wants' and not just their 'needs'.

5 *Make the intended outcomes personal rather than remote.* For example, it is worth making the most of 'you' and 'your' in the outcomes, rather than simply stating 'participants will be able to ... '.

6 *Don't state too many intended learning outcomes at a time.* Five or six such outcomes are enough! If the list of intended outcomes is too long, the programme will appear too formidable – especially if it is just a two-hour training event!

7 *Make sure that the intended learning outcomes are not just 'aims'.* The outcomes should be sufficiently specific, so that participants will be clearly aware of the extent to which they have actually achieved them by the end of the training event. With 'aims', it is usually only possible for participants to have begun to work towards them during an event, rather than have actually achieved them. Intended learning outcomes should be quite specific and self-contained.

8 *Check that the intended learning outcomes do not appear trivial.* This sometimes happens as a result of well-intentioned efforts to make sure that the outcomes are specific, achievable and measurable, rather than broad or general. Each intended learning outcome should be seen as worthwhile in its own right by members of the target audience for the training event.

9 *Work out what you really mean by the intended outcomes!* It can be very worthwhile to look at each outcome in turn, and apply the phrase 'what it really means is ... ' and then draft out two or three alternative versions of the original outcome. Very often, at least one of these alternatives will be much better than the original version.

10 *Road-test your intended learning outcomes with members of the target audience.* Ask them to tell you what they think that the intended outcomes actually boil down to in practice. This can help you to fine-tune the outcomes even further, so that they are as understandable and self-explanatory as possible to the target audience.

11 *Always check your participants' views of their achievement of the intended learning outcomes.* For example, if you've designed three intended learning outcomes for a particular training event, list them on the workshop feedback pro forma, with boxes or columns for participants to tick, indicating which outcomes they feel they have 'completely achieved', 'partly achieved' or 'not yet achieved'. This can help you to refocus the workshop next time round, for example to go further into aspects of the workshop which led to 'not yet achieved' views from participants.

12 *Continue to evolve better intended learning outcomes.* For example, after running a successful training workshop, ask participants to jot down on Post-its what they feel they have actually achieved at the event. Some of their responses are likely to be worth using in the future as a basis for the intended learning outcomes of the same event next time round.

Planning the programme itself

The title, rationale and intended learning outcomes are, of course, important elements of the overall workshop description. In addition, the outline programme needs to present a realistic yet flexible map of the overall event. In particular, it's important to get the timing right. Workshops are normally self-contained discrete training elements, typically spanning a half-day or whole day, and if things go wrong with the timing, there is not usually any opportunity to catch up on a later occasion.

Any experienced workshop facilitator will confirm that, however experienced you become at designing workshops, the most difficult thing to manage remains the timing. This is not least due to the fact that a training workshop is not just a lecture or a performance by the trainer, where every aspect can be pre-planned and pre-timed. Part of the trick of designing an outline timetable is to provide a suitable skeleton which can be fleshed out in reality in a number of different ways, depending on exactly what a particular group of participants do on the day.

Let's look at designing such an outline by comparing two ways of going about the task, for a half-day training event, and thinking about the implications of the design. (Many of the same factors continue to apply to longer – or shorter – training events.)

Programme 1		Programme 2	
		0915	Coffee and registration
0930	Introduction, workshop aims	0930	Introduction, participants' expectations
1000	Exercise 1 – individual then pairs	1000	Exercise 1 – individuals then pairs
1030	Discussion arising from exercise 1	1030	Discussion arising from exercise 1
1100	Tea/coffee	1100	Tea/coffee break
1110	Presentation on topic 2	1120	Setting the scene for group exercise 2
1130	Exercise 2	1130	Exercise 2
1200	Plenary report back and discussion, matters arising, workshop evaluation, action planning,	1200	Report back from groups – two minutes each, then discussion
1230	Close of workshop	1220	Action planning round
		1225	Workshop evaluation pro forma
		1230	Close of workshop – buffet lunch

Why is Programme 2 better than Programme 1?

- The 0915 'coffee and registration' is likely to ensure that most participants are present and ready to go at 0930. The 0930 session in Programme 1 is likely to be interrupted by people coming in late and settling in.
- 'Participants' expectations' in Programme 2 helps to get the session off to a 'soft start' – in other words anyone coming in late hasn't missed anything crucial from the facilitator, but at the same time people who are punctual and present are being valued by having their own expectations (hopes, fears and so on) taken into account and listened to by the facilitator.

- The tea/coffee break of 20 minutes in Programme 2 is much more realistic than 10 minutes in Programme 1. A short break is likely to be followed by a late re-start; a longer break increases the probability of the overall programme keeping to time rather than slipping. Participants are much more aware than most facili-tators realize, of whether or not a programme is running to time – they may have appointments to go to immediately after the event – or trains to catch, and so on.
- There are too many 'things' in Programme 1 from 1200 to 1230; time slippage is inevitable, and the short but important element of 'action planning' may not get done at all.
- The 'buffet lunch' in Programme 2 is likely to encourage all participants to stay till the end, rather than slip out early to go to appointments or catch trains and so on. Furthermore, the discussion that participants may have over the buffet lunch is likely to be further deepening their learning achievement arising from the workshop, and gives them an opportunity to follow up (with each other and with the facilitator) matters arising which had not already been handled during the session itself.

Finding out what they already know

When working with learners you already know, you are likely to be taking into account everything you know about them as you design each successive element of their ongo-ing learning. In the context of training workshops, however, you may well meet a brand new group of people and find it quite difficult to estimate where to pitch the learning experiences you plan for them. In such cases, it can be really helpful to design a short pre-workshop questionnaire to send or email to intending workshop participants.

Normally, such a questionnaire needs to relate quite specifically to the intended learning you plan for the workshop session.

Making 'learning by doing' happen

Effective training workshops are essentially 'learning-by-doing' occasions, so one of the most important aspects of designing successful workshops is setting suitable tasks for workshop participants. In practice, it is more important for you to plan out the fine detail of what your participants will be doing during a workshop than to focus on what you yourself will be doing. The following guidelines are intended to help you to formulate tasks well and brief workshop participants effectively.

Paper-based, on-screen or verbal briefings?

Each of these ways of briefing workshop participants has both advantages and dis-advantages. These can be summed up as follows.

Paper-based briefings – for example, in handout materials, or separate sheets or slips of paper

Advantages	Disadvantages
Participants have the exact words of the briefings in their possession.	If the tasks have not been carefully formulated in the first place, the printed briefings may become dated or inappropriate.
Participants can carry the briefings around with them, for example, when going to break-out rooms for syndicate work.	Printed words lack the additional benefits regarding tone of voice, body language, emphasis and explanation, which are associated with oral task briefings.
Participants retain the exact task briefings after the workshop, and can revisit the tasks on their own or cascade them to other people in their organizations.	If it is decided to alter or fine-tune the tasks orally, participants may revert to the printed briefings, particularly when away from the plenary workshop venue, for example, in syndicates.
If there are several different tasks being done in parallel (for example, by different syndicate groups), all participants can carry with them all the briefings, and remain aware of where their own work fits in to the bigger picture.	If it is decided to shorten particular tasks, participants may continue to work on the full version according to their printed briefings, and may end up not doing the principal parts of the intended task.

On-screen task briefings, for example, overhead transparencies or PowerPoint slides

Advantages	Disadvantages
All the workshop participants see the task briefing at the same time, and in the order that is revealed by the workshop facilitator.	When participants go to different locations for syndicate work, they may not remember exactly what the briefings were, unless they also have the briefings on paper (or carry copies of the overhead transparencies containing the briefings with them).
It is easier to fine-tune task briefings on overhead transparencies or slides than to change printed briefings.	If the task briefings have been fine-tuned in a plenary session, any pre-prepared copies of the briefings may be out of date and may be no longer suitable for carrying to break-out rooms for syndicate work.

Participants can question the tasks in plenary before starting work on them, and clarify ambiguities.

This can sometimes lead to unexpectedly long interruptions to the timing allocated to the tasks.

If all participants will be remaining in the plenary location while working on the tasks, the tasks can continue to be displayed (in adjusted forms) while they work.

If the task briefings take more than one overhead or slide, it can be necessary to 'toggle' between separate slides while participants are working on the task.

Verbal briefings

Advantages	Disadvantages
Tone of voice, body language, emphasis and repetition can be used to ensure that all participants know exactly what they are intended to do when working on the tasks.	If participants go away into syndicate groups, their memories of the verbal briefing may diverge between groups, and different groups may end up approaching the tasks in different ways.
Participants may be more likely to ask necessary questions in a verbal briefing, rather than assuming that because they have a task in print, they will be able to work out exactly what it means.	Participants may focus on the particular parts of a task which were the subject of plenary discussion, at the expense of other parts which may be more important in fact.

Getting the timing right for workshop tasks

The following suggestions relating to timing of tasks may help your workshop participants to keep to time when working on tasks, particularly when they may be in separate syndicate groups in different locations while working on the tasks.

- *Break each task into small, separate stages.* Think in terms of the discrete activities involved in each stage of the task, and make sure that key words and phrases are at the start of the briefing for each task, for example 'share your ideas on ... ', 'list five reasons why there could be problems with ... ', 'prioritize the top three problems you have thought of', and so on.

- *Give deadlines rather than durations.* For example, rather than saying 'spend about 10 minutes on ... ' say 'complete this stage by 1015' and so on, and make sure that participants have on paper the agreed deadlines for each stage of the overall task.
- *Don't make deadlines too optimistic.* If participants slip behind an agreed schedule for a task, they may lose heart, and fail to complete later important stages in time for plenary report back sessions. This is particularly a problem when groups are working in separate rooms, as it is easy for one group to slip behind quite quickly without being noticed.
- *Go round the groups reminding them (for example) 'three minutes to go, please, before you move on to stage 3 of the briefing'.* This can reinforce the agreed timetable for the overall task and avoid some groups finishing too soon before others.
- *Consider providing pro formas to be completed as the tasks are done.* These can remind participants exactly what they are intended to be producing as evidence of achievement of each stage of the tasks, and can ensure that separate groups continue to work along the same lines when doing tasks in parallel.

Getting participants into groups

Most training workshops involve at least some group work. It would not be unreasonable to plan to have three small-group episodes even in a half-day training event. If there's more than one small-group episode, it becomes advisable to ensure that participants don't remain in the same group each time. Advantages of deliberately rearranging the group composition include:

- Any domineering (or awkward, or prejudiced, or overly experienced, or other) participant does not remain with the same fellow participants for too long – the influence is distributed rather than contained.
- The amount participants learn from each other is increased when, over a series of group elements, they work with most other people in the room, rather than just a few.
- It can be useful to get as many of the participants as possible to know each other better – especially if they're likely to be working together again, or if they have similar experiences to share and similar problems to address in their work.

One way of pre-planning group composition is to use (for example) three-part codes on name badges or self-adhesive labels, for example, one Greek letter, one Latinate letter and one number, as follows.

αA1	βA2	γA3	δA4	θA5
αB2	βB3	γB4	δB5	θB1
αC3	βC4	γC5	δC1	θC2
αD4	βD5	γD1	δD2	θD3
αE5	βE1	γE2	δE3	θE4

Give these labels out randomly and ask participants to write their names on them with a felt-tip pen – an overhead projector pen or flip-chart marker – especially when it will be useful for them to become more familiar with each others' names. Then you can split them quickly and easily into three entirely different group configurations, each with five groups of five, as follows:

- grouping by Greek letters
- grouping by Latinate letters
- grouping by numbers.

Getting participants to write their own names on labels brings the following additional benefits to workshops:

- You find out what they *prefer* to be called – there are always some participants who prefer a shorter version of their name than you might have on a printed list, or sometimes a quite different name!
- It helps *you* to be able to address participants by name, and to get their names right – very useful for one-off workshops where you've never seen the people concerned before.
- Handwritten name labels are usually more visible from a distance than typed conference badges.
- Name labels move around with the participants – unlike 'place cards' on tables!

Using flip charts

Flip charts are among the most common of visual media used by trainers. They are also useful in other small-group teaching contexts, such as tutorials and seminars, but not so suitable for large-group contexts such as lectures.

Some training venues have 'electronic' flip charts, where at the touch of a button or two a printout of the content can be generated, and then photocopied so that all participants can have a copy. Interactive whiteboards can also serve similar purposes. However, these more sophisticated kinds of marker board have their own limitations, for example:

- Once the thing is full, you've got to erase its content to make more space for further work. This can mean losing thoughts and ideas you'd prefer to keep in participants' view for the rest of the workshop.
- It's all too easy to use the wrong sort of pen on electronic flip charts and marker boards, and mark them permanently!

The traditional straightforward flip chart has distinct advantages over the more sophisticated varieties, including:

- You can stick up finished flip charts on any suitable wall, door or window around the workshop room.
- You can put up completed charts at a height which makes them easy to be seen around the room.
- You can take the charts away with you after the workshop, for transcription or just to aid your own reflection.

The following suggestions may help you get the most out of using flip charts to help to cause learning to happen in your training workshops.

- *Set the flip chart up before you start.* Some flip-chart stands have a will of their own, and seem to come provided with three legs of unequal length. Don't allow your participants to see you struggle with the thing!
- *Bring your own pens.* There's nothing more frustrating than a flip chart without proper pens. Overhead projector pens will do in a crisis, but your lettering will look spidery and may be hard to read at the back of the room.
- *Don't forget your Blu-Tack.* You may often want to display several flip charts at the same time, so make sure you've got that essential means of sticking flip charts to doors, walls and, even, windows. Be careful, however, if walls are wallpapered – with care it's still possible to stick flip charts to such walls as long as you develop the knack of using Blu-Tack sparingly, and gently peel off the chart with the Blu-Tack still sticking to the chart rather than to the wallpaper.
- *Avoid 'now you see it, now it's gone'.* One of the main advantages of flip charts is the way you can use Blu-Tack to stick charts to walls to keep successive charts in view, rather than just folding the sheet over to start a new chart.
- *Capture the 'need' to learn.* Always have a flip chart to remind participants throughout the workshop what it's really supposed to be about. For example, it can be worth using one chart to keep the intended learning outcomes in sight throughout.

- *Capture participants' 'learning by doing'.* Make sure that *their* ideas and questions are made visible, to increase their sense of ownership of the workshop. When you get groups of participants to create flip charts in workshop exercises, make sure that these are displayed suitably for other groups to see and compare.
- *Don't put too much onto a flip chart.* It's best to 'write big' and use broad pens, so that everyone can see all the words without difficulty. Unless your handwriting is unusually good you may find it best to print upper-case letters when writing on flip charts. But remember that whole sentences or bullet points in upper-case letters tend to generate eye fatigue.
- *Make it easy to tear off successive flip charts.* With pads of perforated flip-chart paper, this is straightforward. However, sometimes you will have to make your own arrangements for removing sheets neatly. Often, it helps to simply unscrew the two knobs which secure the chart to the easel, allowing you to make clean, neat tear-offs at the very top of the pad of charts.
- *A sharp knife can be useful.* For example, there are small collapsible razor-knives – but remember not to still have one in your hand luggage when flying! With these, you can (with practice) score along the top of a chart neatly and tear it off leaving a straight edge at the top. Be careful not to cut more than one sheet at a time though!
- *Decide when 'live' flip-charting really is a sensible choice.* Don't end up writing long sentences dictated by participants. Flip charts work best for keywords, for example, in brainstorming sessions.
- *Prepare important flip charts in advance.* For example, if you're going to use flip charts to write up tasks for participants to do in your training event, it's useful to be able to turn straight to a ready-made flip chart rather than write it all out with them watching.
- *Get participants to use flip charts.* For example, giving a syndicate a flip chart as a means of reporting back on the task they are doing can help concentrate their minds on the task in hand, rather than engaging in sophisticated work-avoidance strategies!
- *Always have some rubber bands.* Often, you'll want to take away the flip charts produced at a training event, so you can write up a report on the event, or collate and distribute the products of the event. An armful of loose flip charts is not an easy package to carry away – but rolled up tightly with a couple of rubber bands, is much more manageable.
- *Consider using your digital camera.* It can be quicker to take photos of flip charts rather than having important ones transcribed at a keyboard, especially when they contain flow charts, diagrams and drawings. You can then email the content back to workshop participants as a reminder of what they may have created, or helped you to create.

Coping with the unexpected

Your reputation as a workshop facilitator (or, indeed, a lecturer, tutor, learning sup-
porter and so on) can depend not only on your professional expertise, but on your
ability to be seen to cope with the unexpected, calmly, professionally, with humour
and with dignity. I have adapted the following suggestions from *2000 Tips for Trainers* (2001 ed. Phil Race, Kogan Page, London), and I hope that they may help you to
attain this image when surprises occur during your workshops or teaching sessions.

- *Welcome the unexpected!* Life is full of the unexpected. Almost every training
  workshop will bring with it at least one thing that is entirely unexpected. It is
  only an enemy if we resist it. Look at it this way: a 'competent' trainer works
  within what is expected; a 'professional' trainer can work within whatever
  turns up. Aim to be able to cope with anything. Don't worry that you don't
  succeed every time – no one can.
- *Harness the unexpected.* Don't hide from it, don't pretend it isn't there. Work out
  what it really means. Define it. Put it into words which everyone shares the
  meaning of.
- *Turn the unexpected into 'issues' and 'questions'.* Add these to the questions and
  issues upon which your training event is based. Sometimes, the things that
  arise from unexpected developments are more important than the original
  issues or questions that your training event was meant to address.
- *Seek everyone's views.* When the unexpected turns up, don't feel that you are
  obliged to have all the answers up your sleeve. It can be the ideal opportunity
  to say 'I don't really know – what do you think?' to your participants. They will
  respect you all the more for this.
- *Legitimize the unexpected.* When important matters turn up 'unexpectedly', add
  these formally to the agenda of your training session. Turn them into additional objectives or intended outcomes.
- *Ask for the unexpected.* Keep asking 'what *else* may we need to be able to deal
  with?' When the 'unexpected' comes directly from your training event participants, they already have a sense of ownership of it and are all the more willing to try to work out ways of handling it.
- *Be prepared for the unexpected.* As a training event facilitator, be ready for all the
  things which *could* happen – data overhead projector bulbs blowing, power
  cuts, a pneumatic drill starting up outside the window, coffee not arriving at
  all, and so on. Always have something else in mind which can limit the damage of the unexpected.
- *Capitalize on the unexpected.* Shamelessly, draw learning points from ways that
  the unexpected has been successfully handled. Participants will remember the
  way that you (for example) turned the three fire alarms (due to a fault in the
  circuit) in one morning into a learning exercise!

- *Remember that the unexpected is* shared. The unexpected can help bring you closer to your participants. It can help you confirm your role as 'benevolent leader'. It can help them gain respect for your judgement and decisiveness.
- *Always have 'plan B'!* When it is quite clear that unexpected factors have made your original plan unworkable, let it show that all the time you had in mind an alternative way in which the aims of your training session could be achieved.

Creating an active learning environment – room layout

Many educational institutions have 'conference suites' specifically designed for short, self-contained training elements, whether for learners from the institution itself or from outside. Such venues often have catering provision built in, so that workshop groups can continue to spend time together discussing and sharing ideas over refreshment breaks and meals. Alternatively, workshops for staff in particular are sometimes held as 'away-days' using conference facilities elsewhere, in hotels for example, to minimize the disruption which can occur when participants continue to be under pressure to deal with day-to-day matters arising from their normal work in the institution.

Spending a little time and thought getting the layout of the room into a 'fit for purpose' format can pay huge dividends at training workshops. Suppose, for example, a rectangular room is to contain a projection point and screen, and 24 participants, working in fours, seated at tables.

Figure 11.1 shows how the room may look if the screen is on one of the shorter walls, and the tables are arranged in rows.

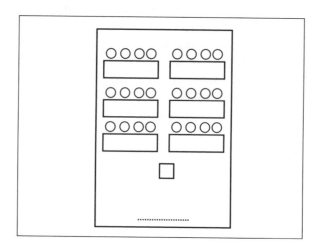

Figure 11.1 An unpromising layout

The problems with this arrangement include:

- The screen is likely to be easily visible only to the participants on the front two tables, who themselves could be in the line of sight of people sitting behind them.
- The participants on the tables at the rear of the room are likely to feel less involved in the workshop than those at the front.
- Participants cannot see each others' faces at all well, in particular those at the front who can't see how others are reacting to the workshop without turning round.

Figure 11.2 shows how the same room could appear simply by altering the position of the screen and projection point.

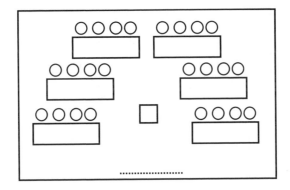

Figure 11.2 The same room, the other way round

This is better in that the facilitator is nearer to more of the participants, and lines of visibility are better, with no participants now being a long way from the screen. However, they are all still sitting in rows, and are not able to see participants' faces at other tables well.

Figure 11.3 shows what the room could look like by turning some of the tables round at an angle. This is an improvement in that participants can see each other considerably better, and the facilitator is less likely to be between most of them and the screen.

Figure 11.4 shows an arrangement with square tables rather than rectangular ones. This is even better, as when working in groups of four, participants are much better able to see each others' faces, and when talking to each other the conversations in one group are less likely to interfere with those of another group. Also the facilitator is much more central, and can interact more easily with any of the groups as necessary.

When deciding upon furniture for training workshop environments, it is useful to order relatively small square tables in the first place. Rectangles can always be made by putting two or more square tables together. For many purposes, round tables are also very suitable, but they don't lend themselves to aggregating when necessary.

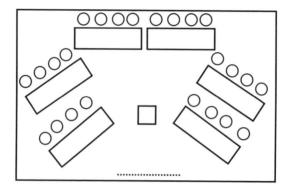

Figure 11.3 The same room, with more opportunity for participation

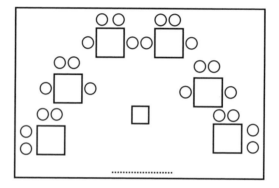

Figure 11.4 The same room, with maximum flexibility

Next, Figure 11.5 shows the extra degree of informality which can be achieved simply by turning all tables so that none is set 'square' in the room. More of the participants can see each other in this layout, and the facilitator is better able to interact equally with each of the groups, and plenary discussion is likely to be far more fluent than in some of the layout options shown by the earlier figures.

A further possibility is putting the tables around the edges of the room, in such a way so that participants can go to the tables when they need to work together in groups at a table, but talk together in clusters in the plenary sessions. These configurations are shown in Figures 11.6 and 11.7.

The discussion above refers to one particular overall group size, 24 participants, but the ideas can easily be extended to other sizes and different numbers of groups. It isn't always possible to have equal numbers of participants in each group, for example, if the total number is 13, it is usually necessary to decide on the relative merits of:

• three groups of three, and one of four
• two groups of four and one of five

and so on. It is best to avoid having any group simply being a pair, however, as there is much more of a difference between the respective dynamics of a pair and a trio, than between those of a trio and a quartet for example. Figure 11.6 shows them in plenary formation, but already clustered in groups of four. It then takes only a short while for them to move their chairs to the respective tables to form working groups round each table as shown in Figure 11.7.

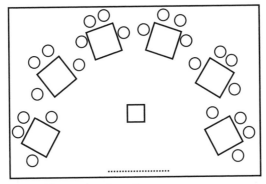

Figure 11.5 The same room, with even less formality

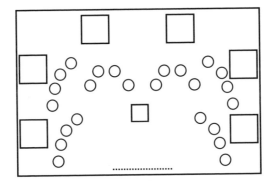

Figure 11.6 Participants working in plenary

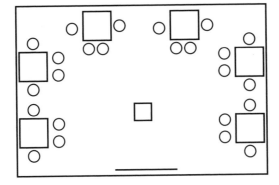

Figure 11.7 Participants working in groups

Workshop room layout – some further suggestions

Participants can become very bored if they are always sitting in the same chair in the same place and with the same neighbours – even in a training event lasting half a day, let alone a full-day workshop. The following suggestions may help you to ensure that your training venue is well chosen and suitably set out.

- *Try to choose rooms which lend themselves to variety.* Training rooms where chairs and tables can be moved around easily are best. Tiered lecture theatres and boardrooms with heavy tables are worst!
- *Don't encourage participants to hide behind tables.* When there is a table between them and you, it is somehow easier for them to sit passively, and lean on the table, and even fall asleep. With nothing to lean on, people are more attentive and involved. Having tables set around the edge of the room can be better.
- *Be kind to bottoms!* Use your own experience to decide what sorts of chairs are best. Remember that participants will be sitting down for longer periods than you will. Concentration spans are less to do with brains, and more to do with bottoms!
- *Don't have too many spare chairs.* Have only a few spare chairs; stack up any others in a secluded corner – or better still, get them out of the room altogether. Spare chairs often become a no-go zone near the trainer (people instinctively sit at the back of a room if there's a back to sit at). Alternatively, spare chairs get occupied by coats, bags or briefcases.
- *Avoid straight lines or rows of chairs.* A circle of chairs, or a U-shape, usually work better for an introductory plenary session (with any tables behind the chairs). Try to arrange the chairs so that all participants have an uninterrupted view of you, and of the projector screen and flip chart. Don't be afraid to move chairs!
- *Consider getting participants to move the furniture themselves.* This is particularly useful when you want to rearrange the layout of the room during a session. It's often far quicker than you doing it yourself (for example, in a coffee break) and it's psychologically useful that participants have a sense of ownership of the environment layout when possible.
- *Help ensure that participants can see each others' faces.* Again, circles and U-shapes work best. When participants can observe each other easily, they get to know each other better and more quickly, and feel more involved in your training event right from the start.
- *Have no safe hiding place!* Have you noticed that in rectangular table layouts, the most awkward participants always seem to establish themselves in one or other of the back corners? If there aren't any corners to start with, this can't happen. (However, when you set out your circle or U-shape, make sure that there are no chairs anywhere near any tables that are in the back corners!).

- *'Now please find a table!'* When you give participants individual or group tasks to do, invite them to move their chairs to any of the tables round the edge of the room (and not the tables to their chairs). This also helps you to be able to circulate freely, and speak to them in groups or individually as necessary.
- *Make full use of any other rooms you have available.* Having additional rooms for syndicate work gives participants a change. Make sure that the same syndicate isn't stuck in the same syndicate room for session after session – ring the changes and give everyone some variety. Consider moving the plenary location around too if there is more than one room big enough.

Finding out how it really went

Feedback or evaluation?

People sometimes confuse feedback and evaluation. Many providers of training workshops use 'evaluation questionnaires' at the end of a workshop, but it can be argued that in fact these are feedback questionnaires, and only part of a wider evaluation context. Evaluation, in its true sense (in the context of training workshops) can not just be achieved through a questionnaire immediately, but needs to be done during the longer timescale of putting into practice what has been gained from a training event. Some argue firmly that 'evaluation takes several years', and needs to embrace a variety of elements, such as:

- how well the learning gained at a training event has been able to be put into practice in day-to-day work contexts
- how well a variety of feedback processes filled in the bigger picture of the success of the event, these feedback elements include more than two or three from the following:
  - structured feedback questionnaire elements
  - open-ended feedback questions
  - face-to-face one-to-one interviews or discussions about the event, at the end of the event and later
  - face-to-face group interviews or discussions about the event
  - testimony from third parties (employers, line managers and so on) in a position to quantify the added-value arising from the participant's attendance at the workshop
  - personal reflections of the participant, relating to the event itself, and the implementation of achievement gained from the event.

Participants themselves often comment at the end of a successful workshop that they do not yet know how useful it will turn out to be, as this, unsurprisingly, depends on the actual relevance to their developing work in a wider context.

Indeed, if the workshop is training them for new or developing work responsibilities, they cannot yet assess its impact or relevance. The same considerations apply, of course, to most aspects of post-compulsory education, not just to workshops. End-of-module or end-of-course questionnaires tell only a limited story.

It is not surprising that feedback questionnaires issued towards the end of a workshop have earned the nickname 'happiness sheets' in many training contexts, as the feedback participants give relates substantially to how they *feel* at the end of the event, rather than on how much the event will turn out to have influenced their practice. Admittedly, happiness and value are connected, and participants are more likely to have gained a great deal from a workshop if they feel inspired and enthused at the end of the event.

Collecting and analysing participants feedback at workshops takes time and energy, not least for the participants themselves who provide the feedback. Therefore, it is important that feedback is not simply planned 'for its own sake' or 'because it is always done in this way'. The checklist which follows should help you to decide *why* you are seeking and analysing feedback, and this in turn will help you to fine-tune *what* feedback you seek and *how* you seek it from participants.

Designing feedback questionnaires

Putting aside for the moment the reservations expressed above about whether questionnaires can be regarded as feedback or evaluation devices, there are some further limitations of questionnaires as a methodology.

- *Questionnaires can induce 'surface' responses.* Since they are normally completed relatively quickly, perhaps, as participants are eager to get on their journeys from the event, there can be a tendency to 'tick the boxes' lightly rather than in a considered manner.
- *Questionnaires can be boring to complete.* Where participants *want* to answer a particular question this isn't a problem, but where they have no strong feelings, giving their answers to routine questions can become a chore.
- *Filling in a questionnaire can be a lonely experience!* At highly participative workshops, the only quiet period may be when everyone fills in the ubiquitous questionnaire, and this can cause the whole event to 'end with a whimper rather than a bang'. It can be worth considering getting small groups of participants to fill in a copy of the questionnaire together, agreeing (or indicating their disagreement appropriately) on their collective responses to the questions and carrying forward their thinking of what has been achieved by the workshop.

Towards purposeful feedback – a checklist

For each of the following feedback purposes, decide the relative importance in the context of your particular workshops.			
Feedback purpose	**Very important**	**Quite important**	**Not really important**
1 To gain participants' feedback on the particular workshop			
2 To fine-tune further workshops in a series of related workshops			
3 To find out more about generic workshop skills and processes to use in future workshops			
4 To determine participants' further training needs			
5 To satisfy organizational requirements to monitor the quality and relevance of training provision			
6 To find out more about particular problem areas, so that they can be addressed in future training provision			
7 To find out more about particular training strengths, so that they can be used to greater effect in future provision			
8 To find out more about a particular cohort of participants, so that future training for them can be fine-tuned			
9 To determine the effect of new or exploratory workshop techniques, so that their future usage can be justified or critiqued			
10 To provide data to be used in the appraisal or monitoring of workshop facilitators			
11 To form the basis of an evaluation report to be written in due course about the particular workshop or training programme			
12 To provide evidence for quality assurance requirements of the organization			

- *Questionnaires can be hijacked by 'happiness' factors.* For example, if a workshop facilitator has inspired and enthused participants, their responses to all the questionnaire elements can be 'rosy' and congratulatory. Similarly, if some participants have found parts of the workshop challenging or difficult, they can be 'blue' in their responses to questionnaire elements. In short, the extent to which they have grown to like or dislike the facilitator can colour their responses even to quite neutral questions about the venue or the catering.
- *Quantitative analysis seems all too easy with structured questionnaires.* For example, it is easy to count up the numbers of ticks in 'excellent' or 'unsatisfactory' boxes, and come to what seems to be a reliable judgement on the success (or otherwise) of a training workshop. However, taking into account the points earlier in this list, we need to ask whether the data is valid enough to make this kind of statistical analysis.

Some ideas for structured questions

Having already stressed that questionnaires should be short, relevant and direct, it is likely in most circumstances that some structured questions should be included, but no more than a single side of A4 in most contexts.

The following examples may give you ideas of your own to develop for your workshops.

Event organization

What is your view of the details you were given before the event commenced?

Excellent ☐   Very good ☐   Good ☐   Satisfactory ☐   Poor ☐

Meeting your expectations

How well did the event meet your own expectations?

Fully met ☐   Partially met ☐   Not met ☐

Specific ratings of elements of the workshop

Workshop aspects	Excellent	Good	Satisfactory	Poor	Comments?
Location					
Refreshments					
Clarity of presentations					
Facilitator's knowledge					
Handling of questions					
Amount of discussion					
Amount of participation					
Relevance to your needs					
Value for your time spent					
Quality of handouts					

Questions about the achievement of learning outcomes

One of the most useful aspects of feedback that we can draw from workshop participants is their feelings about the extent to which they themselves feel that they have achieved the intended learning outcomes of the event. Giving us this feedback is also useful in helping them to reflect on their own learning during the event, and it helps us to see which outcomes we may need to focus more strongly on next time we run a similar workshop. Simple questionnaire elements such as those below can yield a lot of useful information for us.

Achievement of intended outcomes: how well do you feel that the workshop enabled you personally to achieve each of the intended learning outcomes?				
	I feel I've really achieved this now	I feel I've partially achieved this now	I don't feel I've achieved this yet	I had already achieved this before the workshop
(Learning outcome 1)				
(Learning outcome 2)				
(Learning outcome 3)				
(Learning outcome 4)				

Some ideas for open-ended questions

The following example includes a selection of questions which could be useful for finding out in greater depth how individual participants (or, indeed, groups of participants) benefited from a workshop.

Questions about your experience of the workshop	Your responses
What was the most useful thing you personally gained from this workshop?	
What (if anything) do you consider should have been missed out from this workshop?	
What (if anything) do you think should have been added to this workshop?	
To what extent do you feel your time at this workshop has been usefully spent?	
What (if anything) surprised you most about what you learned from this workshop?	
What did you find the most difficult aspect of this workshop?	
What is the most important thing you yourself plan to do directly as a result of this workshop?	
What (if anything) will you personally now try *not* to do as a result of your experience on this workshop?	
To what extent would you recommend that a colleague should take part in a similar workshop?	

Using Post-its for fast feedback

One of the disadvantages of questionnaires is that people tend to fill them in quickly, and give surface responses to the questions, particularly when the questionnaire seems long. A Post-it is a much smaller space and, despite its limited size, can often yield deeper thinking from participants about how they have found your workshop. Better still, you can issue Post-its at a suitable mid-point in your workshop to find out how your participants are *presently* finding your workshop, and you can then make adjustments in the remainder of the workshop to act on what you have learned from their responses.

Using the starter words 'stop', 'start' and 'continue' on a Post-it (Figure 11.8) can bring you a great deal of feedback during or after a workshop, or both. You can ask your participants, for example, 'If I was to run a similar workshop with other people tomorrow, what do you suggest I should stop doing, start doing and continue doing?'

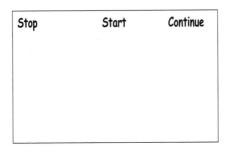

Figure 11.8 'Stop, start, continue' Post-it

The 'stop' entries are the bad news! You will often get much sharper criticisms from this simple feedback method than from detailed questionnaires, because the headings are so open-ended. Participants can tell you just about anything – and they do! There are times when you can't do much about some of the 'stop' entries – for example, if they tell you to stop doing 'health and safety risk assessments' in a workshop where these are essential elements. More often, however, the 'stop' responses can be addressed at least to some extent in your next workshop.

The 'start' entries may give you ideas of things participants found missing from your workshop. Many of these can lead to adjustments to how you would run the same workshop next time round.

The 'continue' responses are the good news. Sometimes you will be surprised by at least some of the things your participants liked about your workshop, and can then use these actions or elements more consciously as you develop your workshop skills.

Normally, there will be contradictions too. Some participants will want you to *stop* something, while others will want you to *continue* the same things. This is where you find out more about the balance to strike next time round.

You can easily keep the findings from 'stop, start, continue' feedback for future reference. For example, you can stick the Post-its eight to an A4 sheet (if the Post-its are the most usual rectangular ones) and photocopy the sheets (manually – don't feed such sheets through mechanical copier feeders – the Post-its detach and cause jams!). Alternatively, you can transcribe the entries to make a feedback summary, and email it back to participants where this is considered a useful thing to do.

References and further reading

Anderson, D. and Race, P. (2002) *Effective Online Learning: The Trainer's Toolkit.* Ely: Fenman.

Ausubel, D.P. (1968) *Educational Psychology: A Cognitive View.* London: Holt, Rinehart and Winston.

Bandura, A. (1997) *Self-efficacy: the exercise of control.* New York: Freeman

Bates, A.W. (1995) *Technology, Open Learning and Distance Education.* London: RoutledgeFalmer.

Bates, A.W. (2002) *National Strategies for e-Learning in Post-secondary Education and Training.* New York: UNESCO.

Biggs, J. (2003) *Teaching for Quality Learning at University.* Maidenhead: Open University Press/SRHE.

Boud, D. (1995) 'Enhancing learning through self-assessment'. London: RoutledgeFalmer.

Bowl, M. (2003) *Non-traditional Entrants to Higher Education: 'They Talk about People Like Me'.* Stoke-on-Trent: Trentham Books.

Brown, S. (2004) 'Formative feedback' – a discussion paper prepared for inaugural professional lecture at Buckinghamshire Chilterns University College, High Wycombe, UK on September 7, 2004.

Brown, S. and Knight, P. (1994) *Assessing Learners in Higher Education.* London: Kogan Page.

Brown, S. and Race, P. (2002) *Lecturing – a Practical Guide.* London: RoutledgeFalmer.

Burge, E.J. and Haughey, M. (eds) (2001) *Using Learning Technologies – International Perspectives on Practice.* London: RoutledgeFalmer.

Burgess, R. (2004) *Measuring and Recording Achievement.* (Burgess Report). London: UUK/SCOP.

Claxton, G. (1998) *Hare Brain, Tortoise Mind.* London: Fourth Estate.

Claxton, J., Mathers, J. and Wetherell-Terry, D. (2004) 'Benefits of a 3-way collaborative learning system: action learning, continuous editing and peer assessment'. Paper presented at the BEST conference 'Reflection on teaching: the impact on learning' Edinburgh.

Coffield, F., Moseley, D., Hall, E. and Ecclestone, K. (2004) *Learning Styles and Pedagogy in Post-16 Learning – A Systematic and Critical Review.* London: Learning and Skills Research Centre (downloadable from www.lsrc.ac.uk). (For a shorter review, see also Coffield, F., Moseley, D., Hall, E. and Ecclestone, K. (2004) *Should We Be Using Learning Styles? What Research Has to Say to Practice.* London: Learning and Skills Research Centre, also downloadable from www.lsrc.ac.uk.)

Cotton, D. (2004) 'Essentials of training design: Part 5: adult learning theories and design', *Training Journal*, May 2004: 22–7.

Curry, L. (1990). 'A critique of the research on learning styles', *Educational Leadership*, 48(2): 50–56.

Gardner, H. (1993) *Frames of Mind: The Theory of Multiple Intelligences*. New York: Basic Books.

Gardner, H. and Hatch, T. (1989) 'Multiple intelligences go to school: educational implications of the theory of multiple intelligences', Educational Researcher, 18(8): 4–9.

Gibbs, G. and Simpson, C. (2002) *'Does your assessment support your students' learning?'*, http://www.open.ac.uk/science/fdtl/documents/lit-review.pdf, Milton Keynes, Open University, accessed September 2004.

Hativa, N. (2000) *Teaching for Effective Learning in Higher Education*. Dordrecht, Boston, MA and London: Kluwer Academic.

Honey, P. and Mumford, A. (1982) *The Manual of Learning Styles*. Maidenhead: Peter Honey Publications.

JISC (2004) *Designing for Learning: An Update on the Pedagogy Strand of the JISC eLearning Programme*. Bristol: JISC.

Knight, P. and Yorke, M. (2003) *Assessment, Learning and Employability*. Maidenhead: SRHE/Open University Press.

Knowles, M. (1975) *Self-Directed Learning*. Englewood Cliffs, NJ: Follet.

Kolb, D. (1984) *Experiential Learning: Experience as the Source of Learning and Development*. Englewood Cliffs, NJ: Prentice Hall.

Kolb, D.A. (1999) *The Kolb Learning Style Inventory*, Version 3. Boston: Hay Group.

Laurillard, D. (2001) *Rethinking University Teaching: A Framework for the Effective Use of Educational Technology: 2nd Edition*. London: RoutledgeFalmer.

Lindsay, R. (2004) book review in *Studies in Higher Education*, 29(2): 279–86.

Litzinger, M.E. and Osif, B. (1993) 'Accommodating diverse learning styles: designing instruction for electronic information sources', in *What Is Good Instruction Now? Library Instruction for the 90s*. L. Shirato (ed.), Ann Arbor, MI: Pierian Press.

MacFarlane, B. (1992) 'The "Thatcherite" generation of university degree results'. *Journal of Further and Higher Education*, 16: 60–70.

McAndrew, P. (2003) 'Can generic models be reused and shared?', LTSN Generic Centre, York, accessed via HEA website, December 2004.

McCarthy, B. (1987) *The 4MAT System: Teaching to Learning Styles with Right/Left Mode Techniques*. About Learning Inc., available from www.aboutlearning.com.

Miller, C.M.L. and Parlett, M. (1974) *Up to the Mark: A Study of the Examinations Game*. Monograph 21. London: SRHE.

Overbye, D. (1991) *Lonely Hearts of the Cosmos: The Scientific Quest for the Secret of the Universe*. London: Macmillan.

Peelo, M. and Wareham, T. (eds) (2002) *Failing Students in Higher Education*. Buckingham: SRHE/Open University Press.

Pellegrino, J., Chudowsky, N. and Glaser, R. (eds) (2003) *Knowing What Students Know: The Science and Design of Educational Assessment*, Washington, DC: National

Academy Press.

Pratt, J.R. (2002) 'The manager's role in creating a blended learning environment', *Home Health Care Management & Practice*, 15(1): 76–9.

Race, P. (2001) *The Lecturer's Toolkit* (2nd edition). London: RoutledgeFalmer.

Race, P. (2004) *500 Tips on Open and Online Learning*. London: RoutledgeFalmer.

Reynolds, M. (1997) 'Learning styles: a critique', *Management Learning*, 28(2): 115–33.

Robinson, A. and Udall, M. (2003) 'Developing the independent learner: the Mexican hat approach', conference proceedings of the 3rd International Symposium on Engineering Education, Southampton.

Robinson, A. and Udall, M. (2004) 'Developing the independent learner: LTSN engineering case study', www.ltsn.ac.uk.

Salmon, G. (2002) *E-tivities: The Key to Active Online Learning*. London: RoutledgeFalmer.

Salmon, G. (2004) *E-moderating: The Key to Teaching and Learning On-line: 2nd Edition*. London: RoutledgeFalmer.

Smithers, R. (2004) *Guardian*, November.

Stowell, N. (2001) 'Equity, justice and standards: assessment decision making in higher education'. Paper presented at the SRHE Annual Conference, University of Cambridge (mimeo).

Thorpe, M. (2003) 'Designing for reuse and versioning', LTSN Generic Centre, York, accessed via HEA website, December 2004.

Wierstra, R.F.A. and de Jong, J.A. (2002) 'A scaling theoretical evaluation of Kolb's Learning Style Inventory-2', in M. Valcke and D. Gombeir (eds), *Learning Styles: Reliability and Validity*. 431–40. Proceedings of the 7th Annual European Learning Styles Information Network Conference, 26–28 June, Ghent. Ghent: University of Ghent.

Yorke, M. (2002) in M. Peelo and T. Wareham (eds), 'Academic failure: a retrospective view from non-completing students', in *Failing Students in Higher Education*. Buckingham: SRHE/Open University Press.

Index